WAITING FOR GODIVA

WAITING FOR GODIVA

A Guide for
Thinking Women and Men
to the Story of Love

Ronald J. Meyers

To order additional copies of this book, contact:
Xlibris Corporation
1-888-795-4274
www.Xlibris.com
Orders@Xlibris.com
12492

FOR RINA

My Molly, Portia, Wife of Bath, Juliet

And our Love's Labour's Won

CONTENTS

THE STORY OF LOVE

Love is an acquired taste.
La Rochefoucauld

It is much easier to accuse one sex than to excuse the other.
It is the old saying, the pot calls the kettle black.
Michel de Montaigne

The love life of a people teaches one more about the people
than its political, social, or economic life.
Pinhas ben Nahum

There is no book on woman by a man that is not a stupen-
dous compendium of posturings and imbecilities.
H.L. Mencken

The true Poet [is] of the Devil's party without knowing it.
William Blake

There is nothing new under the sun.
Ecclesiastes

THE HISTORY OF LOVE • IN COMMON WITH OTHER
SPECIES • HEAVEN'S GREAT NORM • WHAT IS LOVE? •
FEAR AND GALLANTRY • HIGH TRAGEDY • BOOKS AND
MEDIA • THE DECLINE OF LITERACY • TELEVISION SOAPS
AND SIT-COMS • FATHER KNOWS BEST • FROM CROONING
TO ROCK • FEMINISM AND MALE CHAUVINISM • THE WAR
OF THE WORDS (1) •

THE WAR OF THE WORDS (2) • HERESIES, DOGMAS AND
SHIBBOLETHS • THE STORY OF LOVE

THE HISTORY OF LOVE

The history of love is the story of civilization—the account of the
most universal, most irresistible, and most expedient activity of
men and women. Love between the sexes has been marked by
irrationality, dissimulation, anxiety, shame, frustration, disgust,
and suffering. Yet the search for fulfillment through love is not
only the basis of our earthly happiness but the summit of our
biological destiny. The union of man and woman in ecstasy en-
ables us to realize our ultimate purposes—our immortality and
the survival of the species. Although the sex drive is related to our
most primitive character, love is truly the flower of our civilized
achievements.

Moreover, it is an illusion to believe that we can improvise the
script—the motivation and roles have been assigned by nature.
The Renaissance humanist Rabelais praised God's disposition of
this matter:

> Among the gifts, graces, prerogatives with which our sover-
> eign Maker, God Almighty, has endowed and adorned hu-
> man nature from its beginning, the one which seems to me
> most singular and excellent is the one that enables us to
> acquire a kind of immortality and, in the course of this
> fleeting life, perpetuate our name and seed.[1]

For his outspokenness and defense of sexual feeling, he was excommunicated by the Church.

Society's attitudes towards the relationship between the sexes
have evolved through history. The political and religious institutions that govern man affect his behavior and social relations. But
human nature has not changed significantly. The passions that

moved our forebears remain imprinted on our character. The truths that the poets intuited and described through the centuries have received continual confirmation not only through our own experience but also through scientific findings:

Call us what you will, we are made such by love.
John Donne

IN COMMON WITH OTHER SPECIES

The revelations of modern biology, psychology, anthropology and zoology show how closely we are related to other species in our behavior and the organization of our societies. The instinct of aggression is indicative of the more intelligent species, and the survival and territorial imperative is another familiar pattern in both the animal and human kingdom. We are currently demonstrating the ability of higher mammals to conceptualize and reason even without language. The identification and placement of the individual's role within society is common to primitive as well as advanced social structures.

From Maurice Maeterlinck's study of bees in 1901 to his later studies of termites, pigeons and spiders, to Josef and Karel Capek's drama of the twenties, *The World We Live In, The Insect Comedy* and its representation of butterflies and beetles, to Orwell's ant hill society in *1984,* to the original (and sequels) to *Planet of the Apes,* to David Cronenberg horror film, *The Fly,* to the current spate of out-of-control herbivorous and carnivorous reptiles and anthropoid primates—the animal kingdom in the twentieth century has held a mirror up to human society.

Go to the ant thou sluggard; consider her ways and be wise.
Proverbs

However, today's science writers—like, for example, Geoffrey F. Miller in *The Mating Mind,* and Michael Pollan in *The Botany of*

Desire and countless others—to say nothing of those studies deciphering the genome code—have demonstrated how the story of biology is indeed more fantastic than anything ever devised by science fiction in revealing the correspondence between the human, animal, and plant kingdoms.

The process by which animal sexual behavior has assumed social forms was earlier described by Professor Wolfgang Wickler.[2] Male and female are dependent upon each other not only for reproduction but for companionship too. The instinct to mate is very strong indeed in the most primitive organisms to the most complex. The structures of marriage, or just living together, range from monogamous arrangements (the European bearded tit) to polygyny (the cock and his hens) to polyandry (the bee, the wasp, the ant). The care and protection of the young are also widespread in the animal kingdom. The watchful hen, of renown, keeps a sharp eye on her young chicks. The male of the species often seeks forage while the female guards the nest. The care for the old is not usual, but it is not unknown in the kingdom of the wild.

But surely the most fascinating patterns of behavior relate to courtship practices. When love is revealed, each individual species shows its sudden glory. Nature is arrayed in her most gorgeous plumage, the woods and fields are alive with sounds and whistles, and ritual dances abound. The rooster crows early in the morning to impress (please! arouse!) his favorite hen. The woodpecker beats his beak furiously against a hollow limb to attract a mate. The heron displays most striking coloration as its bill metamorphoses from yellow to glowing orange and red. The insect cicada and the penguin woo by singing while the male firefly literally ignites to indicate his availablity, and the female mosquito creates a siren buzz to excite the male. Indeed there are even dialects within individual species, which indicate suitability and biological readiness. The tree sparrow warbles a melancholy dirge, lowers his wings and ruffles his feathers in hopes of acceptance. In the feathered kingdom, the male usually acts as the pursuer, wooing with food and proffering a cozy nest. The rule of thumb here is similar to our own. He proposes; she disposes. The rituals are as elaborate as any seen in our own domain, a lady swaying her hips, a male displaying his biceps, a gentleman bowing and kissing the hand of his true love, she dressing to look good for him, he buying her drinks and dinners, and other fascinating patterns of behavior to be observed at upper class cocktail receptions, singles bars, church socials, and—not least of all—sorority and fraternity parties.

The eagle engages in a dazzling derring-do to impress and captivate his mate. The California gray whale is pursued so ardently by two males that the moving image creates what some had speculated to be a *ménage à trois* so close are the three intertwined with each other; but, in fact, the male bulls are competing for the female's favors right up until the instant of copulation. A dancing fly will offer the female a slaughtered insect of suitable delectation before copulation. The female rarely plays the pursuant role—though the female bullfinch swoops down upon her timorous love with open beak, crying "Chooah, Chooah." Often the male begs the female for the bestowal of favors. Rare is that species which is capable of self-gratification without a partner; but the *Trichonympha*, a unicellular organism, which inhabits the intestines of the wood-eating American cockroach, fulfills both   and

roles; also to be noted is the unique talent of the *Labroides dimidiatus*, a tropical fish, to transform her sex and become a male when required.

Frequently the male engages in individual combat for the attention of the female. In various species, the number of females under his domain acknowledges the status of the male in the pecking order. The stag maintains a harem of deer, and locks horns with any ambitious rival. Jealousy and infidelity also are not uncommon. The cuckoo is famous in story and legend for laying its eggs in the nests of others, and has given its name to the etymology of the cuckold (husband of an unfaithful wife). The male swan can be lured into extra-marital entanglements. The female jackdaw pecks her rival, but the female wasp bites off the head of her antagonist and consumes her mate after copulation. The development of the family unit and bonds between parents and children occur in some higher species. Marital bliss is not typical, but penguins form lasting relationships. The love duet of birds is a well-known song of companionship, and so too the practices of billing, cooing, and preening are gestures of love.

One must be struck by the nobility of love that exists among some species of the finny kind, such as the behavior of the sockeye salmon.[3] After being spawned in fresh waters, the red salmon move out to the open seas of the Northern Pacific, and live there for four years until the time has come to mate. Then they begin a treacherous journey to the home from which they departed. The journey is fraught with hazards—the tiny fish must swim against the current, overcome jagged rocks and steep waterfalls while predators such as bear, eagle, and man lie in wait for them. The few that survive the journey to their spawning ground begin a period of courtship and family life. A male overcomes a rival for the favors of a female, and there is a period of marital bliss while they are bearing their young; when a female loses her bearings on dry land and cannot find her way back to the life-saving water, the male companion will direct her, and, failing that, will come out to save her. After the mating season, there is rapid and agonizing decay—as both male and female die and become part of the food chain, which will nourish their young:

> Nothing of him that doth fade
> But doth suffer a sea-change
> Into something rich and strange.
> Shakespeare

"The Tragedy of the Red Sockeye Salmon" is not unlike the tragedy of humanity—the doom of temporal life and the prospect of immortality through regeneration. Family life is perhaps the greatest source of human fulfillment. Human beings have greater influence in control of their destiny—though the role of fate in the outcome has always been recognized; some societies and individuals are more susceptible to the vagaries of fate than others. The happiness of the individual along with the survival of the species have been acknowledged as an ethical good maintained uniquely in our kingdom; whereas truly ancient species like the ant society have completely submerged the individual personality for the sake of the commonweal.

Loving and the quality of love are truly unique in our species. Men and women have the capacity to sublimate their love into actions of sacrifice, nobility, and creativity. Child bearing for a woman is one such heroic endeavor. Are we not all the seekers and servants of love? The fabulously powerful Shah Jahan built the architectural wonder, the Taj Mahal, in honor of his beloved wife. It can be argued that the supreme achievements of mankind— Napoleon's conquests, the heroic feats of athletes, the triumphs of Wall Street billionaires, and the works of your humblest scriveners—each and all have been the fruit of love.

It also can be argued that actions of villainy have been the bitter fruit of love. Have not the great villains of history been those who were deprived or who wanted love? Satan himself turned to evil because according to Christian teaching, he was rejected by God. Similarly it can be documented that the denial of love in childhood has a critical influence on the development of the young, from the rejected and neglected English King, Richard III to Charles Manson. The Roman Emperor Nero, the dissolute son of a blood-thirsty mother, at age twenty-two himself arranged to have her slain. Consider Yoko Ono's youthful remark that if she had been married to Hitler the Second World War would have been averted.

It often has been noted that behind a great man, there is a woman's influence. I am not suggesting that every politician's wife is affected by a Lady Macbeth complex. But haven't all of the presidents' wives in our recent political history fine-tuned their husband's strings—guiding their actions for both good or evil? If behind every great man there is an influential woman, who is behind a great woman? Obviously a great man or, as some wags say— a surprised man.

In some respects the similarities between men and woman are more significant than the differences. Perhaps men are looking for their other half, and women for the Other—not merely a man but a spirit and a meaning. The male seeks passionate embraces and discovers love, while the female seeks love, considers preludes and consequences, and discovers embraces. For a man erotic desire can be separated from parenthood; and for a woman, notwithstanding the rhythm and the pill, the pleasure of sex, according to Helene Deutsch, extends to the act of birth.[4]

HEAVEN'S GREAT NORM

In the family matrix the role of the mother and the father are critical. The absence of a paternal influence can be a detriment to the development of the child in its quest to find and follow a role model. The lack of maternal concern and love can lead to regression, rejection of others, and even retardation.

The disposition of the child is significantly benefited by harmonious family relations, just as—recent studies confirm—it is damaged by disharmony. The statistics of crime and delinquency offer impressive confirmation of the consequence of broken homes and bad Oedipal resolutions on the maladjustment of the young. Even a mother's unwilling fulfillment of her maternal role often leads to significant psychological consequences. The adjustment of a mother to a positive creative role is related to her success in parenting. The mother who has communicated love and caring will have loving and caring children, while the mother who communicates her discontent will alienate her offspring:

> A wise son maketh a glad father; but a foolish son is the
> heaviness of his mother.
> Proverbs

Recent studies have confirmed that there are distinct male and female stereotypes, though all agree that these characteristics are significantly influenced by social conditioning, and that they are, moreover, generalizations that do not encompass everyone. According to current, popular thinking, men are from Mars and women are from Venus, men are more devoted to power, to generalization and to analytical reasoning, whereas women have a tendency to be more intuitive, expressive, and act on the basis of emotional reasoning. Scholars suggest that men externalize blame, and women internalize it and have difficulty in expressing anger. Men operate out of fear of failure, whereas women are ambivalent about success. Men tend to be more competitive, women cooperative, supportive. Men tend to hide weakness and exhibit strength; women often do not hide weakness. Men define themselves in terms of achievement and success, whereas women are more inclined to define their status on the basis of relationships.[5] The argument about social conditioning cuts both ways, since both sexes can be conditioned to behave according to a socially determined pattern— and many sociologists have noted the trend toward androgyny among contemporary males and females.[6] But the arresting question is what are the optimum conditions leading to the individual's inner harmony?

The harmony of the sexes exists when the male is chivalrous, the woman giving. Helene Deutsch observed: "If woman moves too far away from the instinctual, she loses her specificity." Writing nearly half a century ago, she gently admonished: "trying to reconquer a better social position by the detour of intelligence and by practical achievements that make her more similar to man . . . necessarily involves the danger that she will lose her feminine characteristics."[7] Biology may or may not be destiny; but poor parenting does not serve the young or society. This has been expressed in one of the most ancient and philosophic texts that distinguishes the female (*yin*) and the male (*yang*) principles in the universe and in the family, the *I Ching*:

> Woman's appropriate place is within; men's without. When
> men and women keep to their proper places they act in

> accordance with heaven's great norm. Among the members of the family are the dignified master and mistress whom we term Father and Mother. When father, mother, sons, elder and younger brothers all act in a manner suited to their various positions within the family, when husbands play their proper roles and wives are truly wifely, the way of that family runs straight. *It is by the proper regulation of each family that the whole world is stabilized.* (My italics)[8]

And what of daughters? Alas, the ancient Oriental sages, like the ancients in other lands and cultures, failed to give sufficient recognition to the ideal of equality. Today attitudes are changing; young ladies are in the process of receiving their due, and are moving toward their proper and rightful place outside in society as well as within the home. Discrimination is scorned by society, and progress toward equality is being made throughout the world.

WHAT IS LOVE?

What is love? Is it ideal, or is it physical? Is it better to marry than to remain single? than to burn? Should one marry in youth or in maturity? The Muslims maintain that love which follows marriage is finer than love that precedes marriage. Is experience before marriage necessary? Is it desirable? Is divorce always wrong? Is homosexuality wrong? Should same sex marriages be admitted according to religion and the law? Is deception always wrong? Is friendship the ideal of love?

Is love a mystery, or is it manifest? Is it universal, or is it unique? Are there proper roles for men and women? Are women jealous of men? Are men jealous of women? What is the role of hatred in love? Of ambivalence? Of vindictiveness? The questions have not changed; but the answers have varied.

Human beings have the unique capacity to record their experiences and reflect upon them. One generation passes its knowledge and wisdom on to the other. Therefore, the last generation should be the wisest. But this is not always the case.

> One generation passeth away, and another generation
> cometh; and the earth abideth forever.
> Ecclesiastes

Since the advent of writing, books have served to transmit from one generation to another the delights and mysteries of love. In literature there has been the continual swing between the idealistic and the realistic mode, just as in life there are seasons when individuals give greater emphasis to their idealistic conceptions and other times to their realistic needs. At the same time, literature has affected attitudes—it has been a principal teacher. Literature is then the record of men and women's dependency upon love. It reveals the constancy of feelings as well as the variation of courtship practices. Literature perhaps more than other arts has been able to codify ideas about love. Attitudes toward love have continually shifted between those of repression and freedom. And the stories of love have often been fascinating and even spectacular.

FEAR AND GALLANTRY

There are examples aplenty from life as well as from literature. Montaigne, in the sixteenth century, recounted a story of a young girl who threw herself out of a window to avoid the advances of a soldier who was quartered in her house. She did not succeed in killing herself; and she tried again to cut her throat, unsuccessfully, though she wounded herself seriously. She admitted that the soldier had not attacked her but only pressed his suit with gifts and solicitations. "And all this," Montaigne adds, "with such words, with such expressions, not to mention the blood that testified to her virtue, as would become another Lucrece. Now, I learned that as a matter of fact, both before and since, she was a wench not so hard to come to terms with."[9]

A similar story recorded in *The New York Times* told of a successful lawyer who loved a young lady while he was still married.

When she broke off the liaison, he arranged to have thugs throw lye in her face—so that no one else would want her. He was arrested and served fourteen years in prison for the crime. Released, disbarred, and divorced, he married the young lady—who was nearly blind from the attack; and they live together now. He says: "We laugh together—not too many cries, thank God." "He's a good husband—he still is," she says, "I just find him a workaholic which I resent."[10]

HIGH TRAGEDY

Who can forget the anguish endured by Othello when he is goaded by the malevolent Iago to doubt the fidelity of his wife?

> But yet the pity of it, Iago! O Iago, the pity of it, Iago!

With inexplicable malice, Iago presses his attack with the ferocious, disinterested calm of a hunter trapping his prey:

> If you are so fond over her iniquity, give her patent to offend, for it touch not you, it comes near nobody.

Othello's love is turned to savage anger against the innocent Desdemona as he becomes convinced of her infidelity and deceit:

> Othello: I will chop her into messes! Cuckold me!
> Iago: O, tis foul in her.
> Othello: With mine officer!
> Iago: That's fouler.
> Othello: Get me some poison, Iago, this night. I'll not expostulate with her, lest her body and her beauty unprovide my mind again. This night, Iago.
> Iago: Do it not with poison; strangle her in her bed, even the bed she hath contaminated.
> IV.i.195ff.

After he has committed the unholy deed and discovered the truth of Desdemona's chaste innocence, his anger—turned upon himself—is more savage than toward his defiler:

> I pray you, in your letters,
> When you shall these unlucky deeds relate,
> Speak of me as I am; nothing extenuate,
> Nor set down aught in malice. Then must you speak
> Of one that lov'd not wisely but too well;
> Of one not easily jealous, but being wrought,
> Perplexed in the extreme, of one whose hand
> Like the base Indian threw a pearl away
> Richer than all his tribe.
> V.ii.340-349

BOOKS AND MEDIA

At first glance it is difficult to imagine the practice of love in a non-technological society. How did people get around before the automobile, the bus, the train, the jet? How did they communicate before there were cell phones, chat rooms, and e-mail? How did they entertain themselves before there were television and cable, films, shopping malls, Rock Concerts, MTV, and Playstations? The media have always played a significant role in the dissemination of information on love and influenced practices. La Rochefoucauld thought that without books, people would not know about love, and other media also have fulfilled that function. The earliest poetry that was transmitted orally consisted of legends and histories of heroes and the gods, which often dealt with their amorous experiences and lyrical feelings. Literary culture was originally transcribed on stone, then on papyrus, and finally on paper over the course of several millennia. Theater was another media in the history of love—perhaps the one that has undergone the fewest changes—unless film is seen as an evolution of theatre.

In lyrical poetry, the particular experience has been celebrated and described. In comedy, love has been depicted as calculated deceit by such diverse authors as Aristophanes, Molière, Jane Austen and Nabokov, whereas tragedy has recounted the terrible pain of love.

Today the modern media are playing a dominant role in representing, describing, transcribing and teaching love. Television is far ahead of other influences. And though it has the capacity to present Greek Epic and Shakespearean Tragedy, it often plays to the lower common denominator of its audience. Talk shows explore every moral, social, psychological, theological, and erotic dilemma and present them in the most direct and even shocking format. [11] Though geared to a mass audience, the shows, ranging from the outrageous Jerry Springer to the moralistic and addictive Oprah Winfrey, are not without entertainment value—though often superficial, and invariably titillating. A woman appears on a talk show and discusses her relationship with her husband in raising their infant. She muses that she wishes that her husband had breasts so that he too could share the nursing experience with her; he nods wishfully:

> I have given suck and know
> How tender 'tis to love the babe that milks me.
> Shakespeare

In another respect the young have been overexposed to the stories presented in television popular drama and situation comedies. Indeed they have probably heard all of the variations of the story catalogued by Stith Thompson. In a recent experience in teaching a classic—perhaps *The Arabian Nights*, a student paid, I imagine, the ultimate compliment—he said that he couldn't wait for the television mini-series to be made, and he would remember to catch it then.

THE DECLINE OF LITERACY

This direction in the popularization of culture reflects a condition that has received much consideration. Allan Bloom in *The Closing of the American Mind* (1987) noted the absolute decline in the awareness of the major intellectual influences on Western Civilization, in favor of multi-cultural and post-colonial studies, and this has resulted, in his view, in the current cultural crisis. He argued for an "opening" of the American mind to "self-knowledge mediated by book learning," to the "models first experienced in books as in everyday life," in such classics as the works of Plato and Shakespeare which permit the gratification of "the Delphic command" to 'Know thyself' born in each of us, and answering the eternal question, 'What is man?'" [12] The shift in emphasis of college curriculum to the physical sciences, the social sciences, and computer sciences as well as to vocational training has left many unaware of what they have missed. Marshall McLuhan's similar dire prognostications presented in *Understanding Media* (1964) had projected the demise of book learning, and postulated that the new media would provide new messages as well as new ways of revealing them—and correctly foresaw that Gutenberg's printing press would fall victim to the electronic age.

New times present new opportunities, and such developments as electronic publication and the internet are proving to be a formidable influence, and at the same time it should be acknowledged that editions of the classics are not selling. Indeed many of the editions that I have used here were the same used in my own student days in the fifties, and many others are simply out of print. Romance, Science Fiction novels and Fantasy novels are selling; and these new forms of literature are claiming to inherit the Western tradition.

It seems particularly ironic in view of the fact that the evolution in media a half century ago was the paperback revolution. Indeed I recall professors of literature decrying the vulgarization of the classics through transmission by translations, and their excessive availability in mass printings. At that time, those defenders of culture felt that the classics were the preserve of the specialist and should not be vitiated by being made available cheaply.

As the same time, the classics have become the preserve of the specialist—and the source of exotic and far-fetched semiotic and deconstructionist interpretations. And the classics themselves languish on library shelves.

The new media have usurped the role that literature had in the life of the community—as the significant source of artistic expression and the instructor of the community. Instruction in the lessons of love is still being provided in these diverse media.

TELEVISION SOAPS AND SIT-COMS

The theme of idealistic love seems to be universal in the modern soap operas, which are witnessed by an estimated fifty million viewers a week. The majority of the characters are beautiful people, well dressed, and exuding wholesome feelings. The arch villains are not usually seen—only individuals who are misguided rather than absolutely evil—and they need gentle chastisement and correction; once they can no longer be reformed, they are written out of the series. In the soaps, love is ennobled and marriage sanctified, and geared today to an adolescent audience.

One critic has observed that the messages in the soap operas are very simple—that learning is painful, growing is painful, loving is painful—indeed, perhaps the same message of Greek Tragedy. The stories tend to follow the Aristotelian dictates of a good plot, and provide "storylines and ambiance that reflect old-fashioned, down-home social values," gratify "childhood Oedipal fantasies" relating, for example, to good and bad mother figures, innocent heroines, and triumphant virtue—a world bordering on the fairy tale. It also has been pointed out that there is an attempt to avoid references to society's ills and even to avoid reference to the socio-economic system, unemployment, homelessness, and war. One prevailing characteristic is the idealization of the family and friendship, and the aggrandizement of the good father. This characteristic can be seen in the other popular entertainment form, the Sit-Com, which invariably presents the same idealized father, as the exemplary "Cosby". From "I Love Lucy" and "The Honeymooners" to "All in the Family," "Roseanne" and the "Simpsons", these dramas have celebrated an idealized—albeit dysfunctional—family in which love ultimately prevails among its conflicting members, even when the mother is madcap, and the father a bumpkin. The more recent Sit-Coms and even dramas like "ER", "NYPD", "Seinfeld" and "Friends" celebrate the ideal of friendship and *camaraderie* both within the workplace and without.

FATHER KNOWS BEST

The role of the father in the popular media is undergoing change. In the past he was the quiet hero of the Western film, like Roy Rogers, Gary Cooper, and of the television series, like Lorne Greene, or the consoling voice of Cosby, the quintessential Sit-Com father. Today these authority figures of bygone years are being replaced by the parental figures, the wise omniscient parents like Charlie Rose feeding our appetite for inside gossip and knowledge, and quizmasters like Alex Trebek, Regis Philbin, immaculately tailored, and dispensing great gifts of knowledge and wealth to the lucky few. Orwell thought that television would serve to institute the reign of Big Brother. Big Brother is indeed omnipresent on television, on talk shows, but particularly on Game Shows like *Jeopardy* and *Who Wants to be a Millionaire?* in which he is the source of never-ending bounty. Everyone hopes for a big brother as generous as Regis and Alex!

FROM CROONING TO ROCK

Rock, which derives from the popular music of the fifties, has been the dominant art form of the last half-century particularly among the young and unread. After the Second World War, we listened to Ol' Blue Eyes, Bing Crosby, Perry Como, Dean Martin on the radio, and Johnnie Ray "crying a river" over love. After that, the fantasies of love were captured in the throbbing, pulsating, vibrating rhythms of Rock music beginning with Elvis Presley through Ricky Martin and Britney Spears. The Rock star on MTV often is the antithesis of the paternal figures of contemporary television— the prodigal son, whose outfit, lifestyle and artistic expression evoke a challenge to the status quo.

Elvis was the original Rock star and created the romance of modern music. At the time, he was perceived in his famous pelvic gyrations as reflecting the mood of a sexual revolution. In retrospect, Elvis the Pelvis, was achieving in music what Henrik Ibsen, D.H. Lawrence, James Joyce, Pablo Picasso and others had achieved in literature and art. They all challenged repression, Victorian prudery, and bourgeois morality. Robert Pattison described the rocker as "a vulgar Don Juan, ceaselessly constituting himself out of the energy of his desire, and Kierkegaard was right that 'this energy, this power cannot be expressed in words, only music can give us a conception of it.'"[13]

The Beatles, who were greatly influenced by Elvis, brought a social statement into their work; but it was mainly the message of love that they expressed in such songs as "All You Need Is Love." As their career progressed, they became more involved with mystical experience and Christian love in songs with such titles as "Let It Be."

In the eighties, avant-garde groups like The Grateful Dead called up in their followers the wondrous medieval experience of ambivalence toward death in a celebratory rite, and the Sex Pistols provided a neo-conservative, anti-sex bias—together with a hys-

terical attack on the institutions of society. Love itself was sublimated almost beyond recognition.

FEMINISM AND MALE CHAUVINISM

Every generation has addressed itself to the needs, demands, and
exigencies of love, as has each individual, both thoughtfully and
thoughtlessly. Feminism certainly is not a new phenomenon. And
male chauvinism has been around just as long. Some experiences,
rooted in a particular culture and time, fall into desuetude. Polygamy, which received Biblical sanction, is no longer socially accepted, though still practiced in Muslim societies. Arranged marriages, which existed in many societies over thousands of years, are
becoming rare, though still practiced in India.

The principle of courtliness or *courtoisie* derives from the age of
chivalry where it was believed that the gentle hearted man would
earn the love and favor of his lady—and be motivated to virtuous
deeds. Though chivalry is not idealized today, as it was in the
middle ages, the term gentleman, and the ideal of his gentleness
still applies. Ladies still inspire gentlemen.

In like instance, the battle of the sexes has inspired, and continues to inspire, some of the most farfetched and elegant rhetoric.

THE WAR OF THE WORDS (1)

Ben Jonson, during the English Renaissance, lamented man's dependency upon his wife:

> If you love your wife, or rather dote on her, sir; O, how she'll
> torture you and take pleasure in your torments! You shall lie
> with her but when she lists; she will not hurt her beauty, her
> complexion; or it must be for that jewel or that pearl when
> she does; every half hour's pleasure must be bought anew,
> and with the same pain and charge you wooed her at first.
> *Epicene, or The Silent Woman*

Sir Thomas Browne longed for release from the necessity for such conjunction:

> I would be content that we might procreate like trees, without conjunction, or that there would be any way to perpetuate the World without this trivial and vulgar way of union; it is the foolishest act a wise man commits in all his life; nor is there any thing that will more deject his cooled imagination, when he shall consider what an odd and unworthy piece of folly he hath committed.
> *Religio Medici*

There was also the humorous attack on women in billingsgate:

> The love of woman and a bottle of wine
> Are sweet for a season and lost for all time.
>
> Husbands are in heaven whose wives chide not.

and:

> Wedlock is padlock.
> Age and wedlock bring a man to his nightcap.

and:

> Maids want nothing but husbands; and when they have them they want everything.
>
> Honest men marry soon; wise men not at all.

and:

> Women in mischief are wiser than men.
>
> A man of straw's worth a woman of gold.

and:

Women, wind, and fortune are always changing.

A ship and a woman are ever repairing.

Then there was the advice of the Earl of Northumberland to his son to be firm with women inasmuch as "women's only weapon is the sharpness of their tongues, for they can neither strike nor bite to any purpose." Moreover, "if they get their way they will be froward and perverse." Even Shakespeare was not above the verbal fray, though he usually presented women in a most sympathetic, even feminist light:

> Come on, come on: you are pictures out of doors,
> Bells in your parlours, wildcats in your kitchens,
> Saints in your injuries, devils being offended,
> Players in your housewifery, and housewives in your beds.
> *Othello*

During this period, when Queen Elizabeth occupied the throne and ruled with a gentle but firm hand, there was the vogue of the intellectual woman who was neither reticent in behavior nor ashamed to show her learning. When some men disdained these "ladies, that call themselves the Collegiates, an order between courtiers and countrymadams, that live from their husbands . . . cry down, or up, what they like or dislike in a brain or a fashion, with most masculine . . . authority," the ladies were ready for battle.

Ester Sowernam took up the cudgels in her pamphlet, *Ester Hath Hang'd Haman,* in defense of the virtue, dignity, and worthiness of women. Citing scripture and history, she attacked men for their idleness, lewdness, and inconstancy. When men responded with attacks on the "masculine-women," and argued that women were too manly in their dress and deportment, wore their hair too short, and were neglecting their families, the war heated up. A pamphlet was released under the title, *The Womanish Man, A Dialogue Between the Womanish Man and the Man Woman,* and argued

that men themselves followed fashions of outlandish dress. Moreover, it was a woman's prerogative to follow fancy and choose whatever style of life pleased her. Change was the order of nature—of
the day, of the seasons, of life itself—why should woman be cir-
cumscribed to men's narrowly defined limits? Simple creatures
enjoyed freedom—why should a woman not claim her rights?

Were women better suited to be rulers than men? Charles
Butler, an early naturalist who studied life among the bees, wrote
The Feminine Monarchie, or Historie of Bees.[14] He pointed to the
matriarchal structure of the colony. "For the drones are but vassals
to the Honey Bees; as they excel them in virtue and goodness; so
do they also in power and authority, ruling and over-ruling them
at their pleasure. For albeit, generally among all creatures, the male
is more worthy to master the female, yet in these, the Females have
preeminence and the Feminine gender is more worthy than the
masculine." Nevertheless he eschewed any hasty generalizations.
"He that made these to command their mates commanded them
to be commanded," and suggested alternatively that ladies imitate
the virtue, diligence, industry, chastity and discreet economy of
the female bees.

THE WAR OF THE WORDS (2)

Recent decades have seen the renewed ascendancy of feminist
thought. The descendants of Esther Sowernam are very much in
the forefront of contemporary writing (and on contemporary talk
shows) in defense of the rights of women and social justice. Nevertheless there are lighter moments. Just as in the nineteenth century, evangelical women attempting to reform the women of the
streets were not always successful, so the conflict continues today.
When in the seventies, the feminist movement attempted to establish a dialogue with the ladies in the street in Times Square,
New York City, one hooker screamed that the women's libbers

were jealous of the hold that they had on their husbands and on their boyfriends.

Feminist: You are a disgrace to our sex.

Prostitute: Bug off! You're ruining our action.

When Germaine Greer appeared on a panel at Town Hall, New York City, and invited questions from the audience, one gentleman raised his hand politely and was recognized:

"What is it that women's liberation seeks?" he asked.
"It isn't you honey," she scowled.

Nevertheless some women have shown shrewd humor in attacking the problem of male chauvinism. Phallic fallacy has romanticized anatomy, and many men have treated women as inferiors. Kate Millet wrote: "Lawrence, Miller, and Mailer identify woman as an annoying force to be put down and are concerned with a social order in which the female would be perfectly controlled." [15] Mary Ellman recalled the Marquis de Sade's glum censure: "I believe that the flesh of women, as the flesh of all female animals is necessarily inferior to the male species." She offered an apt comeuppance: "De Sade, of course, seems extraordinarily rude: one does not want to be eaten, but being eaten, one does not want to be thought an inferior dish." And then she conceived an imaginary interview with Hemingway.

"Herr Hemingway, can you sum up your feelings about death?"
"Yes! Just another whore." [16]

But clitoral calumny is really not more worthy than phallic fallacy. Germaine Greer observed: "If you think you are emancipated, you might consider the idea of tasting your menstrual blood—if it makes you sick, you've a long way to go, baby."[17] Kate Millet described the history of injustice against women, and argued that sex is the ultimate oppression: "The sex act is the festival of submission, also the ritual renewal of the feudal contract, whereby the vassal becomes the lord's liegeman." [18] And statements and manifestos abounded protesting that women are enslaved, that women must deny themselves to men, that God must be worshipped as a woman. Jill Johnston wrote in the *avant-garde* seventies:

> The title of this episode is new approach: All women are lesbians except those who don't know it naturally they are but don't know it yet I am a woman who is a lesbian because I am a woman who loves herself naturally who is other women is a lesbian . . . Verily, verily I say unto thee, except a woman be born again she cannot see the Kingdom of Goddess a woman must be born again to be herself her own eminence and grace the queen queenself. [19]

The tone is that of Moll Flanders; the feeling that of Molly Bloom. Shel Silverstein projected in his lyric "Liberated Lady, 1999" his view of the world after women have gained an end to sexual enslavement, job discrimination, control over their own bodies, day care help, and the Equal Rights Amendment:

> She's a liberated lady and she's lookin' out for herself
> And she don't need your protection and she doesn't need
>   your help
> And if you're lookin' for some pretty flower, you better go
>   look somewhere else,
> 'Cause I warn you, she's a liberated lady
>
> She got off work at the foundry she was feelin' kind of beat
> On the bus she had to stand up and let some fellah have her
>   seat
> And she pinched the ass of a guy who passed her walkin'
>   down the street
> When he called a cop, she didn't quite understand
>
> So she stopped off on the corner for her usual shot of rye

When some guy lit her cigarette she punched him in the eye
Then he kicked her in the balls, it was enough to make her
    cry
But she stood there and took it like a man

She's a liberated lady and she smokes them big cigars
You're gonna find her drinkin' boilermakers at the corner bar
And in thirty seconds she'll change a flat tire on your car
Look out—she's a liberated lady

She come home to find her darlin' husband cryin' in distress
She said "Why ain't supper ready and why is this house a
    mess?"
He said "The kids have drove me crazy and I need a brand
    new dress
And how come you don't ever take me dancin?"

She sat down to smoke her pipe and she thought back to the
    time
When she was satin, silk and lace with nothin' on her mind
But now she's gotta mow the lawn and pay the bills on time
And pray to Ms. God, she don't get draft

They got into bed that evening and she strapped her dildo
    on
She climbed on top of him and said "OK, let's get it on"
He said "you know I got my period and my headache isn't
    gone
And he fell asleep—the chauvinistic bastard . . .

But the last word surely belonged to Valerie Solanis who, having gained her notoriety by her attempted assassination of Andy
Warhol, earlier had cut to the heart of the matter in her manifesto
to the Society for Cutting Up Men (SCUM):

Life in this society being, at best, an utter bore, and no
aspect of society being at all relevant to women, there remains to civic-minded, responsible, thrill-seeking females
only to overthrow the government, eliminate the money
system, institute complete automation, and destroy the male
sex.[20]

HERESIES, DOGMAS AND SHIBBOLETHS

The heresies of yesteryear are the dogmas of today, and often the
shibboleths of tomorrow. So it has been with the two characteristic movements of our time: the sexual revolution and the feminist
movement. Hugh Hefner turned a Chicago adolescent's *bon mot*
about the presumed mating tendencies of the bunny rabbit into
Playboy, a magazine and then a cable network that provided a consciousness raising experience for Puritan America; and Gloria
Steinem with another *bon mot* marshaled the recognition due to
Ms America.

Both movements have succeeded in changing perceptions—
and both have grown from outrageous rebels to *grandes dames* of
American culture. When Bobby Riggs, the last "declared" male
chauvinist, was defeated by Billie Jean King on the artificial turf of
the Houston Astrodome in September 1973, the final bastion of
the male chauvinism was felled by the determination and vigor of
the feminist backhand. The seventies turned out to be a period of
education for men about the women's movement, just as the sixties had been a period of education for white society about the
injustice being perpetuated against Blacks.

The eighties saw a consolidation of positions and a reaction of
sorts. Legalized abortion, sex education and casual promiscuity
came under close scrutiny. The defeat of the Equal Rights Amendment, on the other hand, was a reaction on the part of women to
what were perceived as the excessive tendencies of radical feminism. Women were saying that they did not want to deny their
feminine natures or prerogatives. The Moral Majority further chal-

lenged the excesses of pornography, and the Meese commission restricted its distribution much to the consternation of defenders of the constitutional right of free speech. The Christian Broadcasting Networks urged a revival of traditional values—and sought to restore the sagging compliance with the seventh and other commandments. In response, Larry Flynt, proprietor and publisher of *Hustler*, became a leading muckraker for fairness and free speech.

These tendencies continued through to the end of the century. The new woman has declared herself a "heterosexual, ablebodied, American-born feminist .. focused .. on correcting the errors of omission and commission in sexology that pertained to women."[21] The rhetoric of reason was presented for example by Martha Nussbaum, in *Sex and Social Justice* (1999), a philosophical brief for the completion of items on the feminist agenda. It extended from America to the rest of the globe, and its objectives were improving conditions in the workplace, curtailing abusive relationships in which women were victimized, and particularly calling for termination of barbaric practices, principally outside the United States, of slavery and female genital mutilation.

Sarah Blaffer Hrdy, in a thorough, scholarly, anthropological study, *Mother Nature: A History of Mothers, Infants, and Natural Selection*, balances a woman's specific biological role of bearing, lactating, and nurturing the young and her modern role as a dual-career bread winner. She points out that during the Pleistocene period more than ten thousand years ago, "women could carry their babies as they foraged or gathered firewood." "The modern rub," she notes, is that the "factories, laboratories, and offices where women in post-industrial societies go to 'forage' are even less compatible with childcare than jaguar-infested forests and distant groves of mongongo nuts reached by trekking across desert."[22] Through all of this, better understanding of the conditions of all members of our society, men and women, boys and girls, perhaps has been gained. The pressure that adolescent women endure in their maturation process was the subject of Mary Pipher's *Reviving Ophelia, Saving the Selves of Adolescent Girls*(1994), and William Pollack showed the equally strenuous adjustment that adolescent boys undergo in *Real Boys* (1998). Susan Faludi in *Stiffed* presented a sympathetic study of the complexities of adult male adjustment, though warning those who have not accepted the changes that they are in danger of being left behind: "Today it is men who cling more tightly to their illusions. They would rather see themselves as battered by feminism than shaped by the larger culture. Feminism can be demonized as just an 'unnatural' force trying to wrest men's natural power and control from their grasp. Culture, by contrast, is the whole environment we live in; to acknowledge its sway is to admit that men never had the power they imagined."[23]

The Academy Awards of 1999 were given to films that educated and touched the consciousness of America. Both *American Beauty* and *Boys Don't Cry* earned accolades for their creators by dealing with neglected and controversial issues like homophobia, and abuse of women and children, and suggested that in the new century, progress needed to be made.

And so the pendulum shifts between repression and freedom, idealism and realism, equal rights and equal wrongs—"hither and thither, hither and thither," as James Joyce phrased the rhythm so well.

THE STORY OF LOVE

The story of love has occupied a central place in our culture and history from the myth of Adam and Eve and Indra and Maya to the latest Hollywood gossip. The record of these perceptions and observations about love has been recounted through the ages. What is truth itself but a particularly daring insight—or as Nietzsche opined, "illusions about which one has forgotten"—that may exist for an instant, or a century, or a millennium, or throughout the length of a culture or civilization. How long a truth survives perhaps doesn't matter because human begins are uniquely capable of dealing with it when it exists.

The story of love recounted in this book encompasses experiences from the discovery of love to the establishment of relationships, to their evolution into companionship or marriage, and often—sadly—to their termination. From Sappho to Jean-Paul Sartre, poets of love have been amorous adventurers. Literature is the account of these moments, and provides a historical record of these events. Some of the participants in the great love stories have been revered and worshipped; others have been reviled and repudiated. The range of experience has been from happiness and ecstasy to despair and death.

Love has encompassed the pure love of God, or Allah, or Krishna, or Buddha, the sacred love of the Virgin Mary, the flagrant sins of Sodom and Gomorrah, the anguished love of Dido, Christine de Pizan, John Donne, and Dorothy Parker, the jealous love of Medea and Mrs. Claire Zachanassian. Love has been treated graphically in the *Kama Sutra* and *Lady Chatterley's Lover*, bawdily in the works of Catullus, Petronius, Boccaccio and Rabelais. It treats the courtship and discovery of young love in *Romeo and Juliet*, and *Sons and Lovers,* and the flowering of mature love in the *Aeneid.* It describes idealized relationships between mothers and sons and fathers and daughters in the *Arabian Nights*, and the family from classical authors to James Joyce. It describes idealized marriage relationships from those of Prince Rama and his faithful wife Sati, to the great love stories of Shakespeare, to dysfunctional marriages described by Lady Murasaki, and Chaucer, and dramatized by Molière, T.S. Eliot, and Edward Albee.

Sexual desire has been interpreted in the *Dialogues* of Plato, Horaces's *Odes*, the *Essays* of Montaigne, and the writings of Simone de Beauvoir. Love has been idealized by St. Augustine, dichotomized by St. Thomas, symbolized by William Blake, and psychoanalyzed by Sigmund Freud. It has been codified by Andreas Capellanus, deprecated by Juvenal, glorified by Cervantes and Corneille. Joan of Arc was burned at the stake in 1431 for refusing

to wear garments befitting a woman. Sexual desire was the life of
Casanova, brought about the exile of Ovid, the emasculation of
Abelard, the incarceration of the Marquis de Sade and, in our own
recent past, led to the embarrassment and even political destruction of several high profile political and spiritual leaders who have
been caught in their indiscretions.

The story of love will not alleviate the frustration or pain of
the individual experience, though these pages abound with examples of perfect men, perfect women, and perfect relationships—
to which all can aspire. There are both valid insights and moral
guidance derived from a four thousand year tradition, which offer
a better understanding of how others have viewed and answered
the age-old love and marriage questions. The message and the styles
of some of these masters are not so well known. I am indebted to
the scholarship of Denis de Rougemont's *Love in the Western World*
and the historical analysis of sexual relations in studies by Michel
Foucault, the elegant history of the European tradition by Francesco
De Sanctis, as well as Camille Paglia's all-encompassing feminist
study, *Sexual Personae*, all contributing to an understanding of the
dimensions of that elusive "star to every wand'ring bark"; although
its "highth be taken," yet its "worth" can only, by you—gentle
reader—be known.

*Waiting for Godiva, A Guide for Thinking Women and Men to
the Story of Love* is not intended for dummies, but rather for thinking men and women. For some readers, it can provide a cultural
history that traces the theme of love from its beginnings in the
Middle East and the Orient—to Europe and America and the
modern world. For others, it can serve as a review of World Literature, which the inquisitive reader may peruse with pleasure; or
even a reading list in the now-neglected tradition of Great Books;
or for some of the new courses in gender studies, or sexology. This
survey is certainly not all-inclusive, and everyone will no doubt
have his or her own favorite author, style, and story.

Bearing H.L. Mencken's hortatory epigraph cited at the head
of this chapter, as well as the Delphic notation of my one-time

agent Joan Gilbert who had to return to her native England before the placement of the book—"to avoid clucking like a threatened or henpecked husband!" I have tried, and I begin with the ancient world.

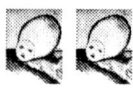

LOVE IN THE ANCIENT WORLD

And God blessed them, and God said unto them: Be fruitful, and multiply and replenish the earth.
Genesis

Apollo: And yet what tie is stronger, joined by Fate and
watched over by Justice, than the joy which Aphrodite has
given to man and woman?
Aeschylus

Jove decreed that virtue was to be in whatever brought us
pleasure.
Ovid

THE OLD TESTAMENT • THE FALLEN WOMAN • EARTHLY AND
HEAVENLY FATHERS • THE SANCTIFICATION OF LOVE • A SONG
OF LOVE

THE GREEKS • THE ILIAD • THE ODYSSEY • SAPPHO •
THE ORESTEIA • MEDEA • ARISTOPHANES • PLATONIC LOVE

THE ROMANS • CATULLUS • HORACE • VIRGIL • ROMAN WIVES
• THE ART OF LOVE • SATYRICON • JUVENAL • MEDITATIONS •
A NEW DAWN

THE OLD TESTAMENT

The myth of paradise in the first book of Genesis is an important source for the Hebrew attitude toward love and offers an early example of the Puritan approach to life. The suppression of sex is a result of the success of the prophets in purifying the religion of Yahweh-Elohim from the influences of the Canaanite tribes. Rather than being born through the uterus, Eve is derived from Adam's rib, denying carnality to the man's progenitors: "she shall be called Woman, because she was taken out of man."[24]

If sex existed in man's condition of blessedness—and there has been controversy on the question—it was not such as would be associated with sin. After the fall, sex is invoked as the curse that God calls down upon Eve, the evil brought into the world by the violation of God's commandment against knowledge: "I will greatly multiply thy sorrow and thy conception: in sorrow thou shalt bring forth children."

The Bible restricts most references to man's libidinous nature and indeed chastises men for possessing this instinct. When the Biblical view is set against other ancient practices, the extent of this denial can be understood. Among many primitive peoples, sex was extravagant in practice and elevated to religious ritual. The thrust of the early prophets was to reform man of these pagan practices as they imprecated evil upon the children of Israel for being impure and "whoring after other gods." Israel was God's wife; in fidelity, she was a virgin bride and had the responsibility to be morally righteous. For Israel to "lust" after another-to be immoral was to be impure-was infidelity and ingratitude, and this behavior incited the wrath of God.

The image of the faithless wife was invoked by the prophet Isaiah to illustrate the moral duplicity of the kingdom of Israel:

How is the faithful city become a harlot! It was full of judgement; righteousness lodged in it; but now murderers.
Isaiah 1:21

The sins and wrongs of the people are likened to pangs of child-birth:

> Like as a woman with child that draweth near the time of
> her delivery, is in pain, and crieth out in her pangs; so have
> we been in thy sight, O Lord.
> *Isaiah*, 26:17

God's mercy and love for his people is like the love of a groom for his bride:

> For as a young man marrieth a virgin, so shall thy sons marry
> thee: and as the bridegroom rejoiceth over the bride, so shall
> thy God rejoice over thee.
> *Isaiah*, 62:5

THE FALLEN WOMAN

The prophet Hosea took to wife an adulteress and harlot to illustrate the patience of God and the anguish of his love for Israel:

> Then said the Lord unto me, "Go yet, and love a woman
> beloved of her friend, yet an adulteress, according to the
> love of the Lord toward the children of Israel, who look to
> other gods, and love flagons of wine." So I brought her to
> me for fifteen pieces of silver, and for an homer of barley,
> and a half homer of barley. And I said unto her, "Thou shalt
> abide for me many days; thou shalt not play the harlot, and
> thou shalt not be for another man: so I will also be for thee."
> *Hosea* 3:1-2

The prophet Jeremiah speaks with God's voice as a husband to his wife:

> "Turn, O backsliding children," saith the Lord; "for I am
> married unto you."
> *Jeremiah* 3:14

Israel was meant to be beautiful and bountiful:

> I have likened the daughter of Zion to a comely and delicate
> woman. The shepherds with their flock shall come unto
> her; they shall pitch their tents against her round about;
> they shall feed everyone in his place.
> *Jeremiah* 6:2-3

But in her evil, Israel will be treated as a fallen woman:

> And when thou art spoiled, what wilt thou do? Though
> thou clothest thyself with crimson, though thy deckest thee
> with ornaments of gold, though thou rentest thy face with
> painting, in vain shalt thou make thyself fair; thy lovers will
> despise thee, they will seek thy life. For I have heard a voice
> as of a woman in travail, and the anguish as of her that
> bringeth forth her first child, the voice of the daughter of
> Zion, that bewaileth herself, that spreadeth her hand say-
> ing, woe is me now! For my soul is wearied because of mur-
> derers.
> *Jeremiah* 4:30-31

Because of the sins of Israel, Jeremiah prophesies the destruction
of Jerusalem:

> And I will make this city desolate, and a hissing; everyone
> that passeth thereby shall be astonished and hiss because of
> all the plagues thereof. And I will cause them to eat the flesh
> of their sons and the flesh of their daughters, and they shall
> eat every one the flesh of his friend in the siege and strait-
> ness, wherewith their enemies, and they that seek their lives,
> shall straighten them.
> *Jeremiah* 19:8-9

The prophecy is fulfilled. Jerusalem is ravaged by the armies of
Nebuchadnezzar, and the temple is destroyed. The poet laments
the devastation, likening the city now to a lonely widow:

> How doth the city sit solitary, that was full of people! How
> is she become as a widow! She that was great among the
> nations, and princess among the provinces, how is she be-
> come a tributary! She weepeth sore in the night, and her
> tears are on her cheeks: among all her lovers she hath none to
> comfort her: all her friends have dealt treacherously with
> her, they are become her enemies.
> *Lamentations* 1:1-2

The didactic attitude prevails throughout the Old Testament, teaching man to serve God rather than his instincts. The patriarchs
married more than one woman; but as with Jacob, the purpose of
sex exclusively was the begetting of many children and strengthening the tribe. Only the kings enjoyed complete license, as the
prophet Samuel warned they would. (*I Samuel*, 8:11-18). David
proved to be unfaithful to God in pursuing his lust. And the excesses of Solomon and his heirs led to internecine strife and even to
the dissolution of the kingdom. The Preacher foreswore earthly
pursuits as "vanity of vanities" and turned rather to the wisdom of
fearing God and keeping his commandments.

EARTHLY AND HEAVENLY FATHERS

The competition for the love and favor of earthly fathers and the
Heavenly Father often undermines the family bond. When the
Lord accused Adam of having sinned, the first husband blamed
his wife for having tempted him. "The woman whom thou gavest
to be with me, she gave me of the tree, and I did eat." Cain slew
his brother Abel when the Lord accepted Abel's offering and rejected Cain's gift.

> And the Lord said unto Cain, "Where is Abel thy brother?"
> And he said, "I know not: Am I my brother's keeper?" And
> He said, "What hast thou done? The voice of thy brother's
> blood crieth unto me from the ground. And now art thou
> cursed from the earth, which hath opened her mouth to
> receive thy brother's blood from thy hand."
> *Genesis* 4:9-11

The rivalry of brothers is a recurrent theme in the Old Testament. Esau and Jacob engaged in conflict even within Rebecca's womb:

> And the children struggled together within her; and she said, "If it be so, why am I thus?" And she went to inquire of the Lord. And the Lord said unto her, "two nations are in thy womb, and two manners of people shall be separated from thy bowels; and the one people shall be stronger than the other people; and the elder shall serve the younger."
> *Genesis* 25:22-23

The boys develop in different ways, Esau becoming a cunning hunter and Jacob remaining at home, a plain man. The father favored Esau, and the mother Jacob. Jacob persuades his brother to sell his birthright for a meal of red pottage when Esau returns from the hunt tired and hungry. The time for the blessing comes, and Isaac sends Esau to bring him some venison; but Rebecca commands her son Jacob to deceive his blind father by dressing in Esau's raiment to receive the blessing intended for the eldest:

> And Rebecca took goodly raiment of her eldest son Esau, which were with her in the house, and put them upon Jacob her younger son. And he come unto his father, and said, "my father": and he said, "Here am I." "Who are thou, my son?" And Jacob said unto his father, "I am Esau, thy firstborn." And Jacob went near unto Isaac his father; and he felt him, and said, "The voice is Jacob's voice but the hands are the hands of Esau."
> *Genesis* 27:15ff

The blessing was given to Jacob.

Joseph is another younger brother who loses favor with his brothers because of the preference shown to him by his father and his own dreams of supremacy. When Joseph is caught alone in the fields, his brothers seek their revenge:

> And when they saw him afar off, even before he came near unto them, they conspired against him to slay him. And they said to one another, "Behold this dreamer cometh. Come now therefore, and let us slay him, and cast him into some pit," and we will say, "Some evil Beast hath devoured him: and we shall see what will become of his dreams."
> *Genesis* 37:18-20

Joseph is, at first, cast into a pit to die, and then sold to a tribe of Midianite merchants:

> And they took Joseph's coat, and killed a kid of the goats, and dipped the coat in blood; and they sent the coat of many colors, and they brought it to their father; and said, "This we have found; and know not whether it be thy son's coat or no." And he knew it, and said, "It is my son's coat; an evil beast hath devoured him; Joseph is without doubt rent in pieces." And Jacob rent his clothes, and put sackcloth upon his loins, and mourned for his son many days.
> *Genesis* 37:31-34

The ultimate filial loyalty is to God, the Father, and even man's lust must be ordered according to God's law. The Old Testament perhaps does not elevate the virtue of chastity to the same degree, as does the New Testament; but it certainly constricts the sexual instinct. The ritual of circumcision is an offering to the Lord, and the basis of the holy covenant. And Joseph most clearly exemplifies the ideal of restraint when he rebuffs the advances of the wife of his master, Potiphar, in Egypt.

> And it came to pass after these things, that his master's wife cast her eyes upon Joseph; and she said, "Lie with me." But he refused, and said unto his master's wife, "Behold, my master wotteth not what is with me in the house, and he hath committed all that he hath to my hand; there is none greater in this house; neither hath he kept back anything from me but thee, because thou art his wife: how then can I do this great wickedness, and sin against God?"
> *Genesis* 39:7-9

The wife revenges herself upon Joseph by seizing his garment and accusing him before her husband of having mocked her virtue. Joseph is placed in prison, where eventually his suffering is vindicated, and he serves Pharaoh and his own people.

THE OEDIPAL TEST

The Oedipal test to supercede the father also occurs in the Bible. Noah's sons, Aaron's sons, and David's son, Absalom, all rebel against their parents. Abram leaves his home in order to serve God's will and is given the name Abraham for his faith. In time he himself becomes the harsh father who is prepared to sacrifice his own son, Isaac, to God. Moses rejects his adopted home when he receives the calling from the Burning Bush. The patriarchs, Moses, Saul, and David make the transition from arrogant rebels to stern (even vindictive) parent and judges. Jephthah actually offers his daughter to satisfy his vow to God that he would sacrifice the first person to greet him after his battle victory. The son is adjured to respect his father and Isaiah prophesies the coming of the Messianic age with the birth of a child, and Malachi admonishes the necessity for reconciliation of father and son in the golden age. "And he shall turn the heart of fathers to the children, and the heart of children to their fathers, lest I come and smite the earth with a curse."

BIBLICAL HEROINES

Though limited by the didactic purposes of the Bible, romance also exists. Abraham sends his eldest servant of the house to seek a wife for his son. And the servant finds a woman who is industrious, kind, and fair to look upon, a virgin. The servant brings Rebecca back to his master:

> And Isaac went out to meditate in the field at the eventide:
> and he lifted up his eyes, and saw, and behold, the camels
> were coming. And Rebecca lifted up her eyes, and when she
> saw Isaac, she lighted off the camel. For she said unto the
> servant, "What man is this that walketh in the field to meet
> us?" And the servant had said, "It is my master": therefore
> she took a veil, and covered herself. And the servant told
> Isaac all things that he had done. And Isaac brought her into
> his mother Sarah's tent, and he took Rebecca, and she be-
> came his wife; and he loved her: and Isaac was comforted
> after his mother's death.
> *Genesis* 24:63-67

Later Jacob, Isaac's son, returns to the home of Rebecca's brother
to seek his fortune. He meets his two cousins, Leah and Rachel,
and he falls in love with Rachel. He presents his suit to his uncle,
Laban:

> And Jacob loved Rachel; and said, "I will serve thee seven
> years for Rachel thy younger daughter." And Laban said, "It
> is better that I give her to thee, than that I should give her to
> another man: abide with me." And Jacob served seven years
> for Rachel; and they seemed unto him but a few days, for
> the love he had to her.
> *Genesis* 29:18-20

But at the end of the tenure of his service, Laban substitutes the
elder daughter Leah for the bride for whom Jacob had indentured
himself. And so Jacob serves yet another seven years for the woman
he loves.

Leah and Rachel bear Jacob many children, and they become
the ancestors of the children of Israel (the name God bestowed
upon Jacob). Later in the Bible, the sister of Moses cares for him
and saves him from the edict of death invoked by the Egyptian
Pharaoh upon the first born of the Hebrews. After the children of
Israel are led across the Red Sea, it is Miriam, now known along
with her brothers as a prophetess, who leads the song of Thanks-
giving:

> And Miriam the prophetess, the sister of Aaron, took a timbrel in her hand; and all the women went out after her with timbrels and with dances. And Miriam answered them, "Sing ye unto the Lord, for he hath triumphed gloriously; the horse and his rider he hath thrown into the sea."
> *Exodus* 15:20-21

After reaching the Promised Land, the Israelites reclaim the land that was assured to them in the covenant between God and Abraham: "And I will give unto thee, and to thy seed after thee, the land wherein thou art a stranger, all the land of Canaan for an everlasting possession, and I will be your God." Now among the Judges of Israel there was Deborah the prophetess, and she called upon the warrior Barak to lead Israel against her enemies; and she accompanied him, and Sisera was defeated; and Sisera escaped to the tent of Jael, where he sought refuge:

> Then Jael, Heber's wife, took a nail of the tent, and took a hammer in her hand, and went softly unto him, and smote the nail into his temples, and fastened it into the ground; for he was fast asleep and weary. So he died.
> *Judges* 4:21

The *Book of Ruth* and the *Book of Esther* are moving romances of women who, through the mystique of their femininity, cast a spell of virtue on their men. Ruth, a poor, widowed proselyte, pursues and marries Boaz, a wealthy landowner and becomes landowner to the royal house of King David. Esther marries the Persian King Ahasuerus and saves her people from the malevolent schemes of his evil-counselor, Haman. The stalwart woman of virtue had her place in legend and history.

SEDUCTRESSES

The other kind of woman in the Bible is the seductress who uses her sexual power over man for evil purposes. Woman as a creature of lust is considered a bane to man, as for example Lot's daughters; Delilah who betrays Samson to his enemies; Bathsheba and Jezebel, both of whom use their power over their husbands for selfish ends. Their examples again serve to illustrate the need for woman, no less than man, to curtail her libidinous nature.

> And I find more bitter than death the woman, whose heart is snares and nets, and her hands as bands: whoso pleaseth God shall escape from her; but the sinner shall be taken by her.
> *Ecclesiastes* 7:26

THE VIRTUOUS WOMAN

The virtuous wife is the image of woman that receives the highest praise in the Bible. Michal saves her husband, David, from the wrath of her father, Saul. The wives of the patriarchs are faithful helpmates to their husbands-even though they often maintain their individuality and point of view. Eve's punishment for sin was that woman's "desire shall be to thy husband and he shall rule over thee." But the Lord also commands Abraham: "In all that Sarah hath said unto thee, hearken unto her voice." The virtuous wife is praised in Proverbs as ministering to the needs of her family and being a pride to her husband "known in the gates when he sitteth among the elders of the land." The implication is that a man will receive credit for his wife's good reputation.

> Who can find a virtuous woman? For her price is far above rubies. The heart of her husband doth safely trust in her, so that he shall have no need of spoil. She will do him good and not evil all the days of her life. Strength and honor are her clothing; and she shall rejoice in time to come. She

openeth her mouth with wisdom; and in her tongue is the
law of kindness.
Proverbs 31:10ff

The *Book of Proverbs* contrasts the good and the bad wife: "A virtuous woman is a crown to her husband: but she that maketh ashamed
is as rottenness in his bones." Furthermore: "Houses and riches are
the inheritance of fathers: and a prudent wife is from the Lord."
Living with a shrew is the deadly bane: "It is better to dwell in the
corner of the housetop, than with a brawling woman in a wide
house." And also: "It is better to dwell in the wilderness than with
a contentious and angry woman." And then again: "A foolish woman
is clamorous: she is simple and knoweth nothing."

THE SANCTIFICATION OF LOVE

The Bible maintains the responsibility of the man for treatment of
a woman. The law reads: "And if a man entice a maid that is not
betrothed, and lie with her, he shall surely endow her to be his
wife. If her father utterly refuse to give her unto him, he shall pay
money according to the dowry of virgins."

The injunction against adultery is severe and repeated even in
two of the Ten Commandments. The law establishes the proce-
dure for testing an adulteress. If a man is jealous of his wife and
thinks that she has been unfaithful, he must bring her to the priest
and make a burnt offering. The priest takes the holy water and
mixes it with dust on the floor of the tabernacle and gives it to the
woman. He offers a curse that if she has defiled her husband the
water will turn poison and the woman will grow sick. She drinks
the brew; if she does not become sick, then she is not guilty. The
husband must then make a jealous offering and receive his wife as
innocent.

The sanctification of the Children of Israel consists in their
separateness from other nations, and their own self-restraint, as is
made clear in *Leviticus*:

And I will set my face against that man, and will cut him off from among his people; because he hath given of his seed unto Moloch, to defile my sanctuary, and to profane my holy name . . . Sanctify yourselves therefore, and be ye holy: for I am the Lord your God. The man that committeth adultery with another man's wife, even he that committeth adultery with his neighbor's wife, the adulterer and the adulteress shall surely be put to death. And the man that lieth with his father's wife hath uncovered his father's nakedness: both of them shall surely be put to death; their blood shall be upon them. And if a man also lie with mankind, as he lieth with a woman, both of them have committed an abomination: they shall surely be put to death; their blood shall be upon them . . . And if a man lie with a beast, he shall surely be put to death; and ye shall slay the beast. Ye shall therefore keep all my statutes, and all my judgements, and do them: that the land, whither I bring you to dwell therein, spue you not out. And ye shall not walk in the manners of the nation, which I cast out before you: for they committed all these things, and therefore I abhorred them. But I have said unto you, Ye shall inherit their land, and I will give it to unto you to possess it, a land that floweth with milk and honey: I am the Lord your God, which have separated you from other people.
Leviticus 20:3ff

A SONG OF LOVE

Despite the emphasis upon those qualities of prudence, wisdom, restraint, chastity, the avoidance of the snares of evil, a single poem survives that expresses of the feeling of libidinal joy. The *Song of Songs* has been studied as an allegory of God's love for his people. But the naturalness of expression, the glorification of physical love between the rose of Sharon, a Black woman, and her lover suggests erotic lyricism that is absent in the Old Testament but quite consistent with expression of similar sentiment found in other literatures. Here there is found a grand celebration of the mysterious and divine beauty of sexual love:

> Let him kiss me with the kisses of his mouth: for thy love is better than wine . . . Look not upon me, because I am black, because the sun hath looked upon me: my mother's children were angry with me; they made me keeper of vineyards, but mine own vineyard have I not kept . . . Behold, thou art fair, my love; behold, thou art fair; thou hast dove's eyes . . . I am the rose of Sharon, and the lily of the valleys . . . I charge you, O ye daughters of Jerusalem, by the roes, and by the hinds of the field, that ye stir not up, nor awake my love, till he please. The voice of my beloved . . . behold, he standeth behind our wall, he looketh forth at the windows, showing himself through the lattice. My beloved spake, and said unto me, "Rise up, my love, my fair one, and come away. For lo, the winter is past, the rain is over and gone; the flowers appear on the earth, the time of the singing birds is come, and the voice of the turtle is heard in the land." . . . I am my beloved's, and his desire is toward me. Come, my beloved, let us go forth in the field; let us lodge in the villages.
>
> *Song of Songs*

THE GREEKS

Sexuality, for the Greeks, was a divine, powerful, and violent force in the universe that exercised an irrational influence on mortals and even on the gods. Greek philosophy taught that the force of Love (Eros) was in contention with the force of Chaos, and Eros was the bond of harmony that held the world together. Eros was necessary concomitant to human happiness.

The Oedipal drive of the son to supplant the father and take his place was seen in the myth of the generations of war among the gods. After Uranus fathered the Titans upon Mother Earth, he was overthrown by his rebellious sons, and Kronos, the youngest of the seven sons, castrated his father with a flint sickle. In turn Kronos was overthrown by his son Zeus, and the Olympian generation of gods established sway over the world.

All creative power was divine, and love itself was divine madness. Aphrodite was the goddess of love, and her son Cupid wielded the arrows that afflicted the victim with the madness. The sexual nature of man overcame his reason and brought him both happiness and misery. Lord Zeus survives in legend and myth as a pursuer of woman, both goddess and mortal, and his amours were a source of continuing jealousy to his wife Hera. In one story, he approached the lovely mortal Leda in the guise of a white swan while she was bathing, and took her. In another, he came to the mortal Alcmena, in the form of her husband, after having summoned Amphitryon away; then he extended the span of the night. Hera sought revenge on anyone who gained her husband's favor; and, for instance, she drove Zeus's paramour, Io, aimlessly around the world pursued by a gadfly. The gods had occasion and opportunity for schemes and counter-schemes. Hephaestus, lame husband of Aphrodite, watched with humiliation while his wife carried on a shameless affair with Ares, the god of war: for this, he earned the reputation as the patron of cuckolds. In revenge, the cunning craftsman constructed a net in which he entrapped his wife with her paramour in the act of intercourse, and vengefully brought the entwined couple to be witnessed by the Olympian family. Thus pornography had its auspicious beginning. The Olympian gods once argued the question of who derived greater pleasure from the sex act. The prophet Teiresias was asked to judge the matter, and he declared that a woman's ecstasy was greater than that of a man. In a feminist rage, Hera blinded him for saying, or knowing, too much.

Pandora, the first woman, was led by curiosity to remove the lid from a jar that her husband possessed, and she loosed all the evils and plagues that confound man. In the *Theogony*, Hesiod compared women's sting to that of mischievous bees: "even so Zeus who thunders on high made woman to be an evil to mortal men, with a nature to do evil. And he gave them a second evil to be the price for the good they had: whoever avoids marriage and the sorrows that women cause, and will not wed, reaches deadly old age without anyone to tend his years, and though he at least has no lack of livelihood while he lives, yet, when he is dead, his kinsfolk divide his possessions amongst them."[25]

THE ILIAD

The Iliad depicts man's heroism in war. The Homeric poem celebrates the social virtues of courage, honor, respect for the gods, reason, and patriotism. The Trojan War was fought to restore Helen to her husband after she had been abducted by Paris from Greece and brought to Troy. Menelaus called upon his brother Agamemnon to lead an expeditionary force across the sea to avenge his dishonor. For nine years the battle was fought to a standoff; but in the tenth year, the Greeks defeated the Trojans, and Menelaus reclaimed his wife.

Hector was a worthy antagonist. Though not responsible for the actions of his brother Paris, he nevertheless was required to defend his homeland from the Greek armies. Perhaps he is the real hero of the *Iliad*, as he accepts his unjust fate courageously and without contumely. He must sacrifice his life for a woman he does not respect while his brother refuses even to assume responsibility for the war he has caused. Such is the irony of Fate!

When first his mother Hecuba, and then his wife try to dissuade him from venturing into battle, Hector insists that he must go. The most moving scene in the *Iliad*, verbally painted with vivid detail and emotion, shows Hector meeting with his wife and his infant son. Andromache argues, and then admonishes her husband for choosing death and leaving her to endure the greater suffering, in being widowed and becoming a prize of war. Though the poem glorifies the virtues of war, there is the underlying theme-that it is less cruel to the dying warriors than to the hapless survivors. As Hector looks with pride at his infant son, Astyanax, she pleads with him to stay his own execution:

> Hector smiled in silence as he looked on his son, but she Andromache, stood close beside him, letting her tears fall and clung to his hand and called him by name and spoke to him: "Dearest, your own great strength will be your death, and you have no pity on your little son, nor on me, ill-starred, who soon must be your widow."
> Book VI, 404-410[26]

Reminding him that Achilles slew her father and brought about the death of her seven brothers as well as her mother, she begs him not to go to certain death. Hector knows that his death is imminent and her captivity will be a disgrace, but he turns a deaf ear to her woeful pleas. His manhood, his self-worth and duty, all compel him to face his fate.

> So speaking, he set his child again in the arms of his beloved wife, who took him back again to her fragrant bosom smiling in her tears; and her husband saw, and took pity on her, and stroked her with his hand, and called her by name and spoke to her:

> "Poor Andromache! Why does your heart sorrow so much for me? No man is going to hurl me to Hades, unless it is fated, but as for fate, I think that no man yet has escaped it once it has taken its first form, neither brave man nor coward. Go therefore back to our house, and take up your own work, the loom and the distaff, and see to it that your handmaidens ply their work also; but the men must see to the fighting, all men who are the people of Ilion, and I beyond others."

> So glorious Hector spoke and again took up the helmet with its crest of horse-hair, while his beloved wife went home-

ward, turning to look back on the way, letting the live tears fall. And as she came in speed into the well-settled house-hold of Hector the slayer of men, she found numbers of handmaidens within, and her coming stirred all of them into lamentation. So they mourned in his house over Hector while he was living still, for they thought he would never again come back from the fighting alive, escaping Achaian hands and their violence.
Book VI, 482-502

The ending occurs as had been foretold: the heroic husband, father, and general perishes bravely in battle. The *Iliad* culminates with a hero's burial upon a fiery pyre:

They piled up the grave-barrow and went away, and thereafter assembled in a fair gathering and held a glorious feast within the house of Priam, king under God's hand. Such was their burial of Hector, breaker of horses.
Book XXIV, 801-804

THE ODYSSEY

The *Odyssey* glorifies the virtues of hearth and home, just as the *Iliad* had glorified martial heroism. The epic relates the efforts of Odysseus to return to his family, who eagerly anticipate his return from battle and the long journey home. Homer tells of his wondrous adventures and his shrewd cunning in meeting the tests that life has set for him. His wife, Penelope, and his son, Telemachus, never lose hope that the head of the household will return when the gods see fit to aid his endeavors. The poem tells of the search for love—the love of a son for his father, a wife for her husband, a man for his home. The poet perceives the human dimension of the family bond:

What a dear welcome thing life seems to children
whose father, in the extremity, recovers
after some weakening and malignant illness:

his pangs are gone, the gods have delivered him.
Book V, 394-397)[27]

Telemachus begins his desperate search, instructed by the goddess Athena. He visits far-away lands and people to learn the whereabouts of his missing father, questions many. When he learns that his father is still alive, the son returns home to await him. Penelope's task is more harrowing. Pressed by her suitors to choose a successor to her husband, she prevaricates, stalls, lies, and puts them off with unfulfilled promises. She declares that she will make up her mind after she finishes weaving a shroud for her father-in-law. But in the evening, she undoes the work that she has completed during the day.

Odysseus is diverted by the whim and anger of unfriendly gods. In the course of his wanderings, he enjoys the generous bounty of the beautiful nymph, Calypso, on the cavernous island of Ogygia. Though he experiences the rare happiness afforded a mortal of enjoying the love and friendship of a goddess, he longs for his own wife; and Lord Zeus, through the messenger, Hermes, finally allows his departure.

Now he comes to the shore of the land of the Phaeacians after his boat has been wrecked in a storm, and even his clothes have been torn by the sea from his body. The goddess Athena has arranged to have to royal princess and her maidens—who have removed to the shore to tend to their laundry—on hand to receive him. The scene, rich with tragic overtones, is not without humor, as the unclothed Odysseus approaches the nubile maidens, protected from his nakedness by an olive branch. He presents his plea on his knees before the princess, and Nausicaa looks benignly upon him and offers to help. Later after relating his sorrows to the royal family, he is aided in constructing a ship that will take him home.

At home, he faces a bleak welcome. Ravaged and unrecognizable, he comes as a beggar to unhouse the guests who have occupied his home. He shows his reputed prowess when he daringly demonstrates that he can string the bow. He then turns his taut weapon on those who have usurped his place, and declares that he is Odysseus and has come to take revenge upon them.

But after this feat, he still confronts the toil of a doubting wife. She commands: if the man who claims to be her husband really is her husband, let him remove his bed from their chamber. The fond husband perceives the test, and reminds his loving wife that her wish cannot be fulfilled, since the husband himself built the bed into a tree trunk in the chamber. Only the true Odysseus could have been privy to such knowledge. Penelope now knows that he has returned, and begs pardon for her seeming restraint at the reunion with her long-absent bed-companion and sharer of life's hardships and misfortunes. The twenty years separation now takes its emotional toll on the weary traveler who has suffered and learned much in crossing the sea:

> Now from his breast into his eyes the ache
> of longing mounted, and he wept at last,
> his dear wife, clear and faithful, in his arms,
> longed for as the sun-warmed earth is longed for by a
> swimmer spent in rough waters where his ship went down
> under Poseidon's blows, gale winds and tons of sea.
> Book XXIII, 231-236

Through sharing love, mortals are permitted the joy of the gods, a fitting reconciliation for a man and his wife:

> The royal pair mingled in love again and afterwards lay
> reveling in stories: hers of the siege her beauty stood at home
> from arrogant suitors, crowding on her sight and how they
> fed their courtship on his cattle, oxen and fat sheep, and
> drank up rivers of wine out of the vats.
>
> Odysseus told of what hard blows he had dealt out to oth-
> ers, and of what blows he had taken—all that story. She
> could not close her eyes till all was told.
> Book XXIII, 301-310

SAPPHO

The poetess, Sappho, who lived on the isle of Lesbos, about the sixth century B.C., also celebrated erotic passion in her poetry. Of an aristocratic family, she is reputed to have been married and to have had a child. A dubious legend is that she committed suicide out of love for the youth Phaon. The fragments that survive deal exclusively with the power of love:

> Desire has shaken my mind
> As wind in the mountain forests
> Roars through the trees.

Her style is realistic, as she evokes the commingling joy and grief in love.

> He seems to be a god, that man
> Facing you, who leans to be close,
> Smiles, and, alert and glad, listens,
> To your mellow voice.
>
> And quickens in love at your laughter.
> That stings my breasts, jolts my heart
> If I dare the shock of a glance.
> I cannot speak,
>
> My tongue sticks to my dry mouth,
> Thin fire spreads beneath my skin,
> My eyes cannot see and my aching ears
> Roar in their labyrinths.
>
> Chill sweat slides down my body,
> I shake, I turn greener than grass
> I am neither living nor dead and cry
> From the narrow betweens.
>
> But endure, even this grief of love.[28]

She enunciates love between women as well as love between man and woman. Her "Ode to Aphrodite" is the most polished work that survives and may have been written for Phaon:

> Guile-weaving child of Zeus, who art
> Immortal, throned in radiance, spare,
> O Queen of Love, to break my heart
>   With grief and care.
>
> But hither come, as thou of old,
> When my voice reached thine ear afar,
> Didst leave thy father's hall of gold,
>   And yoke they car,
>
> And through mid air their whirring ring
> Thy bonny doves did swiftly ply
> O'er the dark earth, and thee did bring
>   Down from the sky.
>
> Right soon they came, and thou, blest Queen,
> A smile upon thy face divine,
> Didst ask what ail'd me, what might mean
>   That call of mine.
>
> "What would'st thou have, with heart on fire,
> Sappho?" thou saidst. "Whom pray'st thou me
> To win for thee to fond desire?
>   Who wrongeth thee?
>
> Soon shall he seek, who now doth shun;
> Who scorns thy gifts, shall gifts bestow;
> Who loves thee not, shall love anon
> Wilt thou or no."
>   So come thou now, and set me free
> From carking cares; bring to full end
> My heart's desire; thyself O be
>   My stay and friend! [29]

Sappho's poetic treatment of love is by no means typical in Greek literature. Love between the unmarried and the romance that precedes marriage are not idealized. True love, for the Greek, derived from the marriage bed; it was based on friendship and the sense of mutual dependency—ripened through association and understanding. This love both was sanctioned and was exemplified by the Olympian immortals.

THE ORESTEIA

The respect for the marriage bond is as a sacred duty was a prominent theme in the Greek drama of the Golden Age. The fifth century tragedians, Aeschylus, Sophocles and Euripides, all treated the story of the infidelity of Agamemnon's wife, and the restoration of justice by the son Orestes. In contrast to the love and patience that Penelope demonstrated for Odysseus, Clytemnestra took Aegisthos as her lover while Agamemnon was away in the war. The marriage bond was necessary to the continuity of the aristocratic family line. Its rupture was a most serious crime.

Lord Zeus himself reflected on this circumstance and blamed man, rather than the gods, for bringing about their own disasters. The crime of Aegisthos and Clytemnestra was used as an illustration of man's fatal weaknesses:

> "My word, how mortals take the gods to task!
> All their afflictions come from us, we hear.
> And what of their own failings? Greed and folly
> double the suffering in the lot of man.
> See how Aegisthos, for his double portion,
> stole Agamemnon's wife and killed the soldier
> on his homecoming day. And yet Aegisthos
> knew that his own doom lay in this. We gods
> had warned him, sent down Hermes Argeiphontes,
> our most observant courier, to say:
> "Don't kill the man, don't touch his wife,
> or face a reckoning with Orestes
> the day he comes of age and wants his patrimony."
> Friendly advice-but would Aegisthos take it?
> Now he has paid the reckoning in full."
> *Odyssey.* I. 37-51

The *Oresteia,* by Aeschylus, is the only complete treatment of the legend that survives. The three plays, *Agamemnon, Choephoroe (The Libation Bearers),* and *Eumenides (The Furies)* are a theological pageant of crime and punishment. The slaying of Agamemnon starts a chain reaction of murder that does not end until the gods intervene to stop the killing. In the first play, Clytemnestra receives her husband with the feigned loyalty of a wife who has waited hopefully for her husband's return from war:

> What day is so sweet
> In a woman's life as when she opens the door
> To her beloved, safe home from war? [30]

But after rolling out the purple carpet, she deceitfully and ruthlessly slays him. Justifying her action, she maintains that she has harbored hatred for him because he murdered their daughter, Iphigenia, at the outset of the expedition to Troy, in order to assure divine favor. Aegisthos, her lover, at her side, also delights in the culmination of his own revenge for an age-old feud between their families and in his assumption of Agamemnon's throne.

> But now, I'll try my hand at monarchy, and all
> who disobey me shall be put in irons
> and starved of food until they submit.

Crime breeds crime, and injustice injustice. There can be no salvation for the state until the evil has been purged, the tyrant removed. In the *Choephoroe,* Orestes returns to Argos, upon the instructions of Apollo, and together with his sister, Electra, conspire to slay and depose the usurper. The mother too must be slain according to Apollo's order.

> Clytemnestra: I brought you up-let me grow old with you!

> Orestes: What, live with you, my father's murderess!

Clytemnestra: Fate had a hand, my son, in your father's end.

Orestes: Yes, the same fate which now decrees your own.

Clytemnestra: Have you no dread of a mother's curse, my child? . . . Beware of the hellhounds of a mother's curse! . . . Ah me, I gave birth to a snake and not a son.

After the dreadful deed, Orestes is pursued by the Furies. The hounds of a mother's curse, wearing filthy rags, dripping ooze from their eyes, bearing the smell of blood in their breath, pursue the matricide. After wandering for a year to expiate his crime, Orestes returns to Delphi to face his accusers in the third play of the trilogy, *Eumenides*. The case is brought to trial. Apollo himself defends Orestes, and he maintains the justice of the son's action because of the violation done by Clytemnestra to the sanctity of the marriage bed.

> And yet what tie is stronger, joined by Fate
> and watched over By Justice, than the joy which
> Aphrodite has given to man and woman?

Athena, the patron goddess of Athens, casts the tie breaking vote after the twelve man jury is split on the decision, and she vindicates Orestes. The law is the will of Zeus, a religious duty. The obligation to revenge the violation of the murderer of a father is greater than the filial obligation to a mother. The furies accept the divine decision, and become neutralized as *erinyes*, friendly spirits. The grim lesson is not necessarily that paternity claims a greater loyalty than maternity, but that the marriage bed possesses the highest sanctity.

MEDEA

Medea treats the marriage question in one of the most ardently feminist plays ever written. It can be seen as an attack on the double standard that holds men less accountable than woman for infidelity. Euripides depicts the human and psychological perspective in the trial and revenge of the wronged wife. Jason abandons Medea after she had helped him in his quest for the golden fleece, betrayed her family, killed her brother, and left her homeland. She married him, bore him sons, and lived as an émigré in Greece. But Jason announces his decision to leave her in order to marry the daughter of the king of Corinth. With duplicitous sophistry, he insists that his action is best for her and for the children since he is marrying so well.

Medea's love for her husband turns to bile as she reflects on his mistreatment of her.

> For though a woman is
> Timid in everything else, and weak, and
> Terrified at the sight of a sword: still:
> When things go wrong in this thing of love,
> No heart is so fearless as a woman's;
> No heart is so filled with the thought of blood.
> ll. 337-342

She laments the injustice-with the outrage and helplessness of a woman whose love and innocence has been betrayed-and she perceives the waste of her life. There could be no more despicable wrong than his behavior towards her:

> There was one man through which I came to see
> The world's whole beauty: and that
> Was my husband; and he has turned out
> Utterly evil. O women, of all creatures
> That live and reflect, certainly it is we
> Who are the most luckless. First of all,
> We pay a great price to purchase a husband;
> And thus submit our bodies to a perpetual
> Tyrant. And everything depends on whether.
> Our choice is good or bad—for divorce
> Is not an honorable thing, and we may not
> Refuse to be married. And then a wife is

Plunged into a way of life and behavior
Entirely new to her, and must learn
What she never learned at home.
She must learn by a kind of subtle
Intuition how to manage the man who
Lies beside her.
ll. 283-301 [31]

Methodically plotting her revenge, she tells Jason that she forgives him and requests permission to offer gifts to the bride. Jason foolishly accepts the sham probably out of guilt and the wish to feel absolved from wrong. But the gifts are poisoned, and the bridegroom watches helplessly as his bride is destroyed. Even so, Medea's anger is not yet assuaged-she has one final stroke. She willfully murders her children so that the destruction of her husband will be complete—her bitterness at a husband's infidelity proving to be even greater than a mother's love. Revenge is indeed a kind of wild justice!

There is no question that her actions are outrageous and horrible. Her irrational temper illustrates the Greek abhorrence for *hamartia*, in this instance, excessive jealousy, and the evil of immoderate conduct. But there can be no gainsaying the sympathy that Medea arouses—because she answers with the only means available to her the injustice she has endured. The Chorus, split in its loyalty to Jason as a Greek, and to Medea as a woman, proves to be more sympathetic to the woman:

When love has passed its limits
It brings no longer good:
It brings no peace or comfort to any soul.
Yet while she moves mildly there is no fire
So sweet as that which is lit by the goddess of
Love. Oh never, upon me, Cypris,
Send forth your golden bow
The unerring arrow poisoned with desire!
ll. 829-836

The gods themselves do not condemn her, as illustrated by the final action in the play; a fiery chariot comes to Medea and bears her away to a land where protection will be assured. She is saved, if not vindicated.

ARISTOPHANES

Finally, there is the intellectual, bawdy, idealistic, pagan comedy of Aristophanes (448-380 B.C.). The first comic genius treated sex as he treats the most serious subjects—politics, philosophy, and poetry—with irreverent passion. But underlying the irreverence is his idealism—born of a commitment to humane issues-the preservation of life and the moral responsibilities of man. Where the Bible enjoins moral behavior under the threat of divine wrath, the comedian forces us to recognize our relationship to others and to act on the basis of social and ethical imperatives.

Lysistrata, his best play, written in 411 B.C., takes profound themes—the horror of war and man's sexual nature—and treats them with grotesque exaggeration. The social theme is that women wish to protect their mates from their proclivity to destroy each other. The play is an anti-war sermon, an assault on the Peloponnesian War which was decimating Greece. The Athenian Lysistrata calls together her sisters from Athens and Sparta and proposes that they refrain from sexual intercourse with their husbands until peace has been established. The oath is administered by Lysistrata with the mock seriousness of a religious ritual:

> Lysistrata: Place all your hands on the cup, and one of you repeat on behalf of all what I say. Then all will swear and ratify the oath. I will suffer no man, be he husband or lover.
>
> Calonice: I will suffer no man, be he husband or lover.
>
> Lysistrata: To approach me, all hot and horny. Say it!

Calonice: (*slowly and painfully*) To approach me all hot and horny. Oh Lysistrata, I feel so weak in the knees.

Lysistrata: If I keep this oath, may I be permitted to drink from this cup,

Calonice: If I keep this oath, may I be permitted to drink from this cup,

Lysistrata: But if I break it, may the cup be filled with water.

Calonice: But if I break it, may the cup be filled with water.

Lysistrata: Do you all swear to this?

All: I do, so help me!

Lysistrata: Come then, I'll just consummate this offering.

(*She takes a long drink from the cup.*)

209-238[32]

The play's humor is the exploration of the behavior of the woman under the terms of the interdiction, and it gives the lie to the conventional idea that men are the dominant or sole possessors of the sexual drive. The plot nearly fails because of the subversion by some of the women who try to evade the terms of the resolution. The most amusing scene in the play is the tease put on by Myrrhine as her husband, Cinesias, brings their child to the women's fortress and pleads with her to minister to the exigencies of her family.

Cinesias: O my darling, O Myrrhine honey, why do you do this to me? (*Myrrhine appears on the wall.*) Come down here!

Myrrhine: No, I won't come down.

Cinesias: Won't you come, Myrrhine, when I call you?

Myrrhine: No, you don't want me.

Cinesias: Don't want you? I'm in agony!

Myrrhine: I'm going now.

Cinesias: Please don't. At least, listen to your baby. (*to the baby*) Here you, call your Mamma! (*pinching the baby*)

Baby: Ma-ma! Ma-ma! Ma-ma!

Cinesias: (*to Myrrhine*) What's the matter with you? Have you no pity for your child, who hasn't been washed or fed for five whole days?
ll. 871-880

Myrrhine makes the gesture of reconciliation, fondling their baby, but putting off Cinesias with her preparations for the rites of Aphrodite, raising his temperature and his desire.

Myrrhine: (*returning with a mattress*) Here's the mattress; lie down on it! I'm taking my things of now, but—let's see: you have no pillow.

Cinesias: I don't want a pillow!

Myrrhine: But I do. (*She goes.*)

Cinesias: Cheated again, just like Hercules and his dinner!

Myrrhine: (*returning with a pillow*) Here, lift your head. (*to herself, wondering how to tease him.*) Is that all?

Cinesias: Surely that's all! Do come here precious!

Myrrhine: I'm taking off my girdle. But remember: don't go back on your promise about the truce.

Cinesias: Hope to die, if I do.
ll. 923-932

The plan succeeds, as the men of Sparta and Athens join the serving the nude, voluptuous, joy-endowing Reconciliation. But the pacific hopes that had been urged in Lysistrata were wishful thinking. The play preceded by seven years the deracination of Athens in the civil war.

After Aristophanes and the demise of Athens, the old comedy of passionate social commitment declined; in its place new comedy treated romantic love and puerile attachments. No comedies of Menander survive; but his works were translated and adapted into Latin by the Roman playwrights, Plautus and Terence.

PLATONIC LOVE

There was one other voice that would resonate from Greece through the millennia. An admirer of Aristophanes, a disciple of Socrates, he was smitten by the Muse and served the cause of Beauty throughout his life. There is a tradition that he was a playwright, a writer of comedies in his youth, and he shifted his sights after drama became discredited, and projected his idealistic fantasies in philosophical writings. Little is known of his personal life, virtually nothing of a personal character; the nature of his family life, his personal relationships. Did he ever marry? Did he have children? What psychological circumstances influenced his attitudes? His early biographers mentioned that he was probably born to an aristocratic family, fell under the influence of Socrates in his youth, and took upon himself the Socratic method and teaching. He founded a school called the Academy and later in life advised various princes about affairs of the state.

Plato (427-347 B.C.) explored truth in his Comedy of Ideas, called *Dialogues*, in which he completely submerged his personality to his thought on politics, on morality, on philosophy, on knowledge, on law, and on love. It is somewhat ironic that this most speculative poet should be remembered for his admonition on the danger of poets to the orderly state. It would seem almost sheer heresy to suggest that the comedian Aristophanes after all might have been in the back of his mind.

His approach to writing represents a new style of Western literature as well as Western thought. His characters are historical—his beloved Socrates is the principal character in his works; but he indulges in fanciful rendition of the events in his stories and his dialogues. His work exists on the level of Aristophanes' comedy *Clouds*, mathematical, philosophical, and unquestionably poetical.

It is only his conception of love that concerns us here. Indeed his views on love, represented in his writings, were written over perhaps half a century; and therefore quite understandably there is not the consistency of a single viewpoint. The Dialogue, *Symposium*, describes a drinking party in which the participants discourse on the theme of love.

Aristophanes, a character in the dialogue, presents a rambling discourse about the evolution of love. In the beginning, human beings were whole and contained within themselves both the masculine and feminine selves. But they were strong and ambitious; and Zeus fearing that they would overthrow the Olympian dynasty divided them in their middle so that they would be half as strong as before, and their threat would be neutralized. Thus male and female were created, and their privy parts were now behind them:

> When the original body was cut through, each half wanted the other, and hugged it; they threw their arms round each other desiring to grow together in the embrace, and died of starvation and general idleness because they would not do anything apart from each other. When one of the halves died and the other was left, the half that was left hunted for another and embraced it, whether he found the half of a whole woman (which we call woman now) or half of a whole man; and so they perished. But Zeus pitied them and found another scheme; he moved their privy parts in

front . . . and made generation come between them by the
male in the female; that in this embrace, if a man met a
woman, they may beget and the race might continue and if
a man met a man, they might be satisfied by their union and
rest, and might turn to work and care about the general
business of life. [33]

For some, Platonic love has come to be identified with the attitude
expressed above-as a physical experience between members of the
same (or different) sex. But in the same dialogue, the seer Diotima
of Mantineia proposes that, despite the pleasure that was available
to men and women in the act of love, the beauty of the soul is to
be preferred to the needs of the body—that the individual must
free himself of the tyranny and lust and sublimate love by seeking
"supreme knowledge whose sole object is absolute beauty." In his
utopian vision of the ideal Republic—Plato again reflected on the
relationship between men and women-and even explored the possibility of communal marriage and child-rearing—but he also suggested the centrality of the marriage bond in human relations.
Socrates rhetorically raises the question in Book V of *The Republic*:

Then clearly the next thing will be to make matrimony
sacred in the highest degree, and what is most beneficial will
be deemed most sacred?

Exactly!

He then goes on to consider the means of breeding human beings
in order to create the best possible offspring.

There is the suggestion of an ideal that was constant in Greek
civilization from Homer to Plato. Perhaps it never was more beautifully or nobly expressed than at the end of Book I of the *Iliad*.
Strife occurs between the lord and lady of Olympus and threatens
to divide the gods. Zeus and Hera are obdurate in maintaining
their point of view about the conflict between the Trojans and the
Greeks. Only the intervention of their son Hephaestus saves the
day and prevents serious discord. He counsels moderation—and

compels Hera to recognize that her happiness lies in accepting the authority of Zeus:

> Afterwards when the light of the flaming sun went under,
> they went away each one to sleep in his home where
> for each one the far-renowned strong handed Hephaestos
> had built a house by means of his craftsmanship and cun-
> ning.
> Zeus the Olympian and lord of the lightning went to
> his own bed, where always he lay when sweet sleep came on
> him
> Going up to the bed, he slept, and Hera of the gold throne
> beside him.
> Book I, 605-611

Here the ideal husband and wife are squabbling and settling their differences, drawing apart and then coming together, without harboring animosity and bitterness, to share a bed, and the love which the gods themselves cherished and, without doubt, the poet Plato reflected upon as "sacred in the highest degree."

THE ROMANS

Rome, under the aegis of its patron goddess Venus (known as Aphrodite to the Greeks), established the greatest empire of the ancient world and bequeathed the legacy of modern statecraft. It is no accident that love found so respected a place in this Mediterranean climate and civilization; for one can still read the book of love, chapter and verse, among those who have inherited the land. The rape of the Sabine women accompanied its founding, and its literature paid homage to the fairest goddess. Romance and its cognates derive from the nation that so assiduously served Venus. The philosopher-poet of the first century B.C., Lucretius, paid tribute to the influence of Venus in his invocation to *The Nature of Things*.

> Mother of Aeneas and his race, darling of men and gods, nurturing Venus, who beneath the smooth-moving heavenly signs fillest with thyself the sea full-laden with ships, the earth with her kindly fruits, since through thee every generation of living things is conceived and rising up looks on through the light of the sun: from thee, O goddess, from thee, the winds flee away, the clouds of heaven from thee and thy coming; for thee the wonder-working earth puts forth sweet flowers, for thee the wide stretches of ocean laugh, and heaven grown peaceful glows with outpoured light.[34]

By fate or destiny, Rome was to be master of the world for half a millennium, and its youth was instructed: "Remember thou shalt rule the world." The Roman accepted his responsibility with patriotism and with discipline. It also required the suppression of one's libidinal drive. This rigor, more often than not, remained an ideal rather than an actual achievement.

The conquest of a Roman Empire by Julius Caesar (100-44 B.C.) and its consolidation by his nephew Octavian, entitled Augustus Caesar (63 B.C.-14 A.D.), enabled the citizens of Rome to enjoy unparalleled opportunity for the development of a sublime culture. The empire provided the background for a golden age as well as for excessive luxury and decadence. The Romans served both patriotism and libertinism with sustained devotion, though at different times, in different ways, and by different citizens.

CATULLUS

The patrician poet Catullus glorified the service of love in his lyrical poems. A Veronese by birth, he developed the tradition of erotic love poetry from the Greeks and named the beautiful lady of his life and poetry *Lesbia* in reverence to the poetess of Lesbos whose style he venerated. Though he loved Lesbia, he wrote about many loves realistically, truthfully, and bawdily. He professed the Epicurean philosophy that life was short; therefore one ought to seize the pleasure of the moment. His life confirmed his ideal; he lived well and died early, in his thirtieth year. Love both elevates and reduces grown men to the exuberance of youth and the gibberish of children:

> My Lesbia, let us live and love
> And not care tuppence for old men
> Who sermonize and disapprove.
> Suns when they sink can rise again,
> But we, when our brief light has shone,
> Must sleep the long night on and on.
> Kiss me: a thousand kisses, then
> A hundred more, and now a second
> Thousand and hundred, and now still
> Hundreds and thousands more, until
> The thousand thousands can't be reckoned.
> And we've lost track of the amount
> And nobody can work us ill
> With the evil eye by keeping count.[35]

He recollects an assignation at the Roman forum, and provides a vivid miniature tableau of the time.

> I was in the Forum once at loose end
> When I was seized and hauled off by my friend
> Varus to meet his girl. "A prostitute,"
> I thought at the first glance, "but rather cute,
> In fact quite pretty." Soon talk started flowing
> On various topics. Then: "How are things going

In the province of Bithynia these days?" Is it
Prospering? Are you richer for your visit?"
I told the simple truth: that no one there
Can line his pocket or perfume his hair-
That goes for natives, governors, and staff too,
Especially if you're in the retinue
Of some mean sod who doesn't give a thought
To his employees. "But at least you brought
The local product back," they said—"a litter
With litter-men?" I, trying hard to glitter
In the girl's eyes, said, "Oh things weren't so
bad, despite the rotten province that I had,
That I can't call my own eight sturdy-backed
Good litter-men. (I hadn't one, in fact,
There or in Rome, on whom I could rely
To hoist a broken bed-leg shoulder-high!)
At which the girl, just like a cheeky tart,
Said, "Dear Catullus, could you bear to part
For an hour with them? I only want a ride
To the temple of Serapis." "Steady!" I cried.
"I meant to say . . . well, strictly, I was wrong
To call them my slaves. Actually, they belong
To a friend of mine who purchased them—that is,
To Gaius Cinna. Anyway, mine or his,
It's all the same to me; I have the loan;
I use them just as though they were my own.
But you're a tactless nuisance. It's absurd
To take a man up on a casual word."

The conjecture is that the veritable Lesbia was the voluptuous
Clodia, wife of Metellus Cillar, the Governor of Cisalpine Gaul.
Catullus realistically describes his triumphs and disappointments;
the ardent suitor suffers many setbacks and frustrations on the
way to conquest:

Enough, Catallus, of this silly whining
What you can see is lost, write off as lost.
Not long ago the sun was always shining
And, loved as no girl ever will be loved,
She led the way and you went dancing after.(8)

No one can be compared to his own true love. He can be unfeeling and even cruel when discussing other ladies.

> How do you do, girl with the outsize nose,
> Colorless eyes, stub fingers, ugly toes,
> Coarse conversation and lips none too dry,
> Friend of the bankrupt man from Formiae.
> Are you the lady whom Cisalpine Gaul
> Ranks with my Lesbia and dares to call
> Beautiful? O provincial generation—
> No taste, no culture, no imagination!(43)

HORACE

Horace, on the other hand, abjured vice and excess—he implores Bacchus: "Spare me, oh spare me, thou god to be dreaded for thy mighty thyrsus!"[36] A republican who fought with Brutus at Philippi, he later was exonerated by Augustus, befriended by Virgil, and patronized by the wealthy Maecenas. He urged the rejection of the life of luxury and foreswore the competition for wealth and man's envy for his neighbor's possessions. He remained a bachelor for life and, in his middle years, reflected on his condition:

> The contests long suspended thou, Venus, wouldst renew.
> Be merciful, I beg, I beg! I am not as I was under the sway of
> kindly Cynara. O cruel mother of sweet Cupids, strive no
> more to bend, when nearly fifty years are past, one now
> callous to thy soft commands! Hie thee rather to the place
> where the persuasive prayers of young men call. More suit-
> ably, borne by thy gleaming swans, shalt thou haste to the
> house of Paulus Maximus, if thou dost seek to kindle a
> fitting heart.
> Book IV, Ode I

He credited his strong moral sense to his father's training; he chastened his countrymen for their wrongdoing and instructed them in their obligations as Roman citizens. His poetry, elegantly conceived and written, has survived the ages as a model of decorum, wisdom, and urbanity. "He lives happily upon a little, on whose frugal board gleams the ancestral salt-dish, and whose soft slumbers are not banished by fear or sordid greed."

VIRGIL

P. Vergilius Maro (70-19 B.C.) was the Augustan poet who epitomized the Roman ideal of patriotism. Born to a poor farm family, he aspired to a legal career but his shyness may have impeded his progress; and he remained on his farm and read and wrote and studied. He gained the recognition of the Emperor Augustus as he celebrated the Julian dynasty. The *Aeneid*, modeled on the Greek Epic, was intended to reflect and to influence Roman grandeur as the *Iliad* and the *Odyssey* had reflected the Greek. Out of the historical struggle between the Roman and the Carthaginian peoples, he wrote of the struggle between two empires, and the triumph of the Latin. Aeneas's superior moral character proves to foreshadow the later achievement of his descendants. But the poem is a celebration of the struggle between a man and a woman-perhaps the most beautiful love story ever told. The conquest of Italy proves to be anticlimactic to Virgil's realism and psychological insight into the character of a woman in love.

The gods again are behind the action, as Aeneas and his men, seeking new shores after their defeat at Troy, are engulfed by a storm and forced to seek haven in Carthage. Aeneas is a worthy successor to his kinsman Hector. The pious Aeneas sees a remarkable civilization thriving under the rule of Queen Dido. As the gods aided the heroes in the Greek epics, Venus, the veritable mother of Aeneas, aids her son as he presents himself "in a shining light" before Queen Dido.

The queen immediately becomes infatuated with the stranger, and soon falls in love with him. The laws of her society obligate her to remain faithful to the memory of her dead husband, Sychaeus, and prohibit her from considering remarriage. She is torn by internal conflict. But her reason proves no match for her desire. Virgil captures in purple poetry the great pain of one who has fallen prey to awesome, terrible power of love as she loses authority over herself and her governance. She prays for release, but to no avail.

> Consumed with passion, the ill-fated Dido,
> wanders in frenzy through the city streets;
> Like a doe, struck by a stray arrow,
> which a careless hunter has driven into her,
> The steel shaft deep in her flesh. Frantically
> she escapes, and scampers aimlessly amid the
> Cretan wood, unable to shake off the deadly wound.
> Book IV, 68-73 [37]

Finally, she succumbs, and upon the advice of her sister, Anna, she surrenders to her passion. Again, there is the complicity of Juno who seeks to frustrate the hopes of the descendents of the Trojans. While on a hunt, a thunderstorm forces Aeneas and Dido to seek shelter in a cave; opportunity presents itself, and their love is consummated. Venus now appeals to her father, and the Lord of the gods responds to her entreaty. Mercury is dispatched to remind Aeneas of his necessary duty to seek Latium and a new life for his people.

Aeneas heeds the command of the gods and surreptitiously prepares to depart from Carthage. But Dido hears of the plan, and she confronts her lover with charges of infidelity and disloyalty. Aeneas is adamant to her pleas. Afterwards her sister tries to persuade Aeneas to stay, but without success. Dishonored and abandoned, the noble queen's fury at her lover is turned on herself:

> Confused and distracted by dire purpose,
> with her eyes rolling, and her skin pallid,
> Dido, turning her rage upon herself, rushed into
> the inner courtyard, and climbed the lofty pyre.
> Her heart beating madly, she unsheathed his sword,

a gift tendered for other, more friendly times.
She cast a glance at the pleasure couch, and her
lover's raiment, and paused to think about him; and fresh
Tears welled up as she spoke her final words: "Oh, these
remembrances of things and times dear to me, so long as the
Gods and fates permitted. Now receive my life, and release
me from this anguish. Well I have lived and honorably, and
now make my way to the afterworld. I have built a glorious
        city
fulfilled obligations to a husband deceased, and
punished a brother's enmity, my conscience clear.
Ah me, to think how happy I might have been had not the
        cursed Trojan
ships touched my shores. Now let me die, and through it be
unavenged, at least I shall gain release and pass into the
peaceful world of death. Let him see it from the distance,
my fiery pyre—an ill-omen for his journey's end."
She spoke these words, and her handmaidens
watched with stupefaction as she fell upon her
Sword, and the blood gushed forth from the open
wounds, dripping over her hands and the blade.
Book IV, 642-668

ROMAN WIVES

Cato the Elder observed: "Men usually rule over women and we
Romans rule over all men, but our women rule over us." The wealth
of the empire—whether riches or the poetry of the golden and
silver ages—was placed at the feet of its women. Neither most
men nor women were libertine; Portia possessed the uncommon
nobility of Brutus, her husband. When Seneca the younger was
charged with conspiracy and compelled to sever the vein in his
wrist, his wife soon died of a broken heart. But Romans jested, as

men will jest, over their bondage to women. The epigrammatist Martial deadpanned:

> All the friends she had, Fabianus, Lycoris has buried
> May she become a friend to my wife. [38]

Marriage has its sweets and disappointments, and couples their ups and downs:

> In darkness you lament, Galla, your husband lost.
> For I think, you are ashamed, Galla, to deplore your spouse openly.

But his finest lines were on the pleasures of Eros:

> I have often enjoyed Christina's favors. Do you ask how generously she grants them? Beyond them, nothing is possible.

and on the joyous tyranny of love:

> Refuse me, Galla; love cloys if its pleasures torture not: but refuse not, Galla, too long.

But it was adulterous love that aroused his keenest feeling:

> New to the marriage bed, and yet unreconciled to her husband, Cleopatra had plunged into the gleaming pool, seeking to escape embrace. But the waves betrayed the lurking dame: brightly she showed, though covered by the o'erlapping water. So, shut in pellucid glass, lilies may be counted, so crystal forbids tender roses to lurk hidden. I leapt in, and, plunged in the waters, plucked reluctant kisses: ye, O transparent waters, forbad aught beyond!

Adultery would seem to have been a major pastime among the Romans, ranging from the savants and wits to the nobility and the emperor himself. Cuckoldry was a highly developed sport. At the time of his conquests, there was a lampoon on Julius Caesar:

Ho, watch your wives, you men of Rome;
we bring the bald-headed lecher home.

THE ART OF LOVE

"I have been appointed by Venus as tutor to tender love," Ovid
wrote.[39] Of noble birth, Ovid was trained in the law, but devoted
his energies to poetry. He began his literary career with an adaptation of Euripides' *Medea*; and followed with stories of famous heroines; poems to his mistress Corinna; tracts on gaining love and on
curing love; and his famous mythological history of the world,
Metamorphoses. He was married three times; and spent the last
nine years of his life in exile, by the decree of Augustus, and his
books were banned. He was a superlative story teller and cata-
loguer of women's ways. To the critics in his own time, he declared, "So long as I am celebrated the world over, it matters not to
me what one or two pettifoggers say about me." He survived as
perhaps the most popular author of the ancient world, and his
expertise on his subject has never been surpassed, serving as a primary source for men as diverse as Shakespeare and Lord Chesterfield.

Love is sex and the pleasure of love for man is conquest. "She is
virtuous who has no wooers," he asserted. Ovid was writing for an
aristocratic audience that had both the wherewithal and the time
to devote themselves wholly to the chase. Woman, according to
Ovid, clearly enjoys her ability to attract a man; and she has only
to be brought around to perceiving the great pleasure that awaits
them, if she submits. Even Penelope is vulnerable to a person who
has mastered *The Art of Love*:

> If anyone among this people knows not the art of loving, let
> him read my poem, and having read be skilled in love. By
> skill, swift ships are sailed and rowed, by skill nimble chari-
> ots are driven: by skill must Love be guided.

Though he must be aided by chance, the would-be lover also must possess the rhetorical skills of flattery and persistence:

> Chance and Venus help the brave. Let not your eloquence submit to our poet's laws; see but that you make a start: your eloquence will come of itself. You must play the lover, and counterfeit heartache with words: her belief in that you must win by any device. Nor is it hard to be believed: each woman thinks herself lovable; hideous though she be, there is none her own looks do not please. Yet often the pretender begins to love truly after all, and often becomes what he has feigned to be. Wherefore, you women, be more compliant to pretenders; one day will the love be true which now was false. Now be the time to ensnare the mind with crafty flatteries, as the water undermines an overhanging bank. Nor be weary of praising her looks, her hair, her shapely fingers, her small foot: even honest maids love to hear their charms extolled; even to the chaste, their beauty is a care and a delight.

There is a time to hold back and to advance:

> Yield if she resists; by yielding you will depart the victor; only play the part she bids you play. Blame if she blames; approve whatever she approves. Affirm what she affirms and deny what she denies. If she laughs, laugh with her; if she weeps, remember to weep; let her impose her laws upon your countenance.

Often the loser will end up the winner:

> If she be gaming, and throwing with her hand the ivory dice, do you throw amiss and move your throws amiss; or if it is the large dice you are throwing, let no forfeit follow if she lose; see that the ruinous dogs often fall to you; or if the piece be marching under the semblance of a robbers' band, let your warrior fall before his glassy foe.

You must show tenacity to gain the ultimate victory.

> Love is a kind of warfare; avaunt, ye laggards! These banners
> are not for timid men to guard. Night, storm, long journeys,
> cruel pains, all kinds of toil are in this dainty camp.

Nor does Ovid lack confidence in his teaching:

> Whoso loves wisely will be victorious, and by my art will
> gain his end.

Ovid followed *The Art of Love* with *The Remedies of Love*, a less popular work. To cure love, it is necessary to take one's mind off the object. Hunting and hard work are two effective means. Absence also serves the same purpose. "It is also useful to surprise your lady in the morning before she has completed her toilette."

Ovid's exile is attributed to his implication in the cause of the profligacy and banishment of Julia, the daughter of Augustus. Perhaps the poet committed some "crime" with her or witnessed something he should not have seen—but more probably, the emperor blamed his daughter's licentiousness on the influence of Ovid's writings. It is doubtful that the greatest love poet of the age should have been accountable for this. The histories of Suetonius and Tacitus and others are far more lurid than literature. The deconstruction of political enemies, such as the decapitation and display of a rival's head while still alive and breathing, or the additional indignity of removal of the tongue from the malefactor as a mockery for misuse of that organ against rivals; or the debaucheries of the daughter and granddaughter of Augustus, of Livia and her son Tiberius, of Caligula, Nero, Messalina, and two Agrippinas, have been ascribed as the reason for the decline and fall of the Roman Empire. The Emperor's absolute power—that often served the gratuitous cruelty and its handmaiden, lust—is more pertinent to the excesses of the age than Ovid's poetry. Nevertheless the image of man and the example that poetry projects can be an important influence for good or evil on the life of a people.

SATYRICON

Petronius, who has been identified with a high court official in Nero's court, depicts the decadence of his society in *Satyricon*. He too was charged with conspiracy and compelled to die in the Roman way. The title suggests that the work was intended to satirize folly; yet its revelation of gross degeneracy seems to deprive it of moral value. The work is not without a philosophic vision. The hero Encolpius, seeking to find meaning in his life through debauchery, finds that such a life leads to a climax of impotence! His most interesting adventure occurs at a dinner party of self-made tycoon Trimalchio who, satiated with food and drunk with wine and power, engages in a boorish domestic quarrel with Fortunata, his wife:

> Our hilarity was somewhat dampened soon after, for a boy, who was by no means bad looking, came in among the fresh slaves. Trimalchio seized him and kissed him lingeringly, whereupon Fortunata, asserting her rights in the house, began to rail at Trimachio, styling him an abomination who set no limits to his lechery, finally ending by calling him a dog. Trimalchio flew into a rage at her abuse and threw a wine cup at her head, whereupon she screeched as if she had had an eye knocked out and covered her face with her trembling hands. Scintilla was frightened, too, and shielded the shuddering woman with her garment. An officious slave presently held a cold-water pitcher to her cheek and Fortunata bent over it, sobbing and moaning. But as for Trimalchio, "What the hell's next?" he gritted out, "this Syrian dancing-whore don't remember anything! I took her off the auction block and made her a woman among her equals, didn't I? And here she puffs herself up like a frog and pukes in her own nest; she's a blockhead, all right, not a woman. But that's the way it is, if you're born in an attic you can't sleep in a palace!" . . . And furthermore, that she may know I can repay a bad turn, I won't have her kissing me when I'm laid out! [40]

JUVENAL

The most vociferous satirical voice of the first and second centuries belonged to Juvenal. The poet, probably banished from the court for irritating some favorite, lived on the fringe of poverty. He decried the depravity of the age—attacking the corruption of courts and venality of public officials.

> Luxury, more deadly than any foe, has laid her hand upon us, and avenges a conquered world. Since the day when Roman poverty perished, no deed of crime or lust has been wanting to us. [41]

He also reflected on the hardships of urban life—the danger of being mugged or of having one's home burglarized—and on the vanity of human wishes. All in all, his writings are vivid and even contemporary. But, like many idealists, he flouted his deepest scorn on members of the opposite sex, his sixth satire being a classic anti-feminist tract:

> Why tell of love poems and incantations, of poisons brewed and administered to a stepson, or of the grosser crimes to which women are driven by the imperious power of sex? . . . Their sins of lust are the least of all their sins. . . . If you are honestly uxorious and devoted to one woman, then bow your head and submit your neck ready to bare the yoke. Never will you find a woman who spares the man who loves her; for though she be herself aflame, she delights to torment and plunder him. . . . Give up all hope of peace so long as your mother-in-law is alive. It is she that teaches her daughter to revel in stripping and despoiling her husband. . . . There was never a case in court in which the quarrel was not started by a woman. What modesty can you expect in a woman who wears a helmet, abjures her own sex, and delights in feats of strength? Yet she would not choose to be a man, knowing the superior joys of womanhood.

He was avowedly attempting to dissuade his friend Postumus from marrying and raising a family. Even if a worthy wife were to be found:

> Well, let her be handsome, charming, rich and fertile; let her have ancient ancestors ranged about her halls; let her be more chaste than the disheveled Sabine maidens who stopped the war—a prodigy as rare upon earth as a black Swan! Yet who could endure a wife who possessed all perfections?

The common lot is not so fortunate:

> So the better the man, the more desirable he be as husband, the less good by far will he get out of his wife. No present will you ever make if your wife forbids; nothing will you ever sell if she objects; nothing will you buy without her consent. She will arrange your friendships for you; she will turn your now-aged friend from the door which saw the beginning of his beard.

MEDITATIONS

The second century Emperor, Marcus Aurelius, ruled with compassion and wrote his *Meditations*—a profound rendition of Stoic philosophy. Stoicism, which like Epicureanism was derived from the Greeks, taught resignation and repression of emotions. Foreshadowing the Christian faith, he argued that one must withdraw from the world to avoid its snares:

> Never esteem of anything as profitable, which shall ever constrain thee, either to break thy faith, or to lose thy modesty; to hate any man, to suspect, to curse, to dissemble, to lust after anything, that requiereth the secret of wall or veils. But he that preferreth before all things his rational part and spirit, and the sacred mysteries of virtue which issueth from it, he shall never lament and exclaim, never sigh; he shall never want either desire or fear. And as for life, whether for a long or short time he shall enjoy his soul thus compassed

about with a body, he is altogether indifferent. For if even
now he were to depart, he is as ready for it, as for any other
action, which may be performed with modesty and de-
cency. For all his life long, this is his only care, that his mind
may always be occupied in such intentions and objects, as
are proper to a rational sociable creature . . . Whosoever therefore in either matters of pleasure and pain; death and life,
honor and dishonor (which things nature in the adminis-
tration of the world, indifferently doth make use of), is not
as indifferent, it is apparent that he is impious. [42]

Between Catullus and Marcus Aurelius there existed a body of
literature that gave expression to the spectrum of human feeling
from self-indulgence to self-denial. Still, more often than not, the
desires from the flesh were upheld over the claim of the spirit.

A NEW DAWN

But a new sun was dawning on the eastern horizon. Ranging from
Palestine, a distant outpost of the Roman Empire, nameless le-
gions of missionaries—at the beginning few in number—asserted
their true faith, sought to convert the heathen, and established
their churches in every community that would allow them. Usually they were persecuted and martyred; but other zealots would
replace them and carry on the teaching.

They were known to the court of the Romans—and these
Christians were even humiliated and ridiculed at the public cir-
cuses. In the fourth century, they gained an important convert.
The Emperor Constantine at first disdained them; but he changed
his mind-after a dream vision, which preceded a battle victory
under the banner of the Cross of Christ: *In hoc signo vinces (By this
sign, you will conquer)*. He conquered or rather Christianity tri-
umphed. In 313, he issued an Edict of Toleration and himself
became the defender of the faith; he established the New Rome at
Constantinople. On his deathbed, he was baptized. In short order, the churches already in place, Christianity became the unify-

ing force of Western Civilization—and extended its dominion throughout the entire world. Now indeed the spirit was to become flesh, even as the flesh once had become spirit.

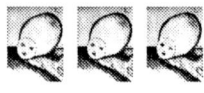

LOVE IN THE CHRISTIAN WORLD

"Verily, verily, I say unto you except a corn of wheat fall into the ground and die, it abideth alone; but if it die, it bringeth forth much fruit." St. John

"God and soul, that is what I desire to know. Nothing else. Absolutely nothing." St. Augustine

The expense of spirit in a waste of shame
Is lust in action, and till action, lust
Is perjur'd, murd'rous, bloody, full of blame,
Savage, extreme, rude, cruel, not to trust,
Enjoy'd no sooner but despised straight,
Past reason hunted, and no sooner had,
Past reason hated as a swallowed bait
On purpose laid to make the taker mad.
Shakespeare

The knowledge of God without that of man's misery causes pride. The knowledge of man's misery without that of God causes despair. The knowledge of Jesus Christ constitutes the middle course, because in Him we find both God and our misery.
Blaise Pascal

JESUS OF NAZARETH • ST. PAUL • THE FATHERS OF THE CHURCH • ST. AUGUSTINE • WOMEN, ART, AND MONASTERIES • THE CONSOLATION OF PHILOSOPHY

THE MIDDLE AGES • HÉLOÏSE AND ABELARD •
MEDIEVAL ROMANCE • AUCASSIN AND NICOLETTE •
JONGLEURS AND TROUBADORS •
QUEEN ELEANOR OF AQUITANE • THE ART OF COURTLY LOVE
• MARIE OF FRANCE • THE CITY OF LADIES •
THE RULE OF NUNS OR RECLUSES • FEMINIST LYRICISM •
THE ALLEGORY OF LOVE • DANTE ALIGHIERI

THE RENAISSANCE • DECAMERON • GEOFFREY CHAUCER •
THE WIFE OF BATH • REFORMATION • RABELAIS •
MONTAIGNE • WILLIAM SHAKESPEARE • ROMEO AND JULIET •
HAMLET • PORTIA AND LADY MACBETH • OTHELLO •
ANTONY AND CLEOPATRA • JOHN DONNE •
MONARCHY AND CHIVALRY • DON QUIJOTE •
FRENCH CLASSICAL DRAMA • CORNEILLE •
MOLIÈRE'S SCHOOL FOR WIVES • PARADISE LOST •
THE COUNTRY WIFE

THE ENLIGHTENMENT • SAMUEL RICHARDSON • CANDIDE •
LES LIAISONS DANGEREUSES • LORD CHESTERFIELD •
CASANOVA • MARQUIS DE SADE

JESUS OF NAZARETH

"In the beginning was the Word, and the Word was with God and the Word was God," begins the *Gospel According to St. John*. The world of the ancients was one in which the supernatural, dreams, and magic were real; and the real world was transitory. Men walked and talked with the gods. Christianity preserves this close encounter with the divine presence until man's conquest of nature—abetted by materialism—undermined the foundation of mystical faith. Salvation is the promise of rich reward in the eternal future for the suffering and impoverishment of this mundane world.

The rock of St. Peter is renunciation of worldly pleasure. The interdictions against excess and the commandment to "sanctify yourselves" and "be ye holy" contained in the Old Testament are corporified into a formal renunciation of the body in the New Testament. Jesus personifies the life of perfect holiness; he never married: "There are eunuchs born that way from their mother's womb; there are eunuchs who made themselves that way for the sake of the Kingdom of Heaven. Let anyone accept this who can." He denied his own family ties:

> While he yet talked to the people, behold, his mother and his brethren stood without, desiring to speak with him. Then one said unto him, "Behold thy mother and thy brethren stand without, desiring to speak with thee." But he answered and said unto them that told him, "Who is my mother? And who are my brethren?"
> *Matthew* 12:46-48

The miracle of parthenogenetic birth rendered in the Dogma of the Immaculate Conception (1854) represents if not the repudiation of the physical act of intercourse, at the very least the Nazarite diminution of the flesh. Jesus comes to represent the Son in Oedipal conflict with his Hebrew father: "All things are delivered to me of my Father." Christianity holds the triumph of the Son in mercy over the stern authority of the Father—even as, for example, the myth of the seasonal cycle represents the displacement of the old king (winter) with the young and vigorous god (spring).

Women do not figure significantly in the New Testament. The dichotomy in the Old Testament between woman as a paragon of virtue and as a temptress and sexual being is carried into the New Testament, the goodness of Mary the Virgin as opposed to the mythical Whore of Babylon, "arrayed in purple and scarlet color, and decked with gold and precious stones and pearls, having a golden cup in her hands full of abominations and filthiness of her fornication. . . . For all nations have drunk of the wine of the wrath of her fornication, and the kings of the earth have committed fornication with her, and the merchants of the earth are waxed rich through the abundance of her delicacies."

Jesus warns against the exercise of the libidinal drive in the prohibition against remarriage:

> What therefore God hath joined together, let not man put asunder. . . . Whosoever shall put away his wife, and marry another, committeth adultery against her. And if a woman shall put away her husband, and be married to any other, she committeth adultery.
> *Mark* X: 9-12

Yet in the parable of the foolish virgins, he identifies the appearance of the Messiah with the coming of a bridegroom and salvation as a holy marriage:

> Then shall the kingdom of heaven be likened unto ten virgins, which took their lamps, and went forth to meet the bridegroom. And five of them were wise, and five were foolish. They that were foolish took their lamps, and took no oil with them: But the wise took the oil in their vessels with their lamps. While the bridegroom tarried, they all slumbered and slept. And at midnight there was a cry made, "Behold, the bridegroom cometh; go ye out to meet him." Then all those virgins arose, and trimmed their lamps. And the foolish said unto the wise, "Give us your oil; for our lamps are gone out." But the wise answered, saying, "Not so; lest there be not enough for us and you: but go ye rather to them that sell, and buy for yourselves."

> And while they went to buy, the bridegroom came; and they that were ready went in with him to the marriage; and the door was shut. Afterward came also the other virgins, saying, "Lord, Lord, open to us." But he answered and said, "Verily I say until you, I know you not. Watch therefore; for ye knew neither the day nor the hour wherein the Son of Man cometh."
> *Matthew* 25: 1-13

Jesus taught compassion for the sinner, and in a famous dispute with the Pharisees argued against the harshness of Mosaic law when he sought to forgive the repentant prostitute: "Seest thou this woman? . . . She hath washed my feet with tears, and wiped them with the hairs of her head. Wherefore I say unto thee, Her sins, which are many, are forgiven; for she loved much: but to whom little is forgiven, and same loveth little." *Luke* 8: 44-47

ST. PAUL

St. Paul formulated the structure of Christianity, in describing the relationship of Jesus to man and men's obligations to God. He was dogmatic in insisting upon the suppression of the libido:

> Know ye not that your bodies are members of Christ? Shall I then take the members of Christ, and make them the members of a harlot? God forbid. What? know ye not that he which is joined to a harlot is one body? For two, saith he, shall be one flesh. But he that is joined unto the Lord is one spirit. Flee fornication. Every sin that a man doeth is without the body; but he that committeth fornication sinneth against his own body. What? know yet not that your body is the temple of the Holy Ghost which is in you, which ye have of God, and ye are not your own? For ye are bought with a price: therefore glorify God in your body, and in your spirit, which are God's.
> *I Corinthians* 6:15-20

In this famous *apercu*, he derided deviation from the letter of the law:

> It is good for a man not to touch a woman. Nevertheless, to avoid fornication, let every man have his own wife and let every woman have her own husband. Let the husband render unto the wife due benevolence: and likewise also the wife unto her husband. The wife hath not the power of her own body, but the husband: and likewise also the husband hath not the power of his own body, but the wife. Defraud

ye not one the other, except it be with consent for a time, that ye may give yourselves to fasting and prayer; and come together again, that Satan tempt you not for your incontinency. But I speak this by permission, and not of commandment. For I would that all men were even as I myself. But every man hath his proper gift of God, one after this manner, and another after that. I say therefore to the unmarried and the widows, it is good for them if they abide even as I. But if they cannot contain, let them marry: for it is better to marry than to burn.

I Corinthians 7:1-9

THE FATHERS OF THE CHURCH

The early Fathers of the Church taught the virtue of chastity and the celibate life. These clergymen denied their sexual needs and defended the purity and sanctity of life. St. Jerome, in the fourth century, asserted that "for mortals this life is a race: we run it on earth that we may receive our reward elsewhere." Christ and the Church were bridegroom and bride; their union, one flesh. Origen, St. Basil the Great, St. Ambrose, and St. Augustine wove the fabric of a beautiful culture that gave form and meaning to life. Origen effected his own emasculation as a rite of enforced celibacy in a fit of religious fervor. Missionaries like St. Patrick, St. Gregory, and St. Boniface brought the gospel to the unconverted states of Europe, which in turn were joined to the Holy Empire.

The Fathers did not find it necessary to reject totally the teachings of the pagans. Much classical thought was adapted and allegorized into Christianity. Aristotle's logic and metaphysics were absorbed. So too Plato's teachings found a ready place in sacred writing. Sublime love was accepted: Plato, after all, had depicted the yearning of the soul for the beautiful and the good. The Idea of the Good was made more concrete in the person of Jesus who lived and died for the sins of men and left a behest of goodness for men to strive to achieve.

Accordingly many of the classics were valued. Greek literature, on the other hand, did not usually survive in the West, except in Latin translation. Homer's work was lost to the Medieval age. Sappho's poetry repeatedly was burned. Ovid's poetry could not readily be assimilated. But Virgil was considered very much a pre-Christian, Christian author. The *Aeneid* was interpreted as having a deeper, allegorical meaning. In his renunciation of Queen Dido, Aeneas, the ideal man, chose purposeful spiritual goals over transient passion and pleasure, and served as a model for all men.

Just as pagan love could be allegorized into religious feeling, so too the individual's own erotic impulses could be glorified as sacred emotion. In the fourth century, St. Ambrose wrote of the soul in mystic detail:

> The soul, raising itself up from the region of the senses and scorning the cares of the earth, aspires to the infusion of the Divine Word. And she bewails herself if he delays his coming; as if she were wounded by love, she can brook no delay and she says with impatience, "Oh, that I may be kissed with a kiss of his mouth!" and she asks herself not for one kiss but for many to appease all her desire. . . . The kiss of the Word signifies that she is illuminated by the knowledge of God. And when she receives this proof of nuptial love, she exclaims in her joy: "I have opened my mouth and I have breathed in his breath!". . . . The soul clings to the Word with a kiss.[43]

ST. AUGUSTINE

St. Augustine (354-430) was the most passionate advocate of Christianity after St. Paul. Born in North Africa, he studied in Carthage and became an academician. His *Confessions* were fired by his own experience. He was profligate in his youth, espousing the heretical Manichean belief, and siring an illegitimate child:

> So for the space of nine years (from my nineteenth to my twenty-eighth year) I lived a life in which I was seduced and seducing, deceived and deceiving, the prey of vicious de-

sires. My public life was that of a teacher of what are called "the liberal arts." In private I went under cover of a false kind of religion. . . . I lived with a woman who was not bound to me by lawful marriage; she was one who had come by way because of my wandering desires and my lack of considered judgment.
Book IV. i,ii[44]

But his penitence was genuine. He rejected carnality and lust as cloying and transitory. He found physical love brimming with pestiferous jealousy; for, he argued, if one wished to indulge in the sight of his beloved in the nude, would not another wish to see her also? He described his own life as "one long temptation" to perfect himself. He presented *The City of God* in which mankind would live in perfect love with the Creator. For him and those of like mind, Christianity was not simply a doctrine or even an allegory of the soul's yearning for God, but an existential rendering of man's need for faith. Had he been a carnal lover, St. Augustine would not have been distinguishable from millions of creatures in the animal kingdom who preceded and followed him and left nothing of themselves. His record reveals man's dimension once he has achieved release from his corporeal prison.

WOMEN, ART, AND MONASTERIES

The image of woman was both an abstraction and a paradox. She was not educated, and enjoyed few prerogatives in her daily existence. Her nature was called into question by the clergy who fostered a misogynistic attitude. At the same time, the Cult of the Virgin was prevalent and apotheosized woman's gentleness, pity, and love. St. Augustine pointed to the paradox that even though it was a woman who brought man to destruction, it was through another woman that salvation was restored. Whereas God exacted retribution, Mary interceded on behalf of the sinner. Mary books and devotional prayers were written. Legends about her goodness emerged. Artists depicted her and glorified her image in ten thousand paintings. She perhaps also served as vindication for the harsh reality of woman's existence.

Art also come to serve Christianity and to educate the non-reading masses in its teachings. Whereas the Old Testament had prohibited idolatry through the creation of graven images after the manner of other religions, Christianity separated itself from Judaism, and celebrated the birth and passion of Jesus, and his relationship with Mary in stark, sensuous iconography. This art has proven to be among the greatest achievements of medieval culture.

The development of monasticism in the fifth century allowed men and women to retreat from the world and to live the ideal of serving Christ. Forsaking imperfect society, they established the ideal family. Oaths of celibacy, poverty, and obedience were required, and a life in isolation was cultivated.

The Sisters pledged themselves as wives of Jesus, recalling the *Song of Songs* as they did so. "The voice of my beloved! Behold, he standeth beneath our wall, he looketh forth at the windows, showing himself through the lattice." They sought to follow his example of goodness and chastity. And paradise would be their reward for their good works. Many notable achievements were derived from this way of life. Education, industry, even commerce existed within many of these orders, which survive almost unchanged today as successful experiments in alternative life styles. Not least among the accomplishments of monastic life was the preservation of medieval culture, the sustenance of a literary tradition, and of literacy itself. Many of the beautifully decorated manuscripts that have survived were written and copied by the clergy-until the printing press was invented.

THE CONSOLATION OF PHILOSOPHY

So long as she was seen apart from her sexual role, woman was venerated as an ideal. The Roman aristocrat and consul, Boethius, who lived in the fifth century, was charged with subversion and listening to evil spirits; and he was sentenced to prison and death. In *The Consolation of Philosophy*, he calls on Lady Philosophy, who offers him wisdom, comfort, and understanding during his incarceration. She banishes the Muses of poetry, terming them "whores from the theatre" who are feeding on his illness.[45] She offers him the consolation of philosophy and the message of sublimated love. The image of the asexual, inspirational woman was to be a significant one in the life and literature of the time.

THE MIDDLE AGES

History and literature record the evolution of Christian life in the Middle Ages. Catholicism pervaded the different nations of Europe and offered a truly international unity within the social political context of feudalism. The Frankish King, Charlemagne, adopted the Roman Church and was crowned Holy Roman Emperor, on Christmas Day 800, by Pope Leo III. He accepted the influence of the Church in spiritual matters, and he fought its religious wars against Islam. In fortress as well as in monastery, in palace as well as in peasant hut, church influence was dominant. The feudal knight served both his lord and the will of God. The lords listened benignly while the sons of the poor performed service as altar boys in church on Sunday mornings.

In spite of serious doctrinal conflicts that continually occurred, the power of the Church proved superior to the throne. The most serious schism occurred between the Roman Catholic and Greek Orthodox Church over the issue of the papal supremacy. But in the same eleventh century, Pope Gregory VII proved to be an able and strong Pope who not only curtailed the corruption and secularism of the clergy but, in his power dispute with Henry IV of Germany, was able to bring the monarch to his knees for forgiveness. The Crusades presented an opportunity for Church and State to join in a common effort against an outside enemy: Islam.

HÉLOÏSE AND ABELARD

The spirit of St. Augustine was dominant, though its demands on human nature were difficult for all and impossible for most. The great love story of the time was the illicit love between the Christian scholar Peter Abelard (1079-1142) and his pupil Héloïse. The birth of a child proved to be their undoing because their society denied them freedom to love—even after they were secretly wed. Peter was emasculated by her angry uncle, and Héloïse was sent to a convent. Death permitted the lovers what life forbade them: their remains were buried together.

The twelfth century however saw a shift toward revivification of erotic passion; or as one scholar has written "L'amour? Une invention du douzième siècle." The Italian Theologian Peter Lombard noted sardonically: "There may hardly be found now any persons experiencing carnal intercourse who do not sometimes come together without the intention of generating offspring." The situation proved to be far more consequential. A new style of love was evolving, and it proved to challenge the sole claim of the spirit.

The feudal court was a physical world in which hunting, fighting, feasting, and worshipping were enjoyed. In the evening, a mixed audience would hear narrative tales. The medieval romance developed strains of ancient romance, epics of the different national states, and reflected feudal as well as Christian ascetic values. The hero was a knight who served his lord with devotion and possessed a Christian soul. His spiritual character called his physical desires into question and the satisfaction of *libido* was purchased at the price of guilt—more so since the hero often formed an adulterous (Oedipal!) liaison with his lord's wife. He would have been better off if he had worshipped his lady from afar.

MEDIEVAL ROMANCE

Tristan and Isolde recounts the feudal loyalty of Tristan and the conflict between his devotion to his lord and his love for Isolde, Mark's wife. The gallant Tristan is a faithful vassal, a heroic slayer of dragons, and a pleasing minstrel. While he accompanies the beautiful, youthful Isolde across the Irish sea to her wedding with Mark, they mistakenly drink a love potion which irrevocably binds them in love. At the court they are forced to conceal their true feelings from others and to suppress their passion because it is sinful and disloyal. Once after court gossip implicates Isolde in an affair with Tristan, she undergoes ordeal by holding a burning iron: but she is not scathed. Even God forgives what man would punish!

The legend of King Arthur and his Knights of the Round Table also developed at this time in folklore, in historical writing, and in romance. Love and honor are the primary themes of these stories; as the knights seek to fulfill their duties as vassals to their king and servants to God. Love ought to be sublimated into holy action and duty; but occasionally, as in the adulterous passion of Sir Lancelot and Queen Guinevere, erotic feeling triumphs.

The romance of *Trolius and Criseyde*, familiar from Chaucer's literary treatment, also tells the sorrow of love. It is set at the time of the Trojan war, but peopled, as all medieval stories were, with knights and ladies who observe feudal and Christian values. Trolius undergoes two trials; first to gain Criseyde's pity and love; then to reconcile himself to her unfaithfulness after she abandons him for another. The lesson is clear. Erotic love is necessary suffering and proper retribution for the betrayal of the soul.

AUCASSIN AND NICOLETTE

There are instances where love brings pleasure and joy as in the pleasing tale of *Aucassin and Nicolette*. It is told in prose with lyrical verse passages. The well born Aucassin, son of Count Garin de Beaucaire, falls in love with the slave girl Nicolette of unknown parentage and pursues her despite his father's objections. When he is chastised by his father for being willful, he answers that he prefers the tortures of hell to being denied satisfaction of his true love.

> In Paradise what have I to do? I care not to enter, but only to have Nicolette, my very sweet friend, whom I love so dearly well. For into Paradise go none but such people as I will tell you of. There go those aged Priests, and those old cripples, and the maimed, who all day long and all night long cough before the altars and in the crypts beneath the churches; those who go in worn old mantles and old tattered habits, who are naked, and barefoot, and full of sores; who are dying of hunger and of thirst, of cold and of wretchedness. Such as these enter in Paradise, and with them I have naught to do. But in Hell I will go. For to Hell go the fair clerks and the fair knights who are slain in the tourney and the great wars, and the stout archer and the loyal man. With them will I go. And there go the fair and the courteous ladies, who have friends, two or three together with their wedded lords. And there pass the gold and the silver, the ermine and all rich furs, harpers and minstrels, and the happy of the world. With these will I go, so only that I have Nicolette, my very sweet friend, by my side.[46]

After forced separations, imprisonments, daring escapes, wars, shipwrecks, Nicolette discovers that she is the daughter of the King of Carthage and returns to find Aucassin. Disguised as a jongleur and playing a viol, she tests Aucassin to see if he still wants her. When he declares his perfect loyalty to his beloved, she reveals herself to him:

When he saw her, Aucassin
Oped both arms and drew her in,
Clasped her close in fond embrace,
Kissed her eyes and kissed her face . . .
In such greeting sped the night,
Till, at dawning of the light,
Aucussin, with pomp most rare,
Crowned her Countess of Beaucaire.
Such delight these lovers met,
Aucussin and Nicolette.
Length of days and joys did win
Nicolette and Aucussin.
Endeth song and tale I tell
With marriage bell.

JONGLEURS AND TROUBADORS

At the same time that romance was flourishing, there developed in
Provence, a new cult of love that was influenced by Arab lyrical
poetry, as well as by Christian asceticism, and idealized woman as
the sole source of goodness and inspiration. The praise was so elaborate that it had a devout nature-and indeed the poetry could be
read as religious hymn to the Blessed Virgin, the praise of a generous benefactress, or the crass flattery of a would-be seducer. The
troubadour Peire Roger wrote:

> I am the truest of lovers; I ask nothing of my lady, neither
> little favors nor a smiling countenance; wherever she may
> be, I am her lover and I court her, hidden, dissimulated, and
> concealed. She does not know the good she does me, nor
> that through her I have joy and merit.[47]

The wandering minstrels were called jongleurs and troubadours.
Nicolette dressed herself as a jongleur when she went through the
courts of Provence to find Aucassin. The jongleur was more like a
vagabond in search of a meal and lodging, whereas the troubadour
enjoyed a higher social status. Many a troubadour found himself

the beneficiary of the favors of the ladies, as has been the continual fortunate lot of men who roam the world, like the rock stars of today, with a song of love on their lips.

QUEEN ELEANOR OF AQUITANE

The court of Queen Eleanor of Aquitane (1122-1204) was the cultural center of the cult of love. She had been married to the English Plantagenet King, Henry II, and brought with her as dowry nearly one third of France. After the murder of St. Thomas à Becket the Archbishop of Canterbury, in the celebrated struggle between the throne and the church—in this instance the king prevailing, she returned to France. She established her famous court, was involved in more than one *affaire de coeur*, and patronized romancers and troubadours. Bernard de Ventadour who was associated with her court at Poitiers wrote:

> It is no wonder if I sing better than any other singer, for my heart carries me closer to love and I am more completely subject to his command. Body and heart and mind and sense, strength and power, I have given them all; the rein draws me so strongly toward love that I have no will to go anywhere else.[48]

The poet credited his inspiration to the lady who owned his heart. Like the bullfighter who offers the great prize, the ear of the bull, to his lady, the medieval hero was proud to acknowledge his inspiration. Like the medieval knight and monk, he served the abstract idea of Love. The literary influences seemed blurred. Were they following the ideal of Platonic love? Were they indebted to St. Augustine? Were they indebted to other literary sources such as Arab mystical poetry? Or were they indebted to Ovid? Did the lover seek a reward for his devotion? Scholars are divided as to whether the love sought was Platonic or passionate; but it is evident that the poets themselves delighted in exploring the ambiguities of the New Style.

Affairs of the heart were discussed with the passionate rigor of scholastic argument. Is a lady to be forsaken because of her age? Or, two knights on a journey to their ladies meet other knights in distress. The one, in honor of his lady, turns from his destination to help; the other continues on his mission. Who has acted more becomingly? Or, which are greater, the joys or sorrows of love? Or, do the eyes or the heart contribute more to preserve love in the avowed lover? Or, conundrums such as: a knight is shut up in a tower with the most beautiful woman in the world; would it be preferable for the knight to love the lady and have her hate him? or hate the lady and have her love him?

THE ART OF COURTLY LOVE

The best description of the code was written by Andreas Capellanus. *The Art of Courtly Love* was set down "to make known . . . the way in which a state of love between two lovers may be kept unharmed and likewise how those who do not love may get rid of the darts of Venus that are fixed in their hearts." Andreas probably intended the book to be a cross between the manual that Ovid had written—he was familiar with Ovid's poetry—and a philosophical disquisition on the subject dear to the hearts of his courtly audience. Love was many things, a diversion, an elaborate pattern of conduct, and the highest ideal of his society. His work has been termed one of those rare documents that explain the secret of a civilization. He defined love as:

> a certain inborn suffering derived from the sight of and
> excessive meditation upon the beauty of the opposite sex,
> which causes each one to wish above all things the embraces
> of the other and by common desire to carry out all of love's
> precepts in the other's embrace.[49]

The code was developed in a feminine environment and reflects some unchanging feelings that women have had and continue to have toward love. It attempted to establish a scientific approach to the subject within the confines of feudal-medieval society. Love was neither an irrational passion nor a divine force which took hold of people as believed by the pagans. The causes of love were as immutable as the laws of the universe, and the pattern of love followed a course as regulated as the seasons. Lovers had responsibilities no less demanding than churchmen and feudal knights—their obligations being as closely ordered as the Canonical Hours of a monk. It was truly holy performance. The standard of conduct required a man to prove his worth in order to earn the love and pity of his lady.

The purpose of love was service, and the reward was secondary. There were four stages: first, the intended lover would worship from a distance; then he would find the courage to declare his love; then his lady would permit him to pay court and perhaps dedicate poems or songs to her; finally he might become her lover. Andreas warned against the easy attainment of one's object. A woman who surrenders too easily will not be worthy of respect. Men appreciate the difficulty of the chase, and competition for the love of a woman only reinforces their desire:

> I will go further and say that even though you know perfectly well that some other man is enjoying the embraces of your beloved, this will make you begin to value her solaces all the more, unless your greatness of soul and nobility of mind keep you from such wickedness.

For all intents and purposes, the woman's role in the experience was a passive one. The great ladies who were served by this code, Dante's Beatrice, Petrarch's Laura, and Shakespeare's Dark Lady never uttered a word—indeed one cannot even know for sure whether they existed for any other purpose than to serve the poetic need for the outpouring of love.

Surprisingly, true love could only be adulterous love as can be seen from the following decision rendered by the Queen. There was a certain knight in love with a woman pledged to another; but she gave him this much hope—that if ever she lost the love of her beloved, then without question, she would confer her love upon him. Soon after, she married her beloved. Now the knight demanded that she give him the fruit of the hope which she had pledged. She claimed she was married and could not do so. The knight brought her to the court of Queen Eleanor. In this affair, the Queen gave her decision that married love was *not* a bar to her oath:

> We dare not oppose the opinion of the Countess of Champagne, who ruled that love can exert no power between husband and wife. Therefore we recommend that the lady should grant the love she has promised.

In the third book Andreas reiterates some of the medieval criticism of woman, that she is fickle, envious, greedy, a slave to her belly, disobedient, deceptive, vainglorious, loud-mouthed, and wanton. The end of the work comes as a surprise, for Andreas advises his friend, Walter, to whom he had dedicated the work, to eschew the pleasures of the flesh and serve the spirit:

> Therefore, Walter, accept this health-giving teaching we offer you and pass by all the vanities of the world, so that when the Bridegroom cometh to celebrate the greater nuptials, and the cry ariseth in the night, you may be prepared to go forth to meet Him with your lamps filled and to go in with Him to the divine marriage; and you will have no need to seek out in haste what you need for your lamps, and find it too late, and come to the home of the Bridegroom after the door is shut, and hear His venerable voice.

It is noteworthy that the cult of love, which evolved in the court of Eleanor, presented a highly structured attitude toward love rather than libertine behavior. Love was essentially a conversation piece for ladies and their admirers sitting together in front of the fire.

Though circumstances have an undeniable influence on the way that people behave, it can be learned from medieval society that, given the same opportunities, ladies perhaps are less libertine than men. Even though Eleanor ultimately herself surrendered to the pleasure of love, it can be said that ladies prefer to savor the adulation and rather postpone the ultimate gratification.

The Art of Courtly Love was not only written in the service of women—but women themselves took their part as creators of its literature. There were women jongleurs and troubadours, and storytellers. Indeed their stories drew upon the same themes that men's did.

MARIE OF FRANCE

One such storyteller was Marie of France. Little is known of her personal life, but it is believed that she lived in the thirteenth century and wrote French short stories called *Lays*. One such story, set in Brittany, tells of a damsel "passing fair of body, apt in book as any clerke, and meetly schooled in every grace that it becometh dame to have." If any knight saw her but once, he was smitten. She "gave courtesy and good will to each alike."[50] Now there were four barons of the realm who were handsome and courteous and brave. Setting their hearts upon the fair damsel, they all gave her rich gifts, and she could not choose among them, though she offered each of them tender words. They competed for her affection in jousts and tourneys, and soon were filled with jealous wrath toward each other. The lady watched from her tower one such tourney as all four barons fell in the contest. Three died, and the fourth was woefully mauled. The worthy damsel fainted at the carnage of the ending, and offered mass on their behalf. She tried to comfort the survivor by offering to write a Lay, which she intended to call the Lay of the Four Sorrows. But he begged her to call her work, "The Lay of the Dolorous Knight," for him who survived. And so she acceded to his entreaty; and that is how this Lay came to be written.

THE CITY OF LADIES

A recently discovered medieval work that addressed itself to the issue of the condition of women at the time was an allegory entitled *The Book of the City of Ladies*, written by Christine de Pizan, a Venetian lady who settled in Paris. Her book describes the plight of her heroine who asks why God has discriminated against women by giving them a lower status and a straying temperament. Suddenly three celestial ladies appear to respond to her doubts. Lady Reason, Rectitude, and Justice teach her of woman's real attainments in the world. They observe the lack of virtue on the part of many evil men in history—the Ovids and Neros—and the lack of understanding on the part of men; and they admonish the men who attack women to disguise their own wickedness, vice and dissolution.

The allegory recalls the deeds of host of great women: the Amazons, the Minervas, the Sapphos, the Esthers, the Penelopes, and the Holy Mother. The painful anguish of Medea is recounted, and it is suggested that she would have preferred to take her own life rather than destroy Jason. How Xantippe the wife of Socrates tore the poisoned vile from her husband, Socrates' hands, and poured its contents on the ground even as he chided her for defying the law!

A great city of ladies is built to provide a worthy reward for the many good women who have been so maligned. "In brief, all women—whether noble, bourgeois, or lower-class—be well-informed in all things and cautious in defending your honor and chastity against your enemies! My ladies, see how these men accuse you of so many vices in everything. Make liars of them all by showing forth your virtue, and prove their attacks false by acting well, so that you can say with the Psalmist, 'the vices of evil will fall on their heads!'"[51]

THE RULE OF NUNS OR RECLUSES

Then there was the *Ancrene Riwle*—the Rule of Nuns or Recluses, which expressed the pious sentiments of a woman in her love and devotion to God. The anonymous authoress defends the rules of the Holy Life as "precepts to hold, for as oft as ye hereafter break any of them, it would too soon hurt your heart and make you fall into despair."[52] Just as this period produced the exemplary St. Francis of Assisi and St. Dominic who set an example of poverty and piety and worship and love, women too could write of their holy, mystical feelings.

FEMINIST LYRICISM

In addition to writing in the service of God, medieval women writers wrote realistic love poetry as well as courtly poems. The disparities of marriage, in which the wife—often a child bride—had no freedom of choice in a *mariage de convenance*, produced inequality, unhappiness and righteous anger and the natural desire for release from such an unhealthy bond.

> Sweet and gentle am I, and hence sorely pained
> By my spouse, neither wanting nor desiring him;
> For I am but a child still, a tender young maid
> Sweet and gentle am I!
>
> By all rights there would have been given me,
> A spouse who brings me joy,
> With whom I might disport myself and laugh each day,
> Sweet and gentle am I!
>
> Heaven save me, I shall never be in love with him!
> In no wise do I covet him;

I feel such shame at the mere sight of him;
I pray death come to take him from me.

One thing there be to which I give my free consent . . .
And my friend has shown my love a new path to take:
Therein lies the hope to which I've given all my heart!
A ballad, this, of sweetest praise:
May it be sung by every lady I've thus apprised
Of that friend of mine I love and desire so,
Sweet and gentle am I! [53]

THE ALLEGORY OF LOVE

The allegorical tradition did not disappear, in spite of the fact that realistic love poetry was gaining acceptance. The Gothic style of writing with its intricate artistry and grandiose thought was as profound an expression of the medieval view of life as the Gothic Cathedral. *The Romance of the Rose* was an allegorical dream in which a young lover falls in love with the Rose of Love and is instructed in virtue. St. Thomas Aquinas (1225-1274) elaborated the metaphysical and philosophical foundations of Catholicism for his age, and maintained the distinction between *concupiscent love* (after the fall) and *benevolent love* (between man and God). It remained for one poet to synthesize the religious and ethical thought of Christianity and the new style of love poetry.

DANTE ALIGHIERI

Dante Alighieri (1265-1321) was the finest Christian poet of the middle ages and also its greatest troubadour. His *Commedia*—the sobriquet "Divina" was affixed by later admirers as a tribute to the poet's mastery—is a dream vision and moral discourse that ends happily as the poet attains the realm of paradise. An allegory—it is Dante's spiritual autobiography as he journeys through hell and purgatory, a truculent attack on man's evil nature, and the embodiment of the poet's own attainment of pure Love.

In celebrating his love for Beatrice, Dante offers a rich, lovely encomium to his lady. As the poet's guide and instructress in the realms of paradise, Beatrice is the apotheosis of the lady of our dreams, whose image suffuses and inspires our view of the world. Beatrice Portinari was the real-life model, though he hardly knew her. He probably fell in love with her when he was nine, she eight, and met her noddingly several times afterwards. But there is no evidence that she returned his love, or even knew of it. She died in her twenty fourth year. Dante married and had a family.

He wrote a cycle of poems called *The New Life* describing his feelings for Beatrice. After he was exiled from his native Florence for his political views (1302), he spent the remaining years of his life wandering through courts of Italy and writing his love epic of one hundred cantos.

> I am one who, when Love inspires me take note, and go setting it forth after the fashion which he dictates within me.
> *Purgatorio*, XXIV

In *Inferno*, Dante meets the carnal lovers who have sinned through lascivious desire. Paolo and Francesca recount their tale of adultery—how, in her husband's vineyard, they fell in love, and how they were caught and treacherously slain by the jealous husband. For their lust on earth, they are punished by existing in hell as disembodied floating spirits who can never grasp each other's corporeality. To have indulged as they have in the pleasures of the flesh on earth brings about the frustration of being denied bodily presence in hell. Dante, however, cannot contain his emotional involvement at their plight, and he faints while hearing their story.

The ordeal is a purification for Dante as well. Virgil, his guide in the lower realms, instructs the poet that imperfect love exists as passion; but once it has been perfected, it is directed toward virtue. Indeed this is the principal metaphysical idea of *The Divine Comedy*—the classical idea that the universe is bound together by the force of Eros—but it is virtuous, asexual. Evil, on the other hand, is the perversion of love, of virtue.

Dante's trip through Inferno and Purgatory is a trial of expiation; and after confronting the evil within his own mortal nature, he is ready to behold the realm of Paradise and the radiant beauty of divine love. After rising through the mountain of purgatory, he undergoes penance and purification—he is absolved of his human frailties as he drinks waters of forgetfulness from the river Lethe. After witnessing the evils of human nature—his own nature—in the lower realms, he is rewarded by being permitted the luminous sight of his beloved Beatrice. He reacts to her as a wayward son would behave before an unforgiving mother.

> Queenlike in bearing, yet stern, she continued, like one who speaks and holdeth back the hottest words till the last.
>
> "Look at me well; verily am I, verily am I Beatrice. How didst thou deign to draw nigh the mount? Knewest thou not that here man in happy?"
>
> Mine eyes drooped down to the clear fount, but beholding me therein, I drew them back to the grass, so great a shame weighed down my brow.
>
> So doth the mother seems stern to her child, as she seemed to me; for the savor of harsh pity tasteth of bitterness. *Purgatorio*, XXX

Even the angels on high melt with pity over the pain of the subdued lover.

Beatrice quite properly rebukes her knight of love though she knows of his prodigious effort to be joined with her. The courtier of love must become a Christian mystic before he can be admitted to Paradise. He must confront his fallibility and the taint of his love. Like a faithless lover or husband who, finding pleasure in the arms of another woman, must bear the censure of his mistress or wife when his conduct is discovered, Dante is forced to suffer the acknowledgement of his indulgence in earthly pleasure. He has not sinned as a mortal man; but rather he has been untrue to the image of his beloved Beatrice. Perhaps he should have died with her rather than endure the temptations of the world. Beatrice depicts the painful ordeal of the mistress or beloved lady, who is intent on correcting her lover's faults and goading him to realize his duty to perfect himself. Dante suffers his humiliation submissively and then receives her comforting embrace.

> My enamored mind, which held amorous converse ever with my Lady, burned more than ever to bring back my eyes to her:

> And whatsoever food nature or art e'er made, to catch the eyes and so possess the mind, be it human flesh, be it in pictures,

> If all united, would seem nought towards the divine delight which glowed upon me when that I turned me to her smiling face.

> And the power of which that look made largest to me, from the fair nest of Leda plucked me forth, and into the sweetest heaven thrust me.
> Paradiso [54]

THE RENAISSANCE

The Renaissance was a term first used in the nineteenth century to describe the revival of classical antiquity and the shift from emphasis on the other-worldly to the worldly life. The pagan influence was decisive, and the transition unmistakable. In Italy the

Renaissance emerged in the fourteenth century and attained its peak in the *quattrocento* and *cinquecento*. There were concurrent social and religious changes. The reform of the Church was a significant occurrence. Incipient nationalism undermined the feudal social structure while capitalism undermined the feudal economic structure. The fourteenth century Florentine artist, Giotto, fostered realistic art that emphasized the human dimension. The Virgin and Child would become suffering human beings—thence the great humanist art was born. Romantic (bourgeois) love would soon usurp the courtly-aristocratic-adulterous convention. Marriage for love, rather than for social or economic convenience, became the new mode. The change did not occur in a single age or even in a century. But no poet after Dante so ably described medieval otherworldliness and the courtly love ideal.

DECAMERON

Giovanni Boccaccio (1313-1375), an illegitimate son of a Tuscan merchant by a Frenchwoman, was an admirer and disciple of Dante, a translator of Greek literature, and a story teller of high merit. Though Boccaccio utilized the florid courtly style, he is best remembered for his naturalistic writing. His best work, *Decameron*, is a collection of medieval tales that deal with realistic people in amusing situations. The characters in the stories are committed to indulgence in the joy and pleasures of this life.

The Black Death of 1348 provides the frame for the collection. Ten young people escape from Florence to the country to avoid the ravages of the plague. While their conduct itself is above reproach, they agree to pass the time by telling stories that are erotic and bawdy. Human frailty, deceit, lust, revenge, jealousy, villainy, love, fortune are some themes treated in Boccaccio's human comedy.

In one story, a nobleman languishes for love of his lady and wastes his wealth in trying to win her favor. Reduced to poverty and the possession of a falcon, he prepares it as a dainty delicacy and serves it to her when she comes to his home for dinner, unaware that she is seeking the falcon as a present for her sick child. When she realizes his sacrifice, the lady is moved to pity, marries him, and they live happily ever after.

The cuckold is a familiar figure. Fiametta tells a tale of a trick played on a jealous husband. "Whatever a woman does to a husband who is jealous without reason, should not be condemned, but on the contrary, commended." The jealous husband poses as a priest to hear his wife's confession. She tells him that she loves a priest who comes to lie with her every night. While the husband guards the door against the intruding cleric, she admits her real lover and passes many a night with him. Later she lessons her husband, omitting but one detail of the truth. He cries:

> "Tell me who this priest is, and hurry about it!" His wife smiled and began, "It gives me the utmost satisfaction to see how a clever man can be led by the nose by a mere woman, like a ram taken by the horns to the slaughterhouse . . . I told you I was in love with a priest. Well weren't you, the man I love—the more fool I!—weren't you a priest at the time? I told you that no door of my house could remain locked, whenever he wished to lie with me. What door of your house was ever shut against you, when you had a mind to join me? I told you the priest would lie with me every night. Can you mention a night you did not lie with me?"[55]

The scholar also is distinguished for his wit and shrewdness. In one story Rinieri falls in love with a widow, Helen, who has another lover. Helen callously compels the scholar to spend the night in the freezing cold waiting to be admitted while she makes love to her gallant. Later her gallant leaves her, and she mistakenly trusts the scholar to help her regain his love. He fools her into exposing herself naked on a tower during a hot July day at the mercy of the sun and vermin who tear at her flesh, and remains intransigent to her pleas for mercy and aid.

Perhaps the most famous story in the collection is "Patient Griselda." The Marquis of Saluzzo, Gualtieri, is urged by his subjects to marry and agrees on condition that he be free to make his own decision. The right granted, he chooses Griselda, a poor country girl who lives in a hamlet near his estate. He comes to her home and declares that he will marry her if she promises to please him and be obedient to his wishes.

When she agrees, he strips her naked and dresses her with bridal clothes and a crown he has brought with him; and he takes her back to his palace. She proves to be an obedient wife and mother to their children. Afterwards Gualtieri decides to test her love. He first deprives her of their daughter; a few years later he deprives her of their son. Then he finally tells her that he has received special dispensation from the Pope and has decided to take another wife. True to her word, this wronged wife, this medieval Medea bears all. When he finally casts her out, she asks only to be permitted to return with the shift that she had on when they had met. And he further demands that she attend his imminent wedding. After this humiliating test, Gualtieri realizes that he has found his version of the perfect wife, and he loves her more than ever.

> "Griselda, it is now time your long-suffering patience were rewarded, and that all those who have looked upon me as a cruel, iniquitous monster should know that all I did was done with an end in view—namely to teach you to be a wife, and them to know how to choose and keep one. At the same time I strove to procure myself enduring peace while I lived with you—a thing I was afraid I should never have, if I married. It was to this end that I tortured and tormented you in all the ways you have borne. I am convinced now that you can give me the bliss I sought, for never, either by word or deed, have you deviated from my desires. Therefore, Griselda, it is my intention soon to restore to you all at once the joys I took from you at various times, and to reward you with supreme happiness for the many torments I have made you suffer. Take, then, Griselda, take with a joyful soul this girl whom you think my bride, and this little lad,

> her brother—take them, your children and mine! Ay, for
> they are those whom you and many others believed I had
> cruelly murdered. Take me, your husband, who loves you
> above everything in the world, for truly, I can well boast
> there is no man alive who has better reason to be satisfied
> with his wife!"

Marital bliss? Social satire? A glorification of male dominance? An allegory of Christian suffering? The tale of a medieval Job, Medea? A satire on female subservience? Is Gualtieri the ideal husband? Is he the typical husband? Is Griselda the ideal wife? Is she the typical wife? Is the tale a paradigm of feminine enslavement, or is it an example of wish fulfillment, fantasy? Or is it work of imaginative truth?

GEOFFREY CHAUCER

Geoffrey Chaucer (1345-1400), "the father of English literature," wrote in the realistic style and concerned himself with the man's moral and libidinous nature. Like Boccaccio, he also wrote in the allegorical-courtly style; but he is best remembered for his rendition of the English character in *The Canterbury Tales*. Chaucer was a pious Catholic, though he perhaps went further than Dante or Boccaccio in depicting the worldly interests and the corruption of the clergy. Of middle class origins, he was part of the court retinue, married a lady-in-waiting, undertook diplomatic missions abroad, and served in various civil service positions at home, most notably as Controller of Customs for the Port of London. He entertained the court audience and was highly esteemed, but he projected in his work his own middle class prejudices.

Chaucer was a peerless comedian. He was a foremost portrayer of the vagaries of human behavior—which he captured both in bold detail and in subtle nuance. The frame of *The Canterbury Tales* is an imaginary pilgrimage to the shrine of St. Thomas à Becket at Canterbury. The twenty nine pilgrims agree to exchange

stories on the three day journey. There is the drama of the itiner-
ant pilgrims as well as of the recounted tales. Chaucer also in-
cludes himself as a pilgrim and assigns to himself, with characteristic British self-deprecating wit, the least engaging story.

In "The Knight's Tale," Chaucer presents a medieval romance;
and at the same time, he ridicules the convention of courtly, idealistic love. Two Theban noblemen, Palamon and Arcite are taken
prisoners after a war between Athens and Thebes and are placed in
a tower. Year after year these cousins peer out of the window of
their cell. One day, Palamon, "blanched and gave a cry as though
he had been stabbed," and confesses to his cousin that he has
fallen in love with a goddess, Emily, the lovely sister-in-law of
Duke Theseus. His friend Arcite looks out the window, and "is
hurt as much as Palamon or more." Arcite berates his kinsman,
reminding him of their vow of friendship, and of his own prior
claim. But Palamon is unimpressed by the argument, and assever-
ates that Arcite had declared himself in love with a goddess, while
he in love with the mortal Emily. They now bicker over their respected claims to the distant lady.

Though a sudden change in circumstances, Arcite is released
from prison; however, he is sent into exile "doomed," as he thinks,
"to dwell no more in Purgatory but in Hell." The forlorn lover
now declares that he would prefer to remain incarcerated in order
to be near his beloved. Chaucer then suggests that the reader de-
cide who is better off: the imprisoned lover who enjoys the sight of
his beloved, or the lover, freed from his physical bondage, but
undergoing the spiritual torment of being denied the sight of his
lady:

> Yow loveres axe I now this questioun
> Who hath the worse, Arcite or Palamon?
> That oon may seen his lady day by day,
> But in prison he moot dwelle alway;
> That oother wher hym list may ride or go,
> But seen his lady shal he never mo.

In the course of the narrative, Arcite returns and disguises himself as a page in order to be near the unattainable Emily, while Palamon escapes from his cell to pursue his quest. Seven years have only nurtured their idealistic love: and when they meet, their jealousy is at a fever pitch, and the cousins exchange blows. The king Theseus then discovers their identity. After hearing their woeful saga of chivalrous love, he offers them the opportunity to joust for the beautiful Emily.

The conclusion of the story is a triumph for love, though it occurs only after a fateful reversal. On the eve of their battle, Palamon prays to Venus, the goddess of love; Arcite prays to Mars, the god of war. Which deity will prove the more potent? The gods express their will. Arcite wins the battle, but not the maiden; for at the moment of triumph, he falls from his horse and dashes his brains on the ground. Despite energetic efforts to save him, the end draws near. He wills the prize to his one-time comrade in arms and, with his last breath, he wishes Palamon and Emily happiness. King Theseus offers paean to the marvelous power of love:

> "The Firste Moevere of the cause above,
> Whan he first made the faire cheyne of love,
> Greet was th'effect, and heigh was his entente.
> Wel wiste he why, and what thereof he mente;
> For with that faire cheyne of love he bond
> The fyr, the eyr, the water, and the lond
> In certeyn boundes, that they may nat flee."[56]

Amor omnia vincit. (Love conquers all). The pilgrims no less than the characters in their stories are creatures of love. Chaucer's writing possesses psychological validity in its clear recognition of man and woman's sexual nature. The prioress who wears a golden brooch with the above inscription on her breast; the friar who has married off many young maiden at his own cost; and the wife of Bath, who has quintuplicated the marriage vows and is not at all averse to plunging into the well-tried waters again; they all reveal the lineaments of human desire reflected through the prism of comedy.

THE WIFE OF BATH

Chaucer is concerned with the relations between man and woman as the central condition of our existence. What are the proper roles of the sexes? Before this question can be answered woman must be vindicated from her position of inferiority in the medieval scheme. She is neither angel nor devil, and her biological and intellective faculties are coequal with those of men. The wife of Bath observes that marriage is the natural state; for her, the more often, the merrier. She cites her own experience as well as the scriptural example of the oft-married, wise King Solomon, and wishes she could manage her affairs half so well as he did. Once she gets started on her dissertation, she allows herself to pursue the matter, like a doctor of divinity, to its logical conclusion. Virginity is a great perfection, but if there were no marriages, no future virgins could be born. And besides, for what cause were the generative organs made? The Lord gave woman to man and man to woman. And, by God! she intends to have her man and keep him (at bay)!

She describes the methods she has used for gaining the advantage over her husbands and keeping them at her beck. Before providing them with her favors, she would negotiate with them. This brought her many gifts. She also expected to be remembered when they returned from their travels. She would harangue them for their smallest faults, complain that she had no clothes to wear, and accuse them of paying more attention to their neighbor's wife. She declares all this in the spirit of sharing her life's secrets with those who would benefit from them:

> Such mother-wit is granted us at our birth; God has given lies, tears, and spinning by nature to all women while they live. So I can boast of one thing: in the end I got the better of my husbands in every way, by force, cunning, or one means and another, such as keeping up an everlasting grumbling and natter. Especially in bed their luck was out; that's

where I'd scold them and do them out of their fun. When I felt my husband's arm come over my side, I wouldn't stay another moment in the bed until he's ransomed himself to me; and then I'd let him do his foolishness. As I always say, everything has its price. Who can lure home a hawk when he's empty-handed? To get what I wanted, I'd put up with all his lust and even pretend an appetite for it, though I never had much taste for old bacon; and that's really what turned me into a scold. For I wouldn't spare them, even at their own table, though the Pope himself sat next to them; I paid them out word for word I tell you! So help me God Almighty, were I to make my will and testament here and now there's never a word I owe them that isn't paid in full. I managed it so cleverly they found it best to give up; otherwise we'd never have had any rest. He could look like a raging lion, but he wouldn't get his satisfaction. Then I'd say, "Darling, look at Wilkin, our sheep! How tame he is! Come to me, sweetheart, let me kiss your cheek! You should be meek and patient too, and have a gentle scrupulous conscience yourself, since you keep on preaching about Job's patience. Be patient always; practice what you preach, for if you don't, we'll certainly teach you how much better it is to have peace in the house. No doubt one of us must knuckle under: and since a man is more rational than a woman is, you ought to be the one to give way."

Her life's story would seem to support her philosophy. The last time that she had married for love, she suffered untold misery, including a belt on the head that caused her partial loss of hearing. Through the wife of Bath, Chaucer shows the difficulty of marriage, particularly for women. In the end, though, the wife gains mastery even over her last husband, and teaches that winning isn't everything, it's the only thing!

Both sexes have the need to be respected and loved; and this love is a truer basis of a relationship than the artificial social code of chivalry. Chaucer, who devoted so much of his writing to "the marriage question," favors marriage based on the recognition of the differences between the sexes, and motivated by friendship and love. Such a relationship is realized in "The Nun's Priest's Tale" in the marital bliss enjoyed by Chanticleer and the uxorial Pertelote, absent of conflict over who rules the roost:

> She was courteous, tactful, elegant and companionable, and had such pretty ways that Chanticleer's heart had been absolutely in her keeping and firmly locked with hers since she was a week old. How happy he was in his love! And at sunrise what a delight to hear them sing in sweet accord, "My love is gone!" For in those days, I'm told, animals and birds could sing and talk.[57]

It hardly seems to matter that in this divinely mated couple, he is rooster, and she a hen.

REFORMATION

The fifteenth and sixteenth centuries were permeated by humanism and and the desire for knowledge. The human body was rendered divine in the paintings of the Italian masters, Botticelli, Leonardo, and Michelangelo. The austerity and spirituality of the monastic life were in decline. The Renaissance woman emerged—bejeweled, coiffed, corseted, perfumed and bedecked, while the Renaissance man maintained the similar interest in outward garb and, at the same time, also outfitted himself with new learning and new values. The most significant change was in his religious perception of himself, in his individualism and in his desire for freedom. Martin Luther (1483-1546), who had served as an Augustinian friar, sought to reform the church of its abuses; the Lutheran Church succeeded in relieving clergy of the obligation of celibacy. But he affirmed a Puritan ethic that taught Christian suspicion of sexual desire. "Had God consulted me about it, I should have advised Him to continue the generation of the species by fashioning human beings out of clay, as Adam was made."

RABELAIS

The giants of sixteenth-century literature were humanists and usually sympathetic to the new learning. Rabelais, Montaigne,
Cervantes, and Shakespeare all were caught in the whirlwind of
the changing currents and asserted man's freedom. The values of
François Rabelais (1490-4553) were formed in the Franciscan and
Benedictine monasteries, in which he lived as a youth and young
man; from which he broke, but never escaped.

His life's work, *The Five Books of Gargantua and Pantagruel*
describing the adventures of his larger than life heroes, was a classic work of Renaissance humanism, a passionate affirmation of man's
corporeal nature. His writing could be bitingly severe as when he
attacked the clergy for battening on people's sins and performing
no useful service. He showed prejudice against monks, whose manners and behavior he knew so well, by describing them as "lazy"
and "timeserving." Furthermore: the monk "does not plow like the
peasant, defend his country like the soldier, heal the sick like the
doctor, preach and elevate like the teacher, nor, let me add, handle
essential commodities like the merchant. Very good: there lies the
reason for the hatred and revulsion we allot him!" But Rabelais
retained his monastic prejudice against women. Pantagruel's friend,
the clever beggar Panurge, who lost his wealth on women and
lawsuits, often expresses misogyny and fear of marriage. Pantagruel
presents his own beat on the marriage question, a putative response to the Wife of Bath: "Having a wife means having the use of
her in the way ordained by nature, namely for company, help and
pleasure. Not having a wife means to loll and poltroon it uxori-
ously, tied to her petticoats." But it is Friar John who offers the
bawdy advice that Satan's ring—the bond dovetailed by joining
your wife's circlet to your flesh—is the surest prophylactic against
being cuckolded.

Yet the famous Abbey of Thélème (as you like it) was an idealistic monastic community, in which good deeds were undertaken

without strict rules and excessive repression, and where men and women lived together as equals in harmony, peace, friendship, and piety, "according to their free will and pleasure."

> The Thélèmites, thanks to their liberty, knew the virtues of emulation. All wished to do what they saw pleased one of their number. Let some lad or fair maid say, "Let us drink" and all of them drank, "Let us play" and all of them played, "Let us frolic in the fields" and all of them frolicked. When falconry or hawking were in order, the ladies sat high upon their saddles on fine nags, a sparhawk, lanner or merlin on one daintily gloved wrist, while the men bore other kinds of hawks.

> They were so well bred that none, man or woman, but could read, write, sing, play several instruments, speak five or six languages and readily compose verse and prose in any of them. Never had earth known knights so proud, so gallant, so adroit on horseback and on foot, so athletic, so lively, so well trained in arms as these. Never were ladies seen so dainty, so comely, so winsome, so deft at handwork and needlework, so skilful in feminine arts, so frank and so free as these.[58]

MONTAIGNE

The good physician, Michel de Montaigne (1533-1592), scion of a wealthy Catholic father and a mother of Spanish Jewish descent, well educated and urbane, described the nature of love from his own experiences. His *Essays* introduced the personal view in western literature, as Montaigne tested his own attitudes on himself and upon his audience. The relations between men and women elicited some of his most profound observations.

> A young man asked the philosopher Panaetius whether it would be becoming to a wise man to be in love. "Let us leave aside the wise man," he replied, "but you and I, who are not, let us not get involved in a thing so excited and violent,

which enslaves us to others and makes us contemptible to ourselves."
On some Verses of Virgil

Eschewing the medium of fiction, he presented his views directly, and he was not unfamiliar with wives of Bath and elsewhere:

> Wives always have a proclivity for disagreeing with their husbands. They seize with both hands every pretext to go contrary to them; the first excuse serves them as plenary justification. I have known one who robbed her husband wholesale in order, so she told her confessor, to give fatter alms. Just trust that pious almsgiving! No responsibility seems to them to have sufficient dignity if it comes by the husband's concession. They have to usurp it either by cunning or by insolence, and always unjustly, to give it grace and authority. As in the case I am speaking of, when they act against a poor old man and for the sake of children, then they seize this pretext and glory in making it serve their passion, and, as if they were slaves making a common cause, readily conspire against his domination and government.
> *Of the Affection of Fathers for their Children*

Although he maintained the medieval suspicion of the sexual drive, he recognized its importance to human nature.

> Those who flee Venus too much sin no less
> Than those who do pursue her to excess.
> *Amyot's Plutarch*

Finally, though he wonders about the negative affect of passions on the actions of individuals, he glorifies the marriage contract.

> A good marriage, if such there be, rejects the company and conditions of love. It tries to reproduce those of friendship. It is a sweet association in life, full of constancy, trust, and an infinite number of useful and solid services and mutual obligations. No woman who savors the taste of it (*Whom the nuptial torch with welcome light has joined, Catullus*) would

want to have the place of a mistress or paramour to her husband. If she is lodged in his affection as a wife, she is lodged there much more honorably and securely. When he dances ardent and eager attention elsewhere, still let anyone ask him then on whom he would rather have some shame fall, on his wife or his mistress; whose misfortune would afflict him more; for whom he wishes more honor. These questions admit of no doubt in a sound marriage.

The fact that we see so few good marriages is a sign of its price and its value. If you form it well and take it rightly, there is no finer relationship in our society. We cannot do without it, and yet we go about debasing it. The result is what is observed about cages: the birds outside despair of getting in, and those inside are equally anxious to get out. Socrates, when asked which was preferable, to take or not to take a wife, said: "Whichever a man does, he will repent it."

But he withholds further comment:

The bitterness of marriage, like the sweets, are kept secret by the wise.[59]
On some Verses of Virgil

WILLIAM SHAKESPEARE

William Shakespeare (1564-1616) shared Montaigne's humanism and avidly read the translation of the *Essays* published in England in 1603. Like Dante before him, who was representative of the middle ages, and like James Joyce, who showed the fragmentation of the twentieth century, Shakespeare's writing embodied the *Weltanschauung*, the spirit of the time, the breadth, wisdom and humanism of the Renaissance. His attitude toward love was realistic like Montaigne's, rather than courtly, and it was influenced, like Chaucer's, by his middle class background. Shakespeare was the dramatist of the effect of passion on our experience and our knowledge, and a precursor of modern psychology in illuminating the nature of men and women. His plays were entertainment for the stage—but his work has survived because of the validity of his insights into the character of men and women.

"The course of true love never did run smooth," Shakespeare wrote in *A Midsummer Night's Dream.* The theme of his comedies is the game of love—and he knew well its connection to the pain of love, and the battle of the sexes, still the mainstays of comedy. In calling one of his plays *Much Ado About Nothing* and another *As You Like It,* he twitted his audience for preoccupation with their libidinous drives. He also considers the ideal of friendship and happiness between the sexes and concludes that there is a proper role for each sex.

Shakespeare was a traditionalist, and he accepted the ethic of romance culminating in marriage. A proper moralist, Shakespeare who, according to tradition, was a victim of pressure to marry Anne Hathaway while she was bearing his child, taught the categorical imperative of bourgeois morality. In the last play that he wrote, Prospero warns his daughter and his future son-in-law to beware of the sword of Damocles that threatens their future.

> But if thou dost break her virgin-knot before
> All sanctimonious ceremonies may
> With full and holy rite be minister'd,
> No sweet aspersion shall the heavens let fall
> To make this contract go; but barren hate,
> Sour-ey'd disdain and discord shall bestrew
> The union of your bed with weeds so loathly
> That you shall hate it both. Therefore take heed,
> As Hymen's lamps shall light you.
> *The Tempest*

Shakespeare was ambivalent about love. Influenced by the Christian tradition, he expressed repugnance toward sexual love: "The expense of spirit in a waste of shame/ Is lust in action." On the other hand, his sonnets idealize love in poetry that never will be surpassed:

Love is not love
Which alters when it alteration finds,
Or bends with the remover to remove,
O, no! It is an ever-fixed mark
That looks on tempests and is never shaken;
It is the star to every wand'ring bark
Whose worth's unknown, although his highth be taken.
Sonnet 116

ROMEO AND JULIET

The Tragedy of Romeo and Juliet has been to the modern world what *The Art of Courtly Love* and *The Divine Comedy* were to the medieval world. Shakespeare transformed the medieval love ideal into the modern love ethic that holds the inseparability of love and marriage. The romance of Romeo and Juliet teaches that in spite of the objections of parents and the stigma of social ostracism, true love survives. The legitimacy of sexual feelings in love and marriage is recognized as universal in its thousands of analogues and variations down to its modern, popular derivations, such as *West Side Story.*

Before Romeo saw Juliet across a crowded room, he never knew true love. He thought that he loved the fair Rosaline, but he loved her according to the conventions of courtly love, and expressed himself according to the book:

Love is a smoke made with the fume of sighs;
Being purg'd, a fire sparkling in lovers' eyes;
Being vex'd, a sea nourish'd with lovers' tears.
What is it else? A madness most discreet,
A choking gall, and a preserving sweet.
I.i.190-194

He confuses rhetoric with passion because he does not know love. His infatuation with Juliet is a sudden intense experience, love at first sight, which possesses his whole being. His expression becomes more direct:

Did my heart love till now? Forswear it, sight!
For I ne'er saw true beauty till this night.

He pursues Juliet silently and devotedly without even acknowledging his love to his friends. He steals into the Capulet orchard
and confesses his passion most tenderly:

Be soft! What light through yonder window breaks?
It is the east, and Juliet is the sun!
Arise, fair sun, and kill the envious moon,
Who is already sick and pale with grief
That thou, her maid, art far more fair than she.

Unaware of his presence, Juliet also soliloquizes her own despair:

O Romeo, Romeo! wherefore art thou Romeo?
Deny thy father and refuse thy name;
Or, if thou wilt not, be but sworn my love,
And I'll no longer be a Capulet.

As soon as they discover each other's presence, they exchange vows
of love. She declares:

My bounty is as boundless as the sea,
My love as deep; the more I give to thee,
The more I have; for both are infinite.

and then asks him to reveal his intentions:

If that thy bent of love be honorable,
Thy purpose marriage, send me word tomorrow,
By one that I'll be procure to come to thee,
Where and what time thou wilt perform the rite;
And all my fortunes at thy foot I'll lay,
And follow thee my lord throughout the world.
II.ii.iff.

Soon, they are secretly wed, and Juliet prepares to elope with her husband. She anxiously awaits the night that will join them:

> Come, civil night,
> Thou sober-suited matron, all in black,
> And learn me how to lose a winning match,
> Play'd for a pair of stainless maidenhoods.
> Hood my unmann'd blood, bating in my cheeks,
> With thy black mantle; till strange love grow bold,
> Think true love acted simple modesty.
> Come, night; come, Romeo; come, thou day in night;
> For thou wilt lie upon the wings of night,
> Whiter than new snow upon a raven's back.
> Come, gentle night, come, loving black-brow'd night,
> Give me my Romeo; and, when I shall die,
> Take him and cut him out in little stars
> And he will make the face of heaven so fine
> That all the world will be in love with night,
> And pay no worship to the garish sun.
> III.ii.10-25

Her premonition of death of her husband proves all-too-accurate as the tragedy of the "star-cross'd lovers" reaches its culmination. Romeo, who cries that he is "fortune's fool" after he unwillingly slays Juliet's cousin, Tybalt, and must flee Verona as an outlaw, rather than escape with his wife. The lovers have one final meeting to consummate their love before fate decrees their untimely death and ultimate heavenly reunion.

HAMLET

The Tragedy of Hamlet, Prince of Denmark has many themes and levels of meaning. It is tragedy of political intrigue and revenge, it is a family tragedy not unlike Aeschylus's *Oresteia*, where the responsibility to punish his father's murderer and his mother's lover devolves upon the son. The courtier Polonius contends that Hamlet has fallen into melancholy or madness owing to his daughter's

rejection of his amorous suit. This was undertaken by the dutiful
daughter upon his instructions. Polonius recounts:

> And my young mistress thus I did bespeak:
> "Lord Hamlet is a prince and out of thy star;
> This must not be"; and then I prescripts gave her,
> That she should lock herself from his resort,
> Admit no messengers, receive no tokens.
> Which done she took the fruits of my advice.

When Ophelia repelled him, Hamlet

> Fell into sadness, then into a fast,
> Thence to a watch, thence into a weakness,
> Thence to a lightness, and by this declension,
> Into a madness wherein now he raves,
> And all we mourn for.
> II.ii.140-151

Polonius's diagnosis is thought by everyone to be wide of the mark.
Yet it gains credibility in a following scene when Ophelia returns
the love letters that Hamlet gave her:

> Ophelia: My lord, I have remembrances of yours
> That I have longed long to redeliver.
> I pray you now receive them.

> Hamlet: No, not I, I never gave you ought.

> Ophelia: My honor'd lord, you know right well you did,
> And with them words of so sweet breath compos'd
> As made these things more rich. Their perfume lost,
> Take these again, for to the noble mind
> Rich gifts wax poor when givers prove unkind.
> There, my lord.

> Hamlet: Ha, ha! Are you honest?

> Ophelia: My lord?

Hamlet: Are you fair?

Ophelia: What means your lordship?

Hamlet: That if you be honest and fair, your honesty should admit no discourse to your beauty.

His bitterness toward her reaching a pitch, he turns his frustration on her no less than on himself:

What should such fellows as I do crawling between earth and heaven? We are arrant knaves, believe none of us. Go thy ways to a nunn'ry.

And then again:

If thou dost marry, I'll give thee this plague for thy dowry: be thou as chaste as ice, as pure as snow, thou shalt not scape . calumny. Get thee to a nunn'ry, farewell. III.i.92ff.

There is little question that his anger toward Ophelia is a reflection of his anger against his mother, whom he blames for having wedded the murderer of his father: "The funeral bak'd meats/ Did coldly furnish forth the marriage tables," he cries. Ophelia becomes the surrogate for his vengeful feelings against his mother, and this ire drives him into the guise of madness:

I have heard of your paintings, well enough. God hath given you one face, and you make yourselves another. You jig and amble, and you lisp, you nickname God's creatures and make your wantonness your ignorance. Go to, I'll no more on't, it hath made me mad.

His inability to deal with his feelings towards Ophelia underscores his disability; later he turns on his mother and uses the same indiscreet language against her.

PORTIA AND LADY MACBETH

There are bad wives and good wives in Shakespeare's plays. Perhaps the noblest wife is Portia in *The Tragedy of Julius Caesar*, who attempts to use her power of persuasion to learn what mischief her husband is planning so that, like a good helpmate, she can protect him from himself.

> Y'have ungently, Brutus,
> Stole from my bed; and yesternight at supper
> You suddenly arose and walk'd about,
> Musing and sighing, with your arms across;
> And when I ask'd you what the matter was,
> You star'd upon me with ungentle looks.
> I urg'd you further; then you scratch'd your head,
> And too impatiently stamp'd with your foot.
> Yet I insisted, yet you answer'd not,
> But with an angry wafter of your hand
> Gave sign for me to leave you.

In spite of Brutus's plea, "Kneel not, gentle Portia," she presses her suit:

> I should not need, if you were gentle Brutus.
> Within the bond of marriage, tell me, Brutus,
> Is it excepted I should know no secrets
> That appertain to you? Am I yourself
> But, as it were, in sort of limitation.
> To keep with you at meals, comfort your bed,
> And talk to you sometimes? Dwell I but in the suburbs
> Of your good pleasure? If it be no more,
> Portia is Brutus' harlot, not his wife.
> II.i.237ff.

She takes her life horribly, consuming coals after her husband dies in the failed conspiracy. In contrast, Lady Macbeth in *Macbeth* plays upon her husband's manliness to goad him to pursue his conspiratorial ambitions and slay the rightful king:

> Hie thee hither,
> That I may pour my spirits in thine ear,
> And chastise with the valor of my tongue
> All that impedes thee from the golden round.
> I.v.25-28

When he shrinks from doing the deed out of moral scruples, her words are turned to daggers directed against his manhood:

> Was the hope drunk
> Wherein you dress'd yourself? Hath it slept since?
> And wakes it now to look so green and pale
> At what it did so freely? From this time
> Such I account thy love.

Wounded to the quick, Macbeth challenges her:

> Prithee peace!
> I dare do all that may become a man:
> Who dares do more is none.

Gleaning his vulnerability and her conquest, she bores in on impending victory:

> What beast was't then
> That made you break this enterprise to me?
> When you durst do it, then you were a man!
> And to be more than what you were, you would
> Be so much more the man.
> I.vii.35ff.

OTHELLO

The Tragedy of Othello, the Moor of Venice explores jealousy with greater intensity than any play since *Medea* had done. The great soldier Othello has had heroic successes in battle but knows little about human nature; his innocence attracts him to the beautiful

Desdemona. But he falls prey to the manipulations of his wicked ensign, Iago, who is also torn by jealousy toward his superior as well as toward his rival, Michael Cassio. He craftily convinces Othello that Desdemona is unfaithful to him; and with the flimsiest evidence, Othello is brought to destruction and to the murder of his wife. The power of the play lies not only in the study of jealousy, but in the exploration of the frustration of impotence turned on oneself and on others. James Joyce's peculiar and stunning observation that "his unremitting intellect is the hornmad Iago ceaselessly willing that the moor in him shall suffer" supports his outlandish notion that Shakespeare never forgave his own wife for a supposed affair with her brother-in-law. Though there is no compelling evidence to sustain such a viewpoint, the depth of Othello's pain lends some credence to Joyce's interpretation and goes a long way to understand the wound that informs this play.

ANTONY AND CLEOPATRA

The Tragedy of Antony and Cleopatra is Shakespeare's rendition of mature love. Drawing upon Plutarch's Roman history, he dramatizes one of the great love stories of all time. Like another famous African heroine, Virgil's Dido, Cleopatra is a monument to the power of love, as poetry celebrates the eternal power of woman's fascination:

> Age cannot wither her, nor custom stale
> Her infinite variety. Other women cloy
> The appetites they feed, but she makes hungry
> Where most she satisfies; for vilest things
> Become themselves in her, the holy priests
> Bless her when she is riggish.
> II.ii.234-239

In a later seventeeth century adaptation, the play was titled *All For Love, or The World Well Lost*. Antony is part of the triumvirate that rules the world, and yet he pines like a schoolboy for his lady

Cleopatra. Cleopatra, for her part the shrewd and calculating Queen of Egypt, holds herself in power by exploiting the vanities of her Roman conquerors, first Julius Caesar and then Antony. Yet enigmatically, she loves Antony almost beyond control. She orders her servants to spy on him: "Where is he? See where he is, who's with him, what he does/ I did not send you. If you find him sad/ Say I am dancing: if in mirth, report/ That I am sudden sick. Quick, and return." Her loneliness caused by his absence drives her to desperation:

> O Charmian!
> Where think'st thou he is now? Stands he, or sits he?
> Or does he walk? Or is he on his horse?
> O happy horse, to bear the weight of Antony!
> Do bravely, horse! for wot'st thou whom thou mov'st?
> The demi-Atlas of this earth, the arm
> And burgonet of men. He's speaking now,
> Or murmuring, "Where's my serpent of old Nile?"
> For so he calls me. Now I feed myself
> With most delicious poison.
> I.v.17-27

The lovers fall victim to the machinations of Octavius Caesar (later Augustus) whose tenacious pursuit of power leaves him invulnerable to the softening influence of woman's love. After the death of Antony's wife, Antony is free to marry Cleopatra. But Octavius goads Antony into marrying Octavia, his own sister, on the pretext of strengthening the bond within the ruling triumvirate. For fear of showing himself unworthy of his duty as a Roman, he forsakes the love of his African Queen, even as Aeneas had done. Octavius, however, betrays Antony, and the separated lovers are doomed. First Antony succumbs. Then Cleopatra declares, "husband, I come," and she applies the asp to her breast. It is not at all surprising that Shakespeare who bestrode the medieval and modern world should have depicted the transitory nature of mundane love in a society which maintained Christian scruples and could validate the attainment of true love only in the afterworld, as exemplified by the experiences of Héloïse and Abelard, Dante and Beatrice, Romeo and Juliet, Desdemona and Othello, and Antony and Cleopatra.

JOHN DONNE

A young contemporary of Shakespeare, John Donne (1572-1631), who, in his youth, was "a great visitor of ladies," and settled down to become the royal chaplain and Dean of St. Paul's, celebrated erotic feeling in his verse. He influenced both the metaphysical and the cavalier style of poetry long after he surrendered his youthful fancy and took up the ministry. His courtship contained the saga of Romeo and Juliet, as he married out of his class the well-born Anne More and was clapped into prison by her irate guardian; Donne turned the occasion to good wit in his note to his wife from his cell: "John Donne, Anne Donne, Un-Done." He wrote about the discovery of love in a most natural and idealistic manner in the poem, "The Good-Morrow."

> I wonder by my troth, what thou, and I
> Did, till we lov'd? Were we not wean'd till then?
> But suck'd on countrey pleasures, childishly?
> Or snorted we in the seaven sleepers den?
> T'was so; But this, all pleasures fancies bee.
> If ever any beauty I did see,
> Which I desired, and got, t'was but a dreame of thee.[60]

Donne was a first rate stylist and perhaps the best realistic love poet since Catullus. His verse is passionate, clever, and profound as he reveals the struggles of love:

> For Godsake hold your tongue, and let me love,
> Or chide my palsie, or my gout,
> My five gray haires, or ruin'd fortune flout,
> With wealth your state, your minds with Arts improve,

Take you a course, get you a place,
Observe his honour, or his grace,
Or the Kings reall, or his stamped face
Contemplate, what you will, approve,
So you will let me love.

His metaphysical wit reaches its peak in this poem that might have been influenced by the difficulty of his courtship, and he wittily entitled "The Canonization."

Wee can dye by it, if not live by love,
And if unfit for tombes and hearse
Our legend bee, it will be fit for verse;
And if no peece of Chronicle wee prove,
We'll build in sonnets pretty roomes;
As well a well wrought urne becomes
The greatest ashes, as halfe-acre tombes:
And by these hymnes, all shall approve
Us *Canoniz'd* for Love:

He also can be funny, as when he mocks his dependency on his libidinal urge in "The Triple Fool":

I am two fooles, I know,
For loving, and for saying so
In whining Poetry.

Again, he displays "metaphysical wit," in punning on the Elizabethan similitude between death and climax in "The Legacie."

When I dyed last, and, Deare, I dye
As often as from thee I goe,
Though it were an houre agoe.

Or then in a somewhat "cavalier" style:

Sweetest love, I do not goe,
For weariness of thee,
Nor in hope the world can show

> A fitter Love for mee;
> But since that I
> Must dye at last, 'tis best,
> To use my selfe in jest
> Thus by fain'd deaths to dye.

"The Flea" is perhaps the best seduction poem in the language, as Donne points to the congress of blood represented by the Flea's "wall of Jet" to seize the moment (*carpe diem*) and to vindicate his own plea for similarly harmless congress of pleasure with his lady.

> Marke but this flea, and marke in this,
> How little that which thou deny'st me is;
> It suck'd me first, and now sucks thee,
> And in this flea, our two bloods mingled bee.

His profanity reaches its peak in the Elegy "To his Mistris Going to Bed."

> Come, Madame, come, all rest my powers defie,
> Until I labor, I in labor lie.
> The foe oft-times having the foe in sight
> Is tir'd with standing though he never fight.

The classical influence is unmistakable:

> Full nakedness! All joyes are due to thee,
> As souls unbodied, bodies uncloth'd must be,
> To taste whole joyes. Gems which you women use
> Are like Atlanta's balls, cast in mens views,
> That when a fools eye lighteth on a Gem
> His earthly soul may covet theirs, not them.

At the same time, his poetry often contains a double meaning, and the idea of woman provokes his most frequent paradox.[61] In his Third Satyre, he describes the religious quest as the search for the ideal women—"Is not our Mistress faire religion?" The Reformation and Counter Reformation have brought about a deep divide

about the nature of the true religion: Mirreus "seekes her at Rome,"
Crantz loves her only, who at Geneva is called,

> Religion, plaine, simple, sullen, yong,
> Contemptuous, yet unhansome.

Graius thinking that she "Which dwels with us, is onely perfect,
hee embraceth her"; on the other hand,

> Careless Phrygius doth abhorre
> All, because all cannot be good, as one
> Knowing some women whores, dares marry none.

After his conversion to the ministry, he wrote some sermons and
philosophical-religious treatises on love, death, and damnation.
He continued to utilize the sexual metaphor to describe religious
feeling as St. Ambrose had done even as, in his youthful poems,
the sexual metaphor might conceal his religious intent. He identifies his wish to be loved by God with a desire to be violated and
chastised into obedience in Holy Sonnet XIV:

> Batter my heart, three-person'd God; for you
> As yet but knocke, breathe, shine, and seeke to mend;
> That I may rise and stand, o'erthrow mee, and bend
> Your force, to breake, blowe, burn, and make me new.
> I, like an unsurpt tower to'another due,
> Labour to admit you, but Oh, to no end;
> Reason, your viceroy in mee, mee should defend,
> But is captiv'd, and proves weake or untrue.
> Yet dearly I love you, and would be loved faine,
> But am betroth'd unto your enemie:
> Divorce mee, untie, or breake that knot again;
> Take mee to you, imprison mee, for I
> Except you enthrall mee, never shall be free,
> Nor ever chast, except you ravish mee.

MONARCHY AND CHIVALRY

The idealistic tradition persisted in the seventeenth century—particularly in authoritarian societies, like Spain and France, as the glorification of dependency and subservience served to uphold the rule of monarchy. While the Protestant countries tended to develop more liberal tendencies, the Catholic states of Europe usually enforced a more repressive order. The feudal service to the lady, which had been an extension of service to the lord in the age of chivalry, now became the obligation of fidelity to the king and the state, and was symbolized and reinforced through service to the Dona.

DON QUIJOTE

When Cervantes's Don Quijote attempts his self-appointed mission of reforming the world of evil, he seeks a Dona who will inspire and grace his effort. True to his character, the ageing don seeks not reality, but only the comforting illusion of knighthood, and so it matters not that the lady he chooses is a farm wench who resides in the vicinity of La Mancha. The novel is as much about the comforting power of madness as it is a romance of chivalry. It has been noted, that *Don Quijote* is a tragedy to those who feel, a comedy for those who are young and untested by life, a tragedy for those who are middle-aged and have experienced life's disappointments and their own disillusionments, and finally a comedy for the old who have survived with soul and wit nearly intact:

> Well, with his armor scrubbed clean, and his helmet ready, and then his horse christened and himself confirmed, he realized that all he needed and had to hunt for was a lady to be in love with, since a knight errant without love entanglements would be like a tree without leaves or fruit, or a body without a soul. So he said to himself: "Now, if for my sins, or by good fortune, I happen to find a giant right here in this

neighborhood, which after all is something that usually happens to knights-errant, and we have a go at it and I overthrow him, or maybe split him right down the middle, wouldn't it be a good idea to have someone to whom I could send him, so he could go and kneel down in front of my sweet lady and say, his voice humble and submissive, "I, my lady, am the giant Caraculiambro, lord of the island of Malindrania, defeated in man-to-man combat by that knight who can never be too much praised, Don Quijote de la Mancha, who has sent me here to offer myself at your pleasure, to be dealt with however your Grace may happen to think best?"

Oh, how our good knight relished the delivery of this speech, especially once he'd decided who was to be his lady love! It turned out, according to some people, that not too far from where he lived there was a very pretty peasant girl, with whom he was supposed, once upon a time, to have been in love, although (as the story goes) she never knew it nor did he ever say a word to her. Her name was Aldonza Lorenzo, and he thought it a fine idea to bestow upon her the title of Mistress of his Thoughts. Hunting for a name as good as the one he'd given himself, a name that would be appropriate for that princess and noble lady, he decided to call her *Dulcinea del Toboso* [*toboso*=limestone rock], since Toboso was where she came from. To him it seemed a singularly musical name, rare, full of meaning, like all the others he'd assigned to himself and everything that belonged to him.[62]

FRENCH CLASSICAL DRAMA

The idealization of woman and the duty of obedience were maintained in the drama written during the ages of King Louis XIII and King Louis XIV of France. Compared with the Elizabethan drama that was written for an audience composed of all classes, the plays of the French classical theater were written exclusively for the court audience consisting of aristocrats and ladies; the age was characterized by the *savante* Madame de Staël as "the most note-worthy of all in literature."[63]

CORNEILLE

Corneille's *Le Cid* is a notable example of the artificial, but never-theless dramatic conflict between love and honor. Don Roderigo, the Cid, is the ideal hero while Chimene is the ideal of pious femininity. After Chimene's father insults Roderigo's father, Roderigo is called upon to avenge the sully to the family name. Roderigo obeys the call of honor and slays Chimene's father; but now Chimene seeks Roderigo's death and promises herself to which-ever knight avenges the death of her father. When Roderigo in-trudes upon her in order to declare that out of love, he will permit Don Sancho to defeat him in the duel, and accept his own death, Chimene is torn by the conflicting claims of love and honor. She cannot accept his love, and she cannot will his death. She declares the he must observe his honor, even as she has observed hers, and thus she inspires him to valour. Roderigo declares:

> I go to punishment not to a combat.
> Since you desire my death, my faithful heart
> Knows no desire to preserve my life.
> My heart is firm, but I can find no joy
> In saving that which only brings you pain.
> This night already had brought death to me
> Had I been fighting for myself alone.
> But for my king, his people, and my country,
> I have been brave not to defend myself.
> Life is not yet so hateful to my soul
> That I would leave it stained with treachery:
> Now it is only of myself I think,
> You seek my death and I accept the sentence.
> Your anger chose another hand to serve it.
> I was not worthy to meet death at yours.
> They shall not see me giving blow for blow.
> I cannot strike the arm that fights for you.

> I shall rejoice to think his blows are yours.
> Since 'tis your honor that his arms maintain,
> I'll bare my bosom gladly to his sword,
> Worshiping as yours the hand that slays me.

Now Chimene relents as she contemplates her pledge to marry whoever avenges her father's murder. She turns to Roderigo as the only man who can save her from such a loathsome union:

> Since life and honor have no power to stay
> This rush to death, dear Roderigo, if ever
> I loved you, in return defend yourself
> And save me from Don Sancho, fight for me.
> Fight to save me from an odious fate
> That will deliver me to one I hate.
> Shall I say more? Go plan your defense.
> Fulfill my duty, silence my complaints.
> And if you love me still, return as victor
> From this encounter where Chimene is prize.
> Adieu. I blush with shame to tell you this.

The Cid, the slayer of innumerable Moors, is motivated to the peak of heroic endeavor and expression:

> What enemy can daunt me now! Come on,
> Navarre, Castille, Morocco, come, you Knights,
> The bravest of all Spain, join arms against me.
> Oppose a solid army to my hand.
> Against so sweet a hope your strength combined
> Were all too small to conquer me alone.[64]

There is one last *contretemps* in the plot when after Roderigo slays Don Sancho, Chimene again changes her mind yet once again and refuses him. The play ends with the hope that the king will be able to reconcile these "honor-crossed" lovers.

MOLIÈRE'S SCHOOL FOR WIVES

Comedy, by definition, treats situations, in which folly is held up to ridicule, and the characters are exposed in their naked frailty; thus they are "lower" than we are. Jean Baptiste Poquelin, who wrote under the name Molière, revealed man's weakness and failure to live up to the abstract ideal of heroism—though his plays were written for and enjoyed by the same court audience that Corneille served. Through jest and derision, Molière deplored the hypocrisy and affectation of the courtly circle. But comedy also uncovers the deepest and most personal wounds to public view— and so Molière revealed himself.

The relations between men and women are notably treated in these comedies, and *The School for Wives* was written during the first year of his marriage to the bewitching young actress Armande Béjart. (She was the sister of Madeleine Béjart, who also had been Molière's friend, and likely mistress.) The plot concerns the efforts of the forty-two year old Arnolphe to raise and educate his bride, who has been his charge from infancy, to be a suitable wife. His method has been to shield her from the world and teach her only his ideas so that she would be docile and submissive to him. Arnolphe, who has a reputation as a cynic and has always ridiculed and scorned men who have been misused by women, confides to his friend his belief in his own inviolability. He has found the philosopher's stone that assures him of the perfect wife.

> The girl I'll marry is an innocent,
> And her simplicity is my protection.

He gloats over the genius of his success in placing her in a convent to protect her from corruption of the world:

> The other day—and this you'll hardly credit—
> She was much troubled and came to ask me,
> In absolute and perfect innocence,
> If children are begotten through the ear!

The play turns out to be an educational experience for the teacher.
Agnes receives gifts from a suitor closer to her own age, Horace,
allows him to visit her and to profess love to her, exchanges *billets-
doux* with him—protesting all the while her ingenuousness, her
ignorance of any wrong-doing, and her guilelessness. Arnolphe's
discovery of her behavior provides him with a shock bordering on
trauma:

> For twenty years, a sage philosopher,
> I've watched the unhappy destiny of husbands,
> I've counted up the various accidents
> Which bring the most sagacious to their doom;
> I've profited by their calamities,
> And when I chose a wife, I sought for ways
> To guard myself against all interlopers,
> And guarantee that I would be no cuckold.
> And, to my ends, I thought I had employed
> The ultimate in human artfulness!
> But fate no doubt has issued a decree
> That never a husband is to be exempt;
> For after all my study, after all
> The experience I've gained upon the matter,
> After some twenty years of meditation
> On the precautious I proposed to take
> To distinguish myself from all the other husbands,
> I'm caught with them in the universal trap!

Agnes knows her own mind—that woman is rare who will live
solely according to any man's expectations. Arnolphe's rigidity and
egotism alienate her, and the play ends with her marrying Horace
after a fortuitous turn of circumstances.

Arnolphe: So you don't love me, then?

Agnes: Love you?

Arnolphe: Yes, me.

Agnes: Oh, no.

Arnolphe: What, no?

Agnes: You wouldn't have me lie?

Arnolphe: And why not love me, impudent, saucy girl?

Agnes: Oh, dear! It isn't me you ought to blame. Why didn't you make me love you, as he did? I don't think I prevented you at all.

Arnolphe: I did my best; I tried to do my best. But all my efforts clearly came to nothing.

Agnes: He just knows how, assuredly, better than you. He had no trouble at all in making me love him.

Arnolphe: Look how this peasant argues and replies! One of the lady wits could do no better! [65]

In a society which limited a woman's freedom, a civilized lady could take revenge on a tyrannic father or husband and compromise his honor by giving her love to a rival. It was a lesson that required no study and no curriculum leading to a formal degree.

PARADISE LOST

A woman's subservience was maintained according to nature and man's reason, and encouraged by Christian teaching. John Milton's *Paradise Lost* retold the saga of creation and the beginnings of our progenitors according to the biblical account. Written at the end of the Renaissance-Reformation, it was a culminating statement of

Christian humanism. As Michelangelo had depicted the glory of
God's creation in his frescoes on the ceiling of the Sistine Chapel,
Milton captured in poetry the epic of man's fall from grace according to Protestant theology. His most memorable scenes are his
rendition of man and woman in their primordial condition.

> Two of far nobler shape erect and tall,
> Godlike erect, with native Honor clad
> In naked Majesty seem'd Lords of all,
> And worthy seem'd, for their looks Divine
> The image of their glorious Maker shone,
> Truth, Wisdom, Sanctitude severe and pure,
> Severe, but in true filial freedom placed,
> Whence true authority in men; though both
> Not equal, as their sex not equal seem'd;
> For contemplation hee and valour form'd,
> For softness shee and sweet, attractive Grace,
> Hee for God only, shee for God in him:
> His fair large Front and Eye sublime declar'd
> Absolute rule; and Hyacinthine Locks
> Round from his parted forelock manly hung
> Clust'ring, but not beneath his shoulders broad:
> Shee as a veil down to the slender waist
> Her unadorned golden tresses wore
> Dishevell'd, but in wanton ringlets wav'd
> As the Vine curls her trendils, which impli'd
> Subjection, but requir'd with gentle sway,
> And by her yielded, by him best receiv'd,
> Yielded with coy submission, modest pride,
> And sweet reluctant amorous delay.
> Nor those mysterious parts were then conceal'd,
> Then was not guilty shame: dishonest shame
> Of Nature's works, honor dishonorable,
> Sin-bred, how have ye troubl'd all mankind
> With shows instead, mere shows of seeming pure,
> And banisht from man's life his happiest life,
> Simplicity and spotless innocence.
> So pass'd they naked on, nor shunn'd the sight
> Of God or Angel, for they thought no ill:
> So hand in hand they pass'd, the loveliest pair

> That ever since in love's embraces met,
> Adam the goodliest man of men since born
> His sons, the fairest of her Daughters Eve.
> Book IV.288-324[66]

In paradise, Adam and Eve live free from vexation of sin. Satan, the fallen Archangel, looks upon their happiness and compares it to his own degradation. He is driven by envy and hatred to plot their downfall so that they will be no higher than the fallen angels. The unvirtuous are always envious of the blessedness enjoyed by the guiltless. Puritanism teaches that the duty of man is to withstand temptation which will deprive him of salvation. But Milton reflects the Judeo-Christian prejudice against the daughters of Eve—when he describes how Eve was lured by the serpent to eat of the forbidden fruit and then bring Adam down with her to their mutual destruction:

> from the bough
> She gave him of that fair enticing Fruit
> With liberal hand: he scrupl'd not to eat
> Against his better knowledge, not deceiv'd,
> But fondly overcome with Female charm.
> Book IX.995-999

In their disobedience, they have fallen, like Satan, into mortal sin. The delights are indeed real, sensuous as well as sensual:

> As with new Wine intoxicated both
> They swim in mirth, and fancy that they feel
> Divinity within them breeding wings
> Wherewith to scorn the Earth: but that false Fruit
> Far other operation first display'd,
> Carnal desire inflaming, hee on Eve
> Began to cast lascivious Eyes, she him
> As wantonly repaid; in Lust they burn
> Till Adam thus 'gan Eve to dalliance move.
> Book IX.1008-1016

THE COUNTRY WIFE

Another treatment of sin and innocence was presented in the outrageous action of Restoration Comedy, where the frolic of love was
rendered into high art. William Wycherly's *The Country Wife (1675)*
deals with the corruption of a somewhat eager country lady from
her over-protective husband, Pinchwife (not unlike Molière's Agnes
and Arnolphe). Mr. Horner, who pursues her, is a gallant and a
man about town, and poses as impotent to allow his lady friends
free access to visit him. Sir Jasper Fidget even brings his wife to his
chambers for the purpose of taunting and humiliating him. Lady
Fidget, who reprimands her husband when he utters the phrase
"naked truth" is free to come and go without loss of reputation, or
sully to her honor. Likewise Mistress Squeamish competes with
her grandmother Lady Squeamish for private time with him and
his good favors, though these dalliances proves to be his undoing.
Strutting into the room with a piece of China in her hand, Lady
Fidget tells her husband and the assembled gathering: "I have been
toiling and moiling for the prettiest piece of China, my dear." Poor
Horner has surrendered his "last" piece of China to her and has
nothing left for either Mistress Squeamish or Old Lady Squeamish. "Upon my honor," he invokes the coy *double entendre*: "I
have none left now," and Lady Figet declares her sole triumph:

> What d'y think if he had any left, I would have had it too,
> for we women of quality never think we have China enough.

Horner tries to placate his other visitors: "Do not take it ill, I
cannot make China for you all, but I will have a roll-wagon for you
too another time."[67]

The upper class audience, which had regained its power and
influence in England, after the Restoration of King Charles II to
the throne (1660), was not only relishing such scenes of subtle, if
not coarse sensuality, but was intent on thumbing its nose at the
rigid Protestant Ethic that had prevailed during the period of the

Commonwealth under Oliver Cromwell. Thus they savaged middle class morality and the "holier than thou" attitude that had been the hallmark of Puritanism; but the fundamental tenets of the Christian faith were not directly being challenged. However, changes were about to occur.

THE ENLIGHTENMENT

The Enlightenment commenced in the middle of the seventeenth century, and Descartes heralded the period with his dictum: *Cogito, ergo sum* (*I think, therefore I am*). It was the age in which man applied his reason to understand the world rather than rely on sacred authority. Deism taught the necessity of religion without mystery, morality without faith. "First follow nature" became the catch phrase. Sir Isaac Newton demonstrated the mechanistic laws of the universe and, in the eighteenth century, Julien Offroy de la Mettrie argued that man himself was a machine. The extension of literacy brought about a new consciousness, and capitalism created a powerful bourgeoisie. Literature was written for, and even by the middle class. The French Revolution was the ultimate triumph of the Enlightenment.

From Richardson through Diderot, writers of the age of reason taught that the primary function of literature was to inculcate virtue. The author was not bound to choose the grandiose design of Milton, "to justify the ways of God to men," but should follow the Horatian precept that a literary work should be *utile-dulce*, instructive as well as diverting. The usual moral tale of the eighteenth century concerned the efforts of the individual to remain virtuous in the face of temptation; though often the tale was titillating. The revelation that man contained within himself the germ of subversion was not yet established, and so the typical eighteenth century man obeyed an iron-clad reason and moral duty, while the untypical man was often mad.

SAMUEL RICHARDSON

The English printer, Samuel Richardson, found the potential for the sentimental novel in which resistance to the sexual impulse was identified with virtue, particularly if a nubile female was a victim. His ability at impersonation of female characters in the daily rituals and most personal intimacies of their lives is perhaps unexcelled in literature. In *Pamela*, he established the formula of a working girl's resistance to temptation and the rewards of marriage which her virtue brings her.

In his next novel, he moved his heroine, Clarissa Harlowe, a notch up on the social scale and showed that the assault upon her virtue was a subject of sufficient suspense to be maintained for an epic nearly the length of *War and Peace* and with a momentousness nearly equal to *Paradise Lost*. Clarissa herself is not without culpability—for she is in rebellion against her father and against authority without appreciating the dangers that she faces. But the novel is as much a study of a rake; Richard Lovelace, the seventeenth century cavalier poet with a devil-may-care attitude was the literary antecedent. Here Robert Lovelace indulges his fancy in the planning of his strategy of seduction, though he is not entirely without scruple and guilt. He vacillates even as he carries his plot to its nefarious conclusion:

> The moment I beheld her my heart was dastardized; and my reverence for the Virgin Purity, so visible in her deportment, again took place.

He nevertheless recants of these virtuous sentiments and pursues his treachery to the act of defilement. This is recounted by Clarissa herself in a letter to her confidante, Miss Howe, as she describes her defloration:

> He terrified me with his looks, and with his violent emotions, as he gazed upon me. Evident *joy-suppressed* emotions, as I have since recollected. His sentences short, and pronounced as if his breath were touched. Never saw I his abominable eyes look as then they looked—triumph in them!—fierce and wild; and more disagreeable than the women's at the vile house appeared to me when I first saw them; and at times, such a leering, mischief-boding cast! I would have given the world to have been a hundred miles from him. Yet his behavior was decent—a decency, however, that I might have seen to be struggled for—for he snatched my hand two or three times, with a vehemence in his grasp that hurt me; speaking words of tenderness through his shut teeth, as it seemed; and let it go with a beggar-voiced humble accent, like the vile woman's just before; half-inward; yet his words and manner carrying the appearance of strong and almost convulsed passion! O my dear! What mischiefs was he not then meditating!
>
> I complained once or twice of thirst. My mouth seemed parched. At the time, I supposed that it was my terror (gasping often as I did for breath) that parched up the roof of my mouth. I called for water: some table-beer was brought me: beer, I suppose, was a better vehicle (if I were not dosed enough before) for their potions. I told the maid that she knew I seldom tasted malt-liquor: yet, suspecting nothing of this nature, being extremely thirsty, I drank it, as what came next: and instantly, as it were, found myself much worse than before: as if inebriated, I should fancy: I know now how. . . .
>
> I remember I pleaded for mercy. I remember that I said *I would be his—indeed I would be his*-to obtain his mercy. But no mercy found I! My strength, my intellects, failed me—and then such scenes followed—Oh my dear, such dreadful scenes!—fits upon fits (faintly indeed and imperfectly re-

membered) procuring me no compassion—but death was
withheld from me. That would have been too great a mercy![68]

Lovelace ultimately repents of his dastardly deed and offers to marry
her. But she refuses to make amends with her defiler and dies of
degradation and humiliation. He is slain by her cousin, who avenges
the family shame.

CANDIDE

In *Candide*, Voltaire utilized melodrama with a philosophical bite
to explore the conflict in nature between virtue and vice. Candide
discovers the consequences of evil identified with sex when he is
thrown out of his home for exchanging solaces with his half sister,
Lady Cunégonde. He is sustained in his travels through life by the
crutch of philosophy, the teaching of his tutor Pangloss that "All is
for the best in this best of all possible worlds." So long as evil was
external, it could be rationalized as a consequence of fate, which
the man of reason could not be expected to control. After a lifetime of being buffeted by chance, Candide is reunited with Pangloss,
whose own experiences have been ever more luckless:

> "Now, my dear Pangloss," said Candide, "tell me this. When
> you had been hanged, dissected, and beaten unmercifully,
> and while you were rowing at your bench, did you still
> think that everything in this world is for the best?" .
>
> "I still hold my original views," replied Pangloss, "for I am
> still a philosopher. It would not be proper for me to recant,
> especially as Leibniz cannot be wrong; and besides, the pre-
> established harmony, together with the *plenum* and the
> *materia subtilis*, is the most beautiful thing in the world."[69]

Voltaire's conclusion was that the individual should withdraw from
the evils of the worldly existence to "cultivate his garden."

LES LIAISONS DANGEREUSES

In the French variation of the seduction novel established by Samuel Richardson, the French career officer and author Choderlos de Laclos depicted the exquisitely evil intrigues of two aristocrats and lovers, the Vicomte de Valmont and the Marquise de Merteuil, and their schemes against the pure innocent Cecile—exposing the corruption of nobility and showing how love could be perverted to lustful cruelty. *Les Liaisons Dangereuses* (1762) broadened the sensibility of the novel and the age, and raised titillation to the level of high art.

LORD CHESTERFIELD

But it was the Englishman Lord Chesterfield, the very worldly and proper statesman, diplomat, savant, man of letters, who presented the epitome of the aristocratic man of the time. He is famous for his *Letters* addressed to his illegitimate son, whom he did not acknowledge in his lifetime, but for whom he provided and attempted to educate as a gentleman in the manners, customs, and morals of the aristocracy. "You have the means, you have the opportunities. Employ them, for God's sake, while you may, and make yourself that accomplished man that I wish to have you." His letters stand as models of decorum, and Horatian urbanity; they were published after his death by his son's widow, his daughter-in-law, for profit. Though the letters preached piety, policy and propriety, his advice on relations with the opposite sex were not without a tinge of Lovelacian shrewdness and Ovidian fancy.

> What do you mean by your "If I dared!" What keeps you from daring? Dare always when there is hope of success; and nothing is lost by daring, even when there is no hope. A gentleman knows how to dare and when to dare; he opens the siege by effort, care, attentions; if he is not at once turned back, he continues steadily on the attack of the stronghold

itself. After certain approaches, success is infallible, and only blockheads doubt of it or do not attempt it.[70]

CASANOVA

The Venetian born Casanova did not become a lion of letters until later in his life—after he abundantly sowed his wild oats—an ironic counterpart to the paradigm of St. Augustine, who heralded the age of Christianity. The legendary Don Juan occupied a significant place in the history of the Enlightenment. He reflected the will of corporeal man to oppose the authority of the Church in matters of the flesh. The character existed first in Spanish folklore and, in the seventeenth century, Molière treated the sin and punishment of the mythical lover. Casanova lived the life of a rake, and claimed a record of 116 (give or take a few dozen) amorous encounters—and indeed influenced its greatest rendition by Mozart in his opera *Don Giovanni*, which owed a debt to Casanova's life. His life was not without its redeeming moments. Condemned as a sinner, he was imprisoned by the Inquisition, escaped, became in turn a spy for the Church, then a successful entrepreneur, and performed the feat in later life of translating the *Iliad*.

MARQUIS DE SADE

But it remained for the Marquis de Sade to make the frontal assault on rational man. The evil that Voltaire located in the world, De Sade placed squarely in the groin of the man of reason. The recognition of a preponderant sexual nature convinced De Sade of his inalterable villainy for he could not reconcile human nature with Christian teachings. He therefore attacked Christianity and, at the same time, excoriated himself along with all mankind as savage and godless. But perhaps he lived and died a blasphemer rather than a heretic.

In *Justine*, using the pretext of a moral tale, he depicted man as his worst, sensual and bestial. "The scheme of this novel (yet 'tis less a novel than one might suppose) is doubtless new; the victory gained by Virtue over Vice, the rewarding of the good, the punishment of evil, such is the usual scheme in every other work of this species: ah! the lesson cannot be too often dinned in our ears."[71] He eschewed the sentimentality of the other eighteenth century novelists in favor of fantasy and irony.

De Sade was a creature of the Enlightenment in believing that the laws that govern man were as ineluctable as the laws that govern the universe. The roots of licentiousness are poverty and repression. Justine is told by her captors: "You must serve either our pleasure or our interests; your poverty imposes the yoke upon you, and you have got to adapt to it." Her oppressors act out their sexual fantasies that in themselves are derived from forced repression of their libidinal drives. The ground that De Sade covered in his writing was familiar; but it not been treated so openly before. For his crime in writing the book as well as multiple rapes, De Sade was arrested and imprisoned at Sainte-Pélagie (though he even denied authorship of *Justine* in order to gain his release). Through the intervention of his family—agreeing to provide a stipend for his upkeep—he was removed from prison and placed in the Asylum at Charenton, where he spent the last decade of his life. There he was provided with quills and ink, and he continued writing, and even organized theatrical entertainment for the local townspeople.

Justine's faith is vindicated at the end of the novel. But the *deus ex machina* that brings about her redemption remains perplexing. The conclusion of the novel is facile, a parody of the eighteen hundred year Christian configuration of salvation: "May you be convinced, with her, that true happiness is to be found nowhere but in Virtue's womb, and that if, in keeping with designs it is not for us to fathom, God permits that it be persecuted on Earth, it is so that Virtue may be compensated by Heaven's most dazzling rewards." The age of the modern was borne on the fluttering stork-wings of irony.

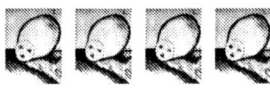

LOVE IN THE MODERN WORLD

For all love, however ethereally it may bear itself, is rooted in the sexual impulse alone, nay, it absolutely is only a more definitely determined, specialized, and indeed, in the strictest sense, individualized sexual impulse. If now, keeping this in view, one considers the important part which the sexual impulse in all its degrees and nuances plays not only on the stage and in novels, but also in the real world, where, next to the love of life, it shows itself the strongest and most powerful of motives, constantly lays claim to half the powers and thoughts of the younger portion of mankind, is the ultimate goal of almost all human effort, exerts an adverse influence on the most important events, interrupts the most serious occupations every hour, sometimes embarrasses for a while even the greatest minds, does not hesitate to intrude with its trash, interfering with the negotiations of statesmen and the investigations of men of learning, knows how to slip its love letters and locks of hair even into ministerial portfolios and philosophical manuscripts, no less devises daily the most entangled and the worst actions, destroys the most valuable relationships, breaks the firmest bonds, demands the sacrifice sometimes of life or health, sometimes of wealth, rank, and happiness, nay, robs those who are otherwise honest of all conscience, makes those who have hitherto been faithful, traitors; accordingly, on the whole, appears as a malevolent demon that strives to pervert, confuse, and overthrow everything;—then one will be forced to cry, Wherefore all this noise? Wherefore the straining and storming, the anxiety and want? It is merely a question of every [Jack] finding his [Jill] Why should such a trifle play so important a part, and constantly introduce disturbance and confusion

into the well-regulated life of man? But to the earnest inves-
tigator the spirit of truth gradually reveals the answer. It is
no trifle that is in question here; on the contrary, the importance of the matter is quite proportionate to the seriousness
and ardor of the effort. The ultimate end of all love affairs,
whether they are played in play or drama is really more
important than all other ends of human life, and is therefore
quite worthy of the profound seriousness with which every
one pursues it.
Arthur Schopenhauer

LOVE IN THE MODERN WORLD • WILLIAM BLAKE •
THE ASCENT OF MAN • CHARLES DARWIN •
THE BYRONIC HERO • JOHANN WOLFGANG VON GOETHE •
MADAME BOVARY • LES MISÉRABLES • CHARLES BAUDELAIRE •
TOLSTOY AND DOSTOYEVSKY • CHARLES DICKENS •
DOMBEY AND SON • QUEEN VICTORIA •
UNCOMMON HEROINES • FLORENCE NIGHTINGALE •
THE SUBJECTION OF WOMEN • PRIDE AND PREJUDICE •
FRANKENSTEIN AND WUTHERING HEIGHTS •
IBSEN AND STRINDBERG • DR. JEKYLL AND MR. HYDE

SIGMUND FREUD AND HIS INFLUENCE • D.H. LAWRENCE •
MARCEL PROUST AND MODERNISM • THE TRIAL •
LUIGI PIRANDELLO • THE TRAGIC SENSE OF LIFE •
FEDERICO GARCÍA LORCA • GEORGE BERNARD SHAW •
PYGMALION • BRAVE NEW WORLD • JAMES JOYCE • T.S. ELIOT •
SIMONE DE BEAUVOIR • ELSA MORANTE •
FREDERICH DÜRRENMATT AND MAX FRISCH •
THREE CONTEMPORARY LATIN AMERICAN WRITERS •
KISS OF THE SPIDER WOMAN • LOVE IN THE TIME OF CHOLERA

LOVE IN THE MODERN WORLD

More than any other influence, the modern world has achieved the transformation of values that accompanied the decline of religion as the most potent moral force in civilization. This loss can be traced in tendencies since the Renaissance and Reformation, and fostered by the Scientific, Industrial, and Information Revolutions—that have enabled men to secure their potential for happiness in this world rather than postpone gratification in the hopes of achieving salvation in the next. The City of Man has replaced the City of God in the hopes and dreams of men.

Nearly all religions established their foundations on the repression of sexuality, teaching that sex is sin, and that the individual who was driven by uncontrolled libidinal instinct was a slave of the Devil. The reassessment accorded to the human sexual drive, however, would prove to be a Trojan Horse in the camp of organized religion.

WILLIAM BLAKE

The prophetic, visionary, mystical English poet, William Blake espoused the cause of freedom and foresaw a society in which man would be released from the shackles of authority and repression. America symbolized the victory of the subjugated—and the expression of the free spirit.

> The Terror answer'd: "I am Orc, wreath'd round the accursed tree:
> The times are ended; shadows pass, the morning'gins to break."[72]

He argued the Devil's point of view in his criticism of organized religion, and favored personal salvation. He was a true visionary—

and asserted that the aim of the future was to reconcile the divided states of Heaven and Hell. As he wrote in "Proverbs From Hell":

> Prisons are built with the stones of Law,
> Brothels with the bricks of Religion.
> The pride of the peacock is the glory of God.
> The wrath of the lion is the wisdom of God.
> The nakedness of woman is the work of God.

In his Gnomic verses, he advocated release from repression:

> Abstinence sows sand all over
> The ruddy limbs & flaming hair,
> But Desire Gratified
> Plants fruits of life & beauty there.

And more to the point in "The Question Answer'd":

> What is it men in women do require?
> The lineaments of Gratified Desire.
> What is it women do in men require?
> The lineaments of Gratified Desire?

In his exquisite short poem, "The Mental Traveller," a psycho-socio-mythical-sexual fantasy, that would prove to be archetypal of modern art, he reveals the unconscious force behind our actions, the desire for power in man and the conflict between the sexes, the genesis and evolution of Oedipal development, and the conflict in society between master and the oppressed—as an expression of an ever continuous cyclical pattern of suppression and freedom.

> I travel'd thro a Land of Men
> A Land of Men & Women too,
> And heard & saw such dreadful things
> As cold Earth wanderers never knew.

For there the Babe is born in joy
That was begotten in dire woe;
Just as we Reap in joy the fruit
Which we in bitter tears did sow.

And if the Babe is born a Boy
He's given to a Woman Old,
Who nails him down upon a rock,
Catches his shrieks in cups of gold.

She binds iron thorns around his head
She pierces both his hands & feet,
She cuts his heart out at his side
To make it feel both cold & heat.

Her fingers number every Nerve,
Just as a Miser counts his gold;
She lives upon his shrieks & cries,
And she grows young as he grows old.

Till he becomes a bleeding youth,
And she becomes a Virgin bright;
Then he rends up his Manacles
And binds her down for his delight.

He plants himself in all her Nerves,
Just as the Husbandman his mould;
And she becomes his dwelling place
And Garden fruitful seventy fold. . . .

The message was couched in symbolism and allegory, an ironic representation of the sacred—in the symbol of Christ suffering until he rises against his oppressor—the woman who has mastered him—and masters her. The nineteenth century would explore the meaning of this conundrum—the attraction of opposites, the force of the sexual drive, the conflict over power and rule. New politics, new science, new imagery, new symbolism would be given new form and expression as, one writer noted, new wine would be poured into old bottles.

THE ASCENT OF MAN

In the West, the force of freedom was unleashed by other nineteenth century philosophers, political leaders, and poets. The French and Napoleonic Revolutions brought the spirit of romanticism to the fore, characterized by Anita Brookner as "infinite longing . . . a longing for what is missing, and an attempt to supply it."[73] Karl Marx protested the evils of industrialism and prophesied that the oppressed classes of society would rise up and overthrow their masters. The revolutions of 1848 that swept through Europe were concrete fulfillment of these ideas. Sigmund Freud revealed the unconscious sources of human energy beneath the controlled external appearance of social man. Arthur Schopenhauer and Friedrich Wilhelm Nietzsche embraced the energy of freedom and attacked the suppression of man's will to freedom. Nietzsche's philosopher hero, Zarathustra, called for recognition of the creative value of man's libidinal drive and the evolution to the Superman (*Übermensch*). "Behold! I teach you the Superman: he is this lightning, he is this frenzy!"

But it was Charles Darwin who perhaps had the greatest impact on his time when he demonstrated the evolution of the plant and animal kingdom not through a mechanistic plan but through free Natural Selection. In questioning the validity of the Biblical myth of Creation, Darwin was not merely rejecting the authority of Church teaching; he was offering an alternative and radically different interpretation of human experience. Whereas the findings of Copernicus relating to the motions of the planets around the sun in the sixteenth century had lain dormant for a century before they were confirmed and accepted—and even then Galileo's demonstrations were challenged by the Church, and he was excommunicated and forced to recant his argument, Darwin's impact was forceful and immediate.

CHARLES DARWIN

The English naturalist Charles Darwin (1809-1892) himself derived from very good stock—his maternal grandfather having been
the artisan and industrialist Josiah Wedgwood and his paternal
grandfather the botanist, man of science, poet, and early evolu-
tionist, Erasmus Darwin. Darwin, who was born on the same day
as Abraham Lincoln, had at one time studied for the ministry; but
after the untimely death of his ten year old daughter, he perhaps
became disillusioned with religion. At all events, he discovered the
fascination and truth of the natural order: plants and animals bound
in a web of complex chemistry, the origin of species and the descent of man and woman in the evolutionary order.

Darwin's theory of Natural Selection was that of sexual selection—and offered another radical account of the significance of
sexuality in human experience. It was through sexual selection that
the main effort of human beings to maintain the selectivity and
variability of the species was to be understood.

Sexual selection was a method by which the species had perpetuated its most desirable traits. In the animal kingdom the competition for the favors of the female allowed the victor to be chosen
for his physical superiority and that led to the improvement of the
species. Thus the stag enjoyed many females and passed on his
virtues to all of them.

Evolution of course raised other disturbing implications at the
time in characterizing the gradual process of the development of
the human species from more primitive forms. A naturalist who
collected information methodically and almost with the zeal of a
monk, Darwin presented his findings to the forum of public opinion—not with the prose of a Jefferson or the drama of Napoleon or
the symbolism of a Blake—but with the irrefutable logic of the
empirical method—and the rational persuasiveness of and even
empathy with the Fathers of the Church:

> Man may be excused for feeling some pride at having risen,
> though not through his own exertions, to the very summit
> of the organic scale; and the fact of his having thus risen,
> instead of having been aboriginally placed there, may give
> him hope for a still higher destiny in the distant future. But
> we are not here concerned with hopes or fears, only with the
> truth as far as our reason permits us to discover it; and I have
> given the evidence to the best of my ability. We must, how-
> ever, acknowledge, as it seems to me, that man with all his
> noble qualities, with sympathy which feels for the most
> debased, with benevolence which extends not only to other
> men but to the humblest living creature, with his god-like
> intellect which has penetrated into the movements and con-
> stitution of the solar system—with all these exalted pow-
> ers—man still bears in his bodily frame the indelible stamp
> of his lowly origin.[74]

He followed tradition in recognizing the differences between men and women; and he saw the particular physical traits as well as mental traits like intelligence, a moral sense, and social awareness as the particular heritage of the human species.

Darwin also presented a radical conception of the institution of marriage by attempting to define it in anthropological terms rather than according to any ordained authority. Thus he defended the social benefit of marriage in terms of the exigent needs of the species. He suggested that monogamy was instigated in human society in order to contain men's sexual jealousy of rivals.

Darwin, along with other anthropologists, mused about the implications of this theory. Some argued that woman herself was asexual—and only responded to man's encouragement. The myth of Adam and Eve was brought into doubt by the theory of evolution, and the question arose as to what kind of relations existed between men and women in the primordial state. Was the natural state matriarchy or patriarchy? Were natural relations between men and women monogamous, polygamous, or polyandrous?

Darwin and then other anthropologists who followed explored and are still continuing to explore different structures of relationships between men and women. But beyond the ancient literatures and the customs of neolithic tribes that have survived until the present time, there has been little beside hypothesis or, more often, wish fulfillment to guide the anthropologist's reasoning. Until the human genome deciphers the code, Darwin surveyed the tree of knowledge and plucked its fruit. In the symbolism of the time, his achievement, like Marx's, was Faustian!

THE BYRONIC HERO

The Romantic writer discovered the self, which actually was not a new literary approach; Montaigne had written his *Essays* from a personal vantage. However the romantic writers opposed the conventions of society—the materialistic and moral standards of the middle class (bourgeoisie). They yearned for aristocratic and courtly values, attacked philistinism and commercial values. They flouted society's rules and flaunted their individuality. All that restrained freedom was intolerable to the Byronic hero.

Lord Byron (1785-1824), the son of a pious Presbyterian mother and a spendthrift rakish father, was a peer of the realm, who fought hard for liberal causes, loved many women, and maintained his right to pursue his homosexual preferences. His vulnerability due to a clubfoot and other glandular problems which afflicted him made him the model of the Romantic hero, and his defiance of society through his iconoclasm and rebelliousness, which included a purported incestuous relationship with his half sister, brought him the condemnation of society and exile from England. He wrote in his epic poem, *Don Juan*:

> I want a hero: an uncommon want,
> When every year and month sends forth a new one,
> Till, after cloying the gazettes with cant,
> The age discovers he is not the true one:
> Of such as these I should not care to vaunt,
> I'll therefore take our ancient friend Don Juan—

We all have seen him, in the pantomime,
Sent to the Devil somewhat ere his time.
Canto I[75]

He indulged in feats of valor, fighting for the independence of modern Greece. He traveled the world in search of experience and passion, found his own life the truest source of epic adventure, and his writings were unabashedly romantic and self-centered. In characteristic fashion, Byron in 1810 imitated the feat of the classical hero Leander, who swam across the Hellespont to visit his Hero. He wrote a poem comparing himself to the legendary lover:

For *me*, degenerate modern wretch,
    Though in the genial month of May
My dripping limbs I faintly stretch,
    And think I've done a feat today.

But since he crossed the rapid tide,
    According to the doubtful story,
To woo,—and—Lord knows what beside,
    And swam for Love, as I for Glory;

Twere hard to say who fared the best:
    Sad mortals! thus the Gods still plague you!
He lost his labour, I my jest:
    For he was drowned, and I've the ague.

"Written After Swimming from Sestos to Abydos"

JOHANN WOLFGANG VON GOETHE

The theme of the Romantic individualist was explored by the originator of modern German literature and creator of the antecedent to the Byronic hero. Johann Wolfgang von Goethe (1749-1832) was a modern Renaissance man, who was adept in science as well as in the arts, in statecraft, as well as in law; and he explored and defined the modern sensibility in his writing. He was secretary of state to Karl Augustus, Duke of Saxe-Weimar and even an early advocate of Darwin's theory of evolution, and his own drawings and studies of plant anatomy confirmed Darwin's findings. He also created modern Romantic literature in *The Sorrows of Young Werther* (1774), which Napoleon reportedly carried in his breast pocket on his military campaigns, as well as in the work of his mature genius, *Faust* (the completed work which was published only after his death).

Werther describes the struggle of a young idealist for realization through love. It is a variation of the medieval romance where the young gallant cherishes an adoration for an unattainable lady. The novel was written before Goethe was twenty-five years old. It was based on a failed love affair with Charlotte von Stein; it challenged the conventions and rules of society, which denied Werther of his wished-for happiness. "It is possible to say a great deal in favor of rules, about as much as can be said in praise of bourgeois society. The person who takes his direction from rules alone will never produce anything in bad taste, in the same way as the person who allows himself to be shaped by rules of social convention can never become an intolerable neighbor or a conspicuous villain."

The problem is that Charlotte is betrothed (and later married) to another man, Albert, and she seeks to discourage his attentions:

> "Werther! Please be reasonable! Your intellect, your knowledge, your talents, should offer such you a variety of satisfactions! Be a man! Get rid of this hopeless attachment to one who can do nothing but pity you." He gritted his teeth and gave her a dark look. She kept his hand in hers. "Think it over calmly, if only for a moment, Werther!" she said. "Do you not feel that you deceive yourself, that you deliberately ruin yourself? Why must it be I, Werther? Just I, who belong to another? Why must that be? I am afraid, very much afraid, that it is only the impossibility of possessing me that attracts you so much."[76]

The modern Palamon will not be dissuaded. When it becomes apparent that he cannot enjoy the fulfillment of his amorous quest, he loses his *raison d'être*. Charlotte is finally used by him to achieve the climax of his Narcissism when he shoots himself in the head with the pistol that she has tendered him.

In his masterpiece, *Faust*, which was called by Pushkin "the *Iliad* of modern life," Goethe dealt with the will to freedom of modern man and the struggle to escape from tyranny. Mephistopheles is both an archetype of the diabolic force that tempts man in order to gain mastery over his eternal soul and, in the dialectic of Karl Marx, the force of money control and capitalistic oppression that enslaves man. Faust's compact with Mephistopheles requires the surrender of soul after a specified term of service by the devil but only after Faust has lost his will to create and succumbed to being content:

> Werd' ich zum Augenblicke sagen:
> Verweile doch! du bist so schön!
> Dann magst du mich in Fesseln schlagen
> Dann will ich gern zugrunde gehn!
>
> (If ever I say to the passing moment,
> "Linger a while! Thou art so fair!"
> Then you may cast me into fetters;
> I will gladly perish then and there.)[77]

MADAME BOVARY

Gustave Flaubert's *Madame Bovary* was as much an assault on the bourgeoisie as a celebration of adulterous love. It is a paradox that the middle class, which had brought about the elimination of the class order and instituted a more conventional moral viewpoint, that had created the wealth of the Industrial Revolution and provided the environment as well as the individuals who created the Scientific Revolution, should have fallen into such opprobrium.

Middle class society, middle class industry, middle class morality, which had been the achievements of the new order, were deprecated with reactionary fervor.

Emma Bovary, who spent a period of her youth in a convent, enjoys a rich imagination and romantic sensibility which glorified the heroic exploits of Joan of Arc, Mary Queen of Scots, Héloïse, and other *femmes fatales*. Her marriage to a doctor provides her with a comfortable standard of living; but she is bored and frustrated. Her affair with a young clerk gives her an opportunity to thumb her nose at society whose rules do not bind her, as she captures the comforting illusion of her youth:

> "I have a lover! I have a lover!" she kept repeating to herself, reveling in the thought as though she were beginning a second puberty. At last she was going to know the joys of love, the fever of the happiness she had despaired of. She was entering a marvelous realm where all would be passion, ecstasy, rapture. She was in the midst of an endless blue expanse, scaling the glittering heights of passion; everyday life had receded, and lay far below, in the shadows between those peaks. She remembered the heroines of novels she had read, and the lyrical legion of those adulterous women began to sing in her memory with sisterly voices that enchanted her.[78]

Whereas Samuel Richardson involved himself in the moral decisions of his heroines, Flaubert remained aloof in treating Emma's behavior; the reader is free to support or condemn her action according to his or her own values. Yet she dies for her sin!

LES MISÉRABLES

Victor Hugo took the plight of the common man in his sprawling epic novel of social injustice in France, *Les Misérables*. In the wake of the French Revolution, Jean Valjean spends nineteen years on the galleys and in prison for the crime of having stolen a loaf of bread. Hugo wrote the novel while he himself lived in political exile for twenty one years. The work lacks the polish or the intelligence of Flaubert's *Madame Bovary*, but it holds the French society up to rebuke and criticism. After escaping from prison, Valjean is able to reintegrate himself into society and become thoroughly bourgeois. The focus of the story is the effort of the police chief, M. Javert, to trap and expose him; and then there is Jean's relationship with the prostitute Fantine and his idealized relationship with her daughter, Cosette, whom he takes into his care after the death of her mother.

CHARLES BAUDELAIRE

The French symbolist poet Charles Baudelaire described the allure of evil and attacked the conventions of society—he even denounced his reader *"Hypocrite lecteur,—mon semblable,—mon frere"* (*hypocrite reader, my double, my brother*). His father, a priest who had given up the tonsure, died when he was a child, and his mother remarried an army colonel. Baudelaire was brought up in the middle class, enjoyed a modest inheritance, and pursued an idiosyncratic life style. He propounded an *avant-garde* view of literature which was presented in the Preface to his major work, *Les Fleurs du Mal* (*The Flowers of Evil*) published in the same year as Madame Bovary (1857):

> It is not for my wives, my daughters, or my sisters that this book has been written; nor for the wives, daughters, or sisters of my neighbors. I leave that to those who have some reason to confuse good deeds with fine language. I know the passionate lover of fine style exposes himself to the hatred of the masses; but no respect for humanity, no false modesty, no conspiracy, no universal suffrage will ever force me to speak the unspeakable jargon of this age, or to confuse ink with virtue. Certain illustrious poets have long since divided among themselves the more flowery provinces of the realm of poetry. I have found it amusing, and the more

pleasant because the task was more difficult, to extract *beauty* from *Evil*. This book, which is quintessentially useless and absolutely innocent, was written with no other aim than to divert myself and to practice my passionate taste for the difficult.[79]

He opposed the false standards of virtue imposed upon him by society and defended the self-realization of the individual, even though it set him against all others. Out of his solitude and his superciliousness the poet forged the truth of his own conscious-ness and lived by its dictates. Though his subtle irony suggests a link to the Marquis de Sade, Baudelaire also looks forward to the aesthetic movement, or art for art's sake, where the techniques, whether symbolism, impressionism, or surrealism, can transcend the meaning. Nevertheless his poems, with such titles as "The Denial of St. Peter," "The Pagan's Prayer," and "Litany to Satan," project immoral and heretical attitudes, and indeed he was fined for heresy. In an autobiographical poem, "The Enemy," he de-scribes the evolution of the poet in his garden of flowers:

> My youth was all a murky hurricane
> Where brilliant suns but rarely burst the gloom;
> So deep the ravages of wind and rain,
> Few crimson fruits my garden-close illume.
>
> And now I've reached the autumn of the mind,
> With spade and rake I needs must toil, to save
> My little seed-plot, torn and undermined,
> Guttered and gaping like an open grave.
>
> And will the flowers that my dreams implore
> Find, in this garden wasted like a shore,
> The mystic food from which their strength must start?
>
> —O grief! O grief! Time eats away our lives,
> And the dark Enemy that gnaws the heart
> Drains the blood from us on which he thrives!

TOLSTOY AND DOSTOYEVSKY

The two great masters of Russian literature, Leo Tolstoy and Fyodor Dostoyevsky, explored the passion of love and its effect upon those who fall into its embrace. In the nineteenth century, Russia was a backward country, in which the promise of science and the elevation of the material lot of mankind were not being realized, as in Europe or in America. Though writing in the humanistic tradition, both Tolstoy and Dostoyevsky ultimately rejected the secular world in favor of primitive, mystical Christianity.

Count Tolstoy, like Lord Byron, was a member of the aristocracy, and after a period of youthful profligacy, he settled down to render in letters the range of the Russian human experience in war and peace, in love and hate. "Happy families are all alike; every unhappy family is unhappy in its own way" begins *Anna Karenina*. The novel focuses on the possibility of mundane happiness within the structure of the family. The location is the upper class society of St. Petersburg. When Anna takes Count Vronsky as a lover, her husband seems willing to go along with the dishonor rather than seek a divorce and create a scandal. Anna is untrue to her class—and even to the code of aristocratic love—in her effort to make permanent her liaison, and she proves as much a traitor to her social status as a victim of love. Once, near to death, she pleads with her husband for forgiveness:

> Don't be surprised at me. I'm still the same . . . But there is another woman in me, I'm afraid of her: she loved that man, and I tried to hate you, and could not forget about her that used to be. I'm not that woman. Now I'm my real self, all myself. I'm dying now, I know I shall die, ask him. Even now I feel—see here, the weights on my feet, on my hands, on my fingers. My fingers––see how huge they are! But this will soon all be over . . . Only one thing I want: forgive me, forgive me quite.[80]

Her husband seems almost prepared to pardon her. "He did not think that the Christian law that he had been all his life trying to follow, enjoined on him to love and forgive his enemies; but a glad feeling of love and forgiveness filled his heart." Likewise, in later years, Count Tolstoy renounced his earthly possessions as well as his literary achievements and lived as a cobbler on his own estate, Yasnaya Polyana, and wrote religious parables.

Dostoyevsky was a social revolutionary as a young man, and faced a firing squad, until a last minute reprieve from the Czar Nicholas I brought about his forgiveness and regeneration. Like Edgar Allan Poe and Charles Baudelaire, Dostoyevsky studied the demonic influence on his notable characters—the criminal, the prostitute, the epileptic (a condition which afflicted him)—all of them sinners who faced the firing squad of life, where only a reprieve from God Almighty could save them.

In perhaps a lighter moment in his life, of which there apparently were not many, he treated the theme of adultery in a most Dostoyevskian manner. *The Eternal Husband* concentrates on the peculiar and profound relationship between the gallant and the husband. In the naturalistic imagery of the century, it was the relationship between the host and its parasite; in the Freudian *Gestalt*—the gallant's passion is directed towards the husband—and the wife is merely the surrogate. Dostoyevsky who offered many stunning psychological insights into the nature of man explored this relationship as well. Velchaninov (the gallant) and Trusotsky (the eternal husband) share a mutual bond, Natalya Vassilyevna; the gallant is dependent upon the husband to provide the wife. The story suggests just how much the eternal husband has the same great need for the services provided by the extra-marital lover. In a most piquant fashion, the cuckold and the gallant meet nine years after the end of the affair. The wife died after she was subjected to mistreatment by her husband, and there is an eight year old daughter, Liza, who also is being abused. The erstwhile lover cannot make up his mind whether to challenge the husband to a duel, or to beg his forgiveness. Yet the cuckolded husband seems unwilling either to acknowledge the affair in any way, or to settle the question of the child's paternity.

Instead he befriends the gallant, drinks champagne with him, lives with him, kisses him, and begs him to advise him on a gift for his future bride. The gallant is taunted by this behavior, by the uncertainty over the paternity claim to his daughter, and by the fear of the husband's revenge. Then the daughter dies of neglect. In a nightmarish fantasy of a duel with Trusotsky, Velchaninov finds himself wounded and bleeding from his own razor blade. The blood wound serves as purgation for guilt, and punishment for his sin. They are eternal brothers, Cain and Abel. Or perhaps in Dostoyevskian terms, they have used each other to punish each other for original sin. They also serve to mitigate each other's fear of woman and guilt over lust. The devout Christian of the Greek Orthodox or Roman Catholic faith must eschew the sins of the flesh; not to do so is to arouse the agents of retribution, blood and suffering. The eternal gallant and the eternal lover happily prey upon each other for their ultimate beneficent salvation.

CHARLES DICKENS

The Englishman Charles Dickens (1812-1870) gave expression to the Victorian moral outlook. For him the perfection of love was more likely to be found in the idealized relationship between man and woman and often between brother and sister as in his best novels, *David Copperfield* and *Great Expectations.* Dickens celebrated the idealized, lost, nostalgic world of childhood, and the gumption of the "innocent" young heroes to survive the macabre and grotesque world of industrial England. Here we find a Shakespearean or, more precisely, a Balzacian canvas that renders, in an almost satiric mode, the life of the time, including the life style of the well born, and the wealthy; but his greatest success was the revelation of the life of the poor, of which his own father and family were constant reminders. Dickens was not only a social historian, but also a strong voice for social reform in the treatment of the weak, the helpless, and the young. He shunned erotic innuendo in his novels.

DOMBEY AND SON

Dickens's novel *Dombey and Son* presents the stereotypes of the roles of men and women in Victorian society. The whole range of the family experience is explored in Dickens and foremost perhaps is the father's yearning for a patrimony for his son. Mrs. Dombey first produces a daughter for Mr. Dombey, and then she dies in childbirth producing a son—the revenge of the gods visited upon him for his uncaring attitude. His daughter Florence has a strained relationship with her father; but she becomes a mother to the orphan Paul, and she loves him in a sisterly way. The young Paul perhaps intimidated by his father turns to his sister Floy for the love and affection as, for example, when he asks her to sing at a family gathering:

> Though Florence was at first very much frightened at being asked to sing before so many people, and begged earnestly to be excused, yet, on Paul calling her to him, and saying "Do, Floy! Please! For me, my dear!" she went straight to the piano, and began. When they all drew a little away, that Paul might see her; and when he saw her sitting there alone, so young, and good, and beautiful, and kind to him; and heard her thrilling voice, so natural and sweet, and such a golden link between him and all his life's love and happiness, rising out of the silence; he turned his face away, and hid his tears.[81]

Soon thereafter the sickly Paul is on his deathbed; but he enjoys one final embrace and fond thought:

> "Now lay me down," he said; "and Floy, come close to me, and let me see you."

> Sister and brother wound their arms around each other, and
> the golden light came streaming in, and fell upon them,
> locked together.

The relationship between father and daughter remains strained.
Later in the novel Mr. Dombey marries a second time, and the
marriage does not meet his specifications. In the formal means of
address used by husbands and wives at the time, Dombey expresses dissatisfaction with the behavior of Mrs. Dombey after she
has embarrassed him before his friends at a dinner party:

> "Mrs. Dombey, I must beg leave have a few words with
> you."

> "Tomorrow," she replied.

> "There is no time like the present, Madam," he returned.
> "You mistake your position. I am used to choose my own
> times; not to have them chosen for me. I think you scarcely
> understand who and what I am, Mrs. Dombey."

> "I think," she answered, "that I understand you very well."

He continues:

> "Your conduct does not please me."

> She merely glanced at him again, and again averted her eyes;
> but she might have spoken for an hour and expressed less.

> "I repeat, Mrs. Dombey, does not please me. I have already
> taken occasion to request that it may be corrected. I now
> insist upon it."

> "You chose a fitting occasion for your first remonstrance, Sir,
> and you adopt a fitting manner, and a fitting word for your
> second. You *insist*! To *me*!"

> "Madam," said Mr. Dombey, with his most offensive air of

state, "I have made you my wife. You bear my name. You are
associated with my position and reputation. I will not say
that the world in general may be disposed to think you
honored by that association; but I will say that I am accus-
tomed to 'insist' to my connexions and dependents."

Somewhat later, Mr. Dombey sends his Confidential Agent, Mr.
Carker, to repeat his message of displeasure, and Mrs. Dombey, as
though to illustrate her appreciation of Mr. Dombey's position,
name, and reputation, runs off with his Confidential Agent.

The picture of the ideal Victorian wife is that of nurturing,
giving, and completely devoting herself to her husband. Later in
the novel Floy marries her sweetheart Walter, and she becomes the
ideal wife as she had been the ideal sister and daughter: "If anything could make me happier in being allowed to see and speak to
you, would it not be the discovery that I had any means on earth
of doing you a moment's service! Where would I not go, what
would I not do for your sake!"

QUEEN VICTORIA

The Victorian age was presided over by a dominant and pious
queen who embodied and fostered that stereotype of the sexually
repressed woman, which the modern world was to oppose. Queen
Victoria, who ruled from 1837-1901, gave her name to the age in
which "the sun never set upon the British Empire" but also to a
standard of prudery that was carried to excess. The Victorians believed that if it weren't seen, like the legs of a piano, which were
decorously covered, then it didn't exist. There were no references
in polite society to a man's trousers (called unmentionables) because of the association that might be adduced. She was an incur-
able romantic who cherished the morality and values of chivalry,
and the memory of her beloved deceased husband, Prince Albert.

The assumptions about the differences between the sexes was
maintained in most nineteenth-century literature. Woman con-

tinued to be adored and celebrated as she had been in earlier ages, as angel and temptress, *femme fatale* and home-maker. She only could be fulfilled in a relationship with a man, in loving and in being loved. Chivalric love was romanticized in the poetry of Keats, Shelley, and the Brownings. Lord Byron wrote: "Man's love is of man's life a thing apart,/'Tis woman's whole existence." Elizabeth Barrett Browning described her love for Robert Browning "to the depth and breadth and height/My soul can reach when feeling out of sight/For the ends of Being and ideal grace." Alfred, Lord Tennyson, poet laureate of the time, reflected on the difference between the sexes:

> Man for the field and woman for the hearth;
> Man for the sword, and for the needle she;
> Man with the head, and woman with the heart;
> Man to command, and woman to obey;
> All else confusion.

He idealized the lady sitting in her turret looking down at Camelot, waiting for her knight, Sir Lancelot, to rescue her and to love her in "The Lady of Shalott":

> Four gray walls, and four gray towers
> Overlook a space of flowers,
> And the silent isle embowers
> The Lady of Shalott . . .
> There she weaves by night and day
> A magic web with colors gay . . .
> His broad clear brow in sunlight glow'd;
> On burnish'd hooves his war-horse trode;
> From underneath his helmet flow'd
> His coal-black curls as on he rode,
> As he rode down to Camelot . . .
> From the bank and from the river
> He flash'd into the crystal mirror,
> "Tirra lirra," by the river
> Sang Sir Lancelot.
> She left the web, she left the loom,

She made three paces thro' the room,
She saw the water-lily bloom,
She saw the helmet and the plume,
She look'd down to Camelot.
Out flew the web and floated wide;
The mirror crack'd from side to side;
"The curse is come upon me," cried
The Lady of Shalott . . .
Heard a carol, mournful, holy,
Chanted loudly, chanted lowly,
Till her blood was frozen slowly,
And her eyes were darken'd wholly,
Turn'd to tower'd Camelot.
For ere she reach'd upon the tide
The first house by the water-side,
Singing in her song she died,
The Lady of Shalott.
Under tower and balcony,
By garden-wall and gallery,
A gleaming shape she floated by,
Dead-pale between the houses high,
Silent into Camelot.
Out upon the wharfs they came,
Knight and burgher, lord and dame,
And round the prow they read her name,
The Lady of Shalott.
Who is this? and what is here?
And in the lighted palace near
Died the sound of royal cheer;
And they cross'd themselves for fear,
All the knights at Camelot:
But Lancelot mused a little space;
He said, "She has a lovely face;
God in his mercy lend her grace,
The Lady of Shalott."

UNCOMMON HEROINES

It is not necessarily true that the momentum of the woman's movement was derived from the dramatic contribution of the leading
theorist of the nineteenth century, Charles Darwin, and his recon-
sideration of the nature of man and woman. It can as likely be
adduced that the activism of the women's movement was inspired
by ideas of freedom derived from the ideals of the Enlightenment
and the American and French Revolutions. At all events, the evolution of woman's role has been an important consequence of the
modern age.

Mary Wollstonecraft's *A Vindication of the Rights of Women* was
addressed and dedicated to the French diplomat and social reformer, Charles Maurice de Talleyrand, and argued for the education of women and the improvement of their status in their relationships with men. Wollstonecraft specifically challenged the
Christian teaching presented, for example, by Milton in *Paradise
Lost*, though she did not reject the role of a woman as helpmate to
her husband, and did not even strongly insist on a woman's right
to vote—but sought a "friendship" in the relations between men
and women, and education for women to achieve this goal.

She also tried her hand at writing novels, but she was more
successful as a polemicist than as an imaginative writer. In *Mary, A
Fiction* (1788), she cited Jean Jacques Rousseau who had emphasized the virtue of the natural man and had contrasted the natural
goodness of the individual with the corrupting influence of society; and she depicted her heroine as an heiress who was unhappy
with her marriage and social class and surrendered her wealth to
serve the poor. *The Wrongs of Woman* (1798) dealt with the frustrations of a woman's life as she continued to explore her rage against
men and society, and argued for divorce from unsuitable marriages;
and she further lamented, in the manner of the heroine of *The City
of Ladies*, that she would have preferred to have been born a man
or, better yet, not at all.

Though the feminist movement was at first identified with the temperance movement—to control the bad habits of men, and later with the suffragist movement—to gain the vote, the nineteenth century revolutionists for women's rights sought equality in their relationships with men. (Later Christabel Parkhurst would campaign on the platform "Votes for Women, Chastity for Men.") The parameters of the movement were limited because of the inability of women to confront the sexual issue frontally. For the open acknowledgement of the sexual impulse would not be tolerated in polite society.

But it was essentially in their personal lives that some women defined their demands for sexual liberation. They sought to be freed from the double standard, which gave man the right to be sexually promiscuous, at least before marriage, but required that a woman maintain her virtue.

For other women, taking or refusing a man's name would be enough of an action. And the lines of demarcation were then, as they are now, drawn on the issues of marriage and the role of the family. Mary Wollstonecraft and George Sand took their stands by living with men, without benefit of marriage. Mary bore a child without benefit of religious ceremony to the social philosopher, William Godwin, and died shortly thereafter, leaving her daughter Mary to be raised by her single parent father.

FLORENCE NIGHTINGALE

Florence Nightingale also campaigned for an expansion of women's roles and wrote an essay, "Cassandra," in which she defended women's rights. The "ministering angel" who established her reputation in serving as a nurse in the Crimean war, went on to reform the British Medical Services, and she also took up the cudgels for women's rights. She argued the social injustice of her time in a prophetic essay with obvious allusions to the Greek visionary, and

complained that women were not free to cultivate their full faculties. She daringly challenged the central structure of the family:

> The family? It is too narrow a field for the development of
> an immortal spirit, be that spirit male or female. The chances
> are a thousand to one that, in that small sphere, the task for
> which that immortal spirit is destined by the qualities and
> the gifts which its Creator has placed within it, will not be
> found.

> The family uses people, *not* for what they are, not for what
> they are intended to be, but for what it wants them for—for
> its own uses. It thinks of them not as what God has made
> them, but as something which *it* has arranged that they
> shall be. If it wants some one to sit in the drawing-room,
> *that* some one is to be supplied by the family, though that
> member may be destined for science, or for education, or for
> active participation by God, *i.e.* by the gifts within.

> As for marriage, it is the only avenue away from the doom of
> "silent misery." Marriage is the only chance (and it is but a
> chance) offered to women for escape from this death; and
> how eagerly and how ignorantly it is embraced![82]

THE SUBJECTION OF WOMEN

Writing, however, was a profession that women could pursue. From
the advent of the printing press and the *Theses* of Martin Luther,
writing had been used as a radical form of social protest and cry for
reform. It was one profession where a woman of sense and sensibility could practice her craft. The French writer Amandine Aurore
Lucie Dupin, Baronne Dudevant, adopted the name George Sand,
Mary Ann Evans became George Eliot, and the Brontë sisters experimented with the names Currer, Ellis and Acton Bell. Jane
Austen, the Brontë Sisters, Mary Shelley, and George Eliot proved
the equals of men in their craft. George Sand posed the distinction: "Men would dare more if only they knew what women dream."

Though most men opposed the insurgency of women, some supported the cause. The libertarian John Stuart Mill attacked the subjugation of women:

> What is now called the nature of women is an eminently artificial thing—the result of forced repression in some directions, unnatural stimulation in others. It may be asserted, without scruple, that no other class of dependents has had their character so entirely distorted from its natural proportions by their relation with their masters.[83]

PRIDE AND PREJUDICE

Even when writing under their own names, many authors reflected a male impersonation. A character in Jane Austen observes that "a woman's only power is the power of refusal." In her most famous novel, *Pride and Prejudice*, she explores through the medium of comedy the painful relationship between the sexes. "It is a truth universally acknowledged, that a single man in possession of a good fortune must be in want of a wife."[84] With five eligible daughters on their hands, the drama of Mr. and Mrs. Bennett's life revolves around the marriage resolution; Mrs. Bennett "was a woman of mean understanding, little information, and uncertain temper. When she was discontented, she fancied herself nervous. The business of her life was to get her daughters married; its solace was visiting and news." Jane Austen herself never married. In her novel she traces the permutations and complications between Mr. Darcy and Elizabeth Bennett who is never quite certain what it takes to capture and hold the male fancy.

FRANKENSTEIN AND WUTHERING HEIGHTS

Mary Shelley's *Frankenstein* has proven to be one of the most popular novels of enduring interest. Mary was the daughter of Mary Wollstonecraft and William Godwin. *Frankenstein*, written when she was in her late teens, is a story of an abandoned monster who kills and destroys out of rage and a need to be loved. Mary's mother died at her birth, and Mary later lived with and married the well-born radical poet, Percy Bysshe Shelley. Indeed the novel was conceived in a retreat in the Alps where Lord Byron, Shelley, and their friends undertook to write horror stories to amuse each other.

Victor Frankenstein is a brilliant young scientist who studies Chemistry and through the secret of electricity is able to regenerate a corpse; it is a peculiar variation on the theme of life after death by an admitted free thinker, and an early example of the science fiction genre, which perhaps has become the eschatology of the modern age. After producing his creation, Frankenstein denies him a home, love, and a mate; in revenge, the man becomes a monster and scourge. Was woman the unwanted monster? Was her rage born out of anger at the status-deprived gender that she felt compelled to accept?

Similarly Emily Brontë in *Wuthering Heights* centers her interest on the enigmatic male character. Heathcliff, a romantic, Byronic hero, has no past, and his relationship with Catherine Earnshaw is idealistic and unreal. The power of love in her book is the fantasy—the ability of Heathcliff to arouse the love of Catherine through his unrepressed emotion. Men can swear, can act, can kill for their love—where woman must be good and wait to be loved.

IBSEN AND STRINDBERG

The marriage question, which occupied a position of importance throughout the century—mainly by feminists, anthropologists, and social reformers—was considered anew at the close of the century. The modern world would question whether differences between men and women were less a result of sacred writ and biology than social conditioning. Was marriage the most salubrious relationship between the sexes? What were the proper roles for men and women? Must there be a master? What are the alternatives to marriage?

Two Scandinavian authors emphatically brought the matter of relations between men and women to the modern consciousness. Henrik Ibsen, a Norwegian playwright, dramatized the social and moral issues of his age. August Strindberg, a Swede who was thrice married, explored his own dependency on love and his fear and abhorrence of the liberated woman.

Ibsen sympathized with new cause of the rights of women. In *A Doll's House* (1879), he boldly argued the natural right of women to be liberated from confining duties to husband and children, and presented the outline of a new morality. The division of labor in a marriage forced a wife to accept an unequal position. Torvald condescends to his wife and fails to treat her as an equal. When he discovers in the course of the play that she forged her father's name on a promissory note and compromised his position, he is indignant at her. Nora, for her part, committed the crime for his sake, when he was ill, and needed the money to go abroad in order to recuperate. Even though the threat of being exposed does not materialize, Nora accuses her husband of failing to stand by her, and she leaves him—in order to be true to herself.

> Helmer: You're insane! You've no right! I forbid you!

> Nora: From here on, there's no use forbidding me anything. I'll take with me whatever is mine. I don't want a thing from you, either now or later, Helmer.

> Helmer: What kind of madness is this!

> Nora: Tomorrow I'm going home—I mean, home where I came from. It'll be easier up there to find something to do.

> Helmer: Oh, you blind, incompetent child!

> Nora: I must learn to be competent, Torvald.

Helmer: Abandon your home, your husband, your children! And you're not even thinking what people will say.

Nora: I can't be concerned about that. I only know how essential this is.

Helmer: Oh, it's outrageous. So you'll run out like this on your most sacred vows.

Nora: What do you think are my most sacred vows?

Helmer: And I have to tell you that! Aren't they your duties to your husband and children?

Nora: I have other duties equally sacred.

Helmer: That isn't true. What duties are they?

Nora. Duties to myself.

Helmer: Before all else, you're a wife and a mother.

Nora. I don't believe in that anymore. I believe that, before all else, I'm a human being, no less than you—or anyway, I ought to try to become one. I know the majority thinks you're right, Torvald, and plenty of books agree with you, too. But I can't go on believing what the majority says, or what's written in books. I have to think over these things myself and try to understand them.[85]

Like Goethe's hero who captured the imagination a hundred years earlier, when a rash of suicides followed—in emulation of the behavior of Young Werther, the departure of Ibsen's heroine had the effect of causing wives to suddenly abandon their families.

Ibsen maintained his fascination with the Byronic hero who was defiant and therefore was perceived as an enemy of the people. Both Ibsen and Strindberg focused on the influence of the sins of the parents on their children. Strindberg's *Miss Julie* is a tragedy in which a mother's hatred of men has become her daughter's birthright and made it impossible for her to love a man. In Ibsen's *Ghosts* the problem of syphilis is dealt with in a tragic story—with strong modern connotations—about a son who falls victim to hereditary syphilis and the sins of his father. Ibsen wrote a drama that sought not merely to sensationalize human experience but to raise disturbing modern issues. Young Oswald Alving not only inherits syphilis from his father—but his father's moral depravity, as well, and has a relationship with the maid who is indeed his father's illegitimate daughter, the result of his debauchery. The modern ghosts of the past are as unremitting as the Greek fates.

Strindberg chastised Ibsen for taking up the cause of the liberated woman. He insisted that woman was out to destroy her mate and rather than support her as the weaker vessel, the male deserves such consideration. The battle of the sexes was not a playful game between men and women—as had been depicted by Ovid, Capellanus, Shakespeare and others—but was a struggle to the death for power between a predatory spider and her mate. Marriage placed man at the disadvantage since a woman was more ruthless than a man. His play *The Father* demonstrated such a confrontation between husband and wife and raised the question as to who has paternity rights over the offspring. A brutal confrontation follows when the wife, Laura, suggests that a man can never be certain of his rights over his child:

> Captain: In this fight, one of us must go under.
>
> Laura: Which?
>
> Captain: The weaker naturally.
>
> Laura: Then is the stronger in the right?
>
> Captain: Bound to be as he has the power.
>
> Laura: Then I am in the right.[86]

In a later play, perhaps as a result of Strindberg's carping influence, Ibsen modified his view of the emancipated woman. In *Hedda Gabler*, he depicted a married woman who was dissatisfied with the role in which nature had cast her. The masculine woman, Hedda, is selfish, cruel, and vicious—a misery to herself and to her husband. She rejected the great romantic love of her life, Eilert Lovborg, because he did not offer her guaranteed status and security. Instead she married a promising scholar who was malleable to her will. Like Madame Bovary, Hedda is restless in her marriage. When she meets Lovborg again, and he is involved in writing a great cultural document, her jealousy is roused. She is frustrated by her own lack of creativity, and she manipulates Lovborg so that he loses his book. It is her tragedy that only through manipulation can she attain her creativity. In an ironic twist, the malevolent Judge Brack, knowing Hedda's secret, tries to blackmail her into becoming his mistress. Rather than give up her freedom, she shoots herself in the head with her father's pistol.

From his attitude of bitterness toward women, Strindberg compromised later in his life, after a religious conversion. In *A Dream Play*, he explored what seemed to him to be the final truth of human existence, that human life is a vale of tears and "human beings are to be pitied." The daughter of the Hindu God Indra descends to earth, becomes a mortal woman, and explores the possibility of happiness in marriage. The wife wants the window open; the husband wants it closed. The maid pastes up the cracks in the structure to warm them and also to insulate them from the outside. He eats cabbage to please her but dislikes fish that she likes. He criticizes her for her untidiness; and she uses his newspaper to light the fire. He observes: "And the child which should be our bond and blessing is our undoing." The daughter of Indra concludes: "It is terribly hard too be married, harder than anything. I think one has to be an angel."

DR. JEKYLL AND MR. HYDE

Sigmund Feud (1856-1939), the great Viennese physician, revolutionized thought in the twentieth century through his discovery of psychopathology. The poets eternally had explored man's psychological nature, but Freud sought to establish a scientific approach toward understanding human behavior. Darwin had presented his evidence on the origin of the species and argued that the prominence of the sexual drive derived from a more primitive nature; the anthropologists and biologists who followed him confirmed his interpretation. Robert Lewis Stevenson in his famous novel, *The Strange Case of Dr. Jekyll and Mr. Hyde* (1886), told the story of a man, Dr. Jekyll, who, by day, was a model of social responsibility and respectability; but, by night, was transformed into a monster, Mr. Hyde. It reflects the dichotomy in human nature of the schizophrenic or bi-polar temperament. Modern science began to trace the progression from ape to man, while Freud explained the duality between the social and the aboriginal man in terms of an internal conflict between conscience and unrestrained desire.

The recognition of the importance of sex and the challenge to traditional thinking about man's nature was considered as pernicious as Darwin's restatement of the Biblical account of Creation. Though both Darwin and Freud explained the duality in human beings caught between bestial heritage and divine nature, their revelations are still being questioned and remain discomforting. Freud himself modestly argued that his discoveries were of limited effectiveness in resolving the causes of our unhappiness, but only pointed to possible sources. No man has been able to affect a cure for human misery, but Freud's invention or discovery of psychology—though it has pretty much been assimilated into our patterns of thought—remains as controversial today as when he set it down. Until current genetic theory provides a Copernican revolu-

tion that better explains human behavior, his views are perhaps
the most persuasive evidence we have.

SIGMUND FREUD AND HIS INFLUENCE

Freud taught the predominance of the *libido*, and confirmed the
poet's truth of the individual's need for love. Society imposes re-
straints upon its members to insure order because, if man's libidinal drives were permitted to run rampant, there would be neither
peace nor social tranquility. Civilization begins with "thou shalt
not." "The substitution of the power of united number for the
power of a single man is the decisive step towards civilization."
Society strikes the necessary balance between its own demands
and the needs of the individual.

> A great part of the struggle of mankind centers round the
> single task of finding some expedient (*i.e.* satisfying) solu-
> tion between these individual claims and those of the civi-
> lized community; it is one of the problems of man's fate
> whether this solution can be arrived at in some particular
> form of culture or whether the conflict will prove irreconcil-
> able.[87]

Culture begins with sublimation. "Sublimation of instinct is an
especially conspicuous feature of cultural evolution; this it is that
makes it possible for the higher mental operations, scientific, artistic, ideological activities, to play such an important part in civilized life." Repression is a significant part of the process. The reward for refraining from instinctual gratification is civilization: art,
science, indeed the progress of society. "It is to the [sexual in-
stinct] alone that we can attribute an internal impulse toward
'progress' and toward higher development!" [88]

Creativity is related to the power of the unconscious, which is projected in fantasy and wish-fulfillment. The artist shares the instinctual nature of his fellows; but through greater need and sensitivity, he projects the feelings of all. As the dream of the individual reveals through condensation and displacement the psychic life of the individual, so art reveals the psychic life of society.

Morality is related to the development of a super-ego—the conscience of the individual that acts as a check on the *id* (instinctual nature) and suppresses it. But where the super-ego's hold is excessively rigid, the individual will fail to make an adjustment between his needs and those of society.

> Thus conscience does make cowards of us all;
> And thus the native hue of resolution
> Is sicklied o'er with the pale cast of thought.
> *Hamlet*

The father or father-figure influences the development of the individual's super-ego, and its efficacy is related to the terror of punishment that it inspires—and ultimately to the psychological fear, in the male, of punishment by castration.

Perhaps Freud's greatest insight was the discovery of the Oedipus complex—the influence played by the individual's parents in the initiation into adulthood. Oedipus was the mythical King of Thebes and the subject of a tragedy by Sophocles. After the oracle revealed to Laius and Jocasta that their son was destined to slay his father and marry his mother, Laius ordered him to put to death. The mother turned him over to a servant who took pity upon him, and left him on the glens of Mount Cithaeron. There, he was found by a shepherd and brought to Corinth where he was raised by King Polybus and Queen Merope, who did not relate the circumstances of his adoption. After Oedipus attained manhood, he consulted the oracle at Delphi and was given the dire prophecy: that he was destined to slay his father and marry his mother. Seeking to evade the horrific prognostication, he chose not to return to

Corinth and to Polybus and Merope. In the course of his travels, he met a traveler on a crossroad, engaged him in an argument and battle, and slew him. He then arrived at Thebes where he solved the riddle of the Sphinx, and married the widowed Queen Jocasta. As a result of the dishonor to his parents, the gods brought a plague on the city. Sophocles' play relates the story of Oedipus' investigation to find the criminal, until he discovers the terrible truth. The chorus draws the moral that man has no free choice and is powerless before the will of the gods.

Freud suggests that the strong appeal of the play is not principally related to the question of fate and free will. Indeed, if Oedipus had been more cautious, he would have made a more exemplary effort to avoid slaying a man who could have been his father, and marrying a woman who could have been his mother. Freud argues that there is a stronger reason for the play to be "capable of moving a modern reader or playgoer no less powerfully than it moved the contemporary Greeks."

> His fate moves us only because it might have been our own, because the oracle laid upon us before our birth the very curse which rested upon him. It may be that we were all destined to direct our first sexual impulses toward our mothers, and our first impulses of hatred and violence toward our fathers; our dreams convince us that we were. King Oedipus, who slew his father Laius and wedded his mother Jocasta, is nothing more or less than a wish-fulfillment—the fulfillment of the wish of our childhood. But we, more fortunate than he, insofar as we have not become psychoneurotics, have since our childhood succeeded in withdrawing our sexual impulses from our mothers, and in forgetting our jealousy of our fathers. We recoil from the person for whom this primitive wish of our childhood has been fulfilled with all the force of the repression which these wishes have undergone in our minds since childhood. As the poet brings the guilt of Oedipus to light by his investigation, he forces us to become aware of our inner selves, in which the same impulses are still extant, even though they are suppressed.[89]

Sexual feeling is both the principal wellspring and tributary outlet of our character, behavior, and emotions. Freud observed the ambivalence of our emotions—conflicting love-hate feelings are apparent in all our deep attachments—whether to parents, companions, husbands, wives and lovers, and even political leaders.

> My only love sprung from my only hate.
> *Romeo and Juliet*

Freud would have been the first to insist that the healthy life of an individual depends not so much upon sexual positions as on sexual roles. The continuity of the species depends not only on physical union but also on the assumption of parental roles. There is no species in the animal kingdom that does not depend upon the aspiration of the young to the roles of their progenitors. Freud observed that every relationship between a man and a woman has "four people" involved—the parents no less than the individuals. Our attitudes—and our value judgments on sex—have been most significantly influenced by those who have had the responsibility for providing for us, and teaching us.

The family is the matrix of all social and emotional adjustment in our society, and the transition from the *Oedipal* (or *Electra*) phase is a necessary condition of adulthood. Inasmuch as Oedipus failed to make this transition, he became the exemplar of the Oedipus complex. "Therefore shall a man leave his father and mother, and shall cleave unto his wife: and they shall be one flesh" *(Genesis)*. The maladjustment of an individual's sexual role—and therefore of his social role—relates the failure of the triangular bond between parent and child. A most damning criticism of any society, therefore—is that the role of parent that the youth must assume in the Oedipal or Electra resolve is rejected, or even scorned.

The empirical proof for Freud's analysis is most convincing. Freud based his observations on years of research, and his reading of literature confirmed what he learned from his patients.. "It can scarcely be owing to chance that three of the masterpieces of the literature of all time—*Oedipus Rex* by Sophocles, Shakespeare's *Hamlet* and Dostoyevsky's *The Brothers Karamazov*—should all deal with the same subject, parricide. In all three, moreover, the motive for the deed is laid bare."[90] All three works then are concerned with evolution of these Oedipal crises, and are instances of neurotic adjustment. Thus, they serve as a catharsis for the audience and reader.

Freud rejected the claim of the feminists that women actually were the same as men, and differences arose because of different conditioning. The behavior of a woman was related to her biological, physiological, psychological nature—and could be changed with as much finesse as a leopard could change its spots. He was supported by poets and contemporary anthropologists, who maintained that men and women were indeed different since the time of Adam and Eve, Zeus and Hera, and Pandora and Epimetheus.

> I cannot escape the notion (though I hesitate to give it expression) that for women the level of what is ethically normal is different from what it is in men. Their superego is never so inexorable, so impersonal, so independent of its emotional origins as we require it to be in men. Character-traits which critics of every epoch have brought up against women—that they show less sense of justice than men, that they are less ready to submit to the great necessities of life, that they are more often influenced in their judgments by feelings of affection or hostility—all these would be amply accounted for in the modification of the formation of their superego which we have already inferred. We must not allow ourselves to be deflected from such conclusions by the denials of the feminists, who are anxious to force us to regard the two sexes as completely equal in position and worth.[91]

His teaching well might have served to emphasize the necessity of establishing strong familial ties. As a matter of fact, the result has been the opposite. Instead of encouraging the stability of the family, Freud's work has been used to degrade the family as the preeminent creator of neurotic character. Moreover, since creative people by and large have come from strong Oedipal conflicts, they have tended to disparage the family as an institution of the conventional bourgeoisie; but they have failed to suggest an alternative that would offer the economic and social stability and sexual identity that the family has offered.

Freud's influence on the liberation of our attitude toward sex has been more notable. He wrote:

> Present-day civilization gives us plainly to understand that sexual relations are permitted only on the basis of a final, indissoluble bond between a man and woman; that sexuality as a source of enjoyment for its own sake is unacceptable to it; and that its intention is to tolerate it only as the hitherto irreplaceable means of multiplying the human race.[92]

A major consequence of his thought in the twentieth century, was in fact the vitiation of Victorian notions of prudery and a change in our mores. The twentieth century witnessed the evolution toward greater acknowledgement of the legitimacy of our libidinal drives—and even the apotheosis of the sexual revolution.

D.H. LAWRENCE

D.H. Lawrence's *Sons and Lovers* is a study of the Oedipal resolve, though Lawrence probably was not familiar with Freud's work. It is a *Bildungsroman*—a novel of a young man's maturity into adulthood, and Lawrence intuitively perceives the significance of parental influence on his hero artist Paul Morel. The son of a coal miner who does not get along with his wife, Paul, a delicate boy, is drawn to his mother's side and pampered by her.

> Paul loved to sleep with his mother. Sleep is still most perfect, in spite of hygienists, when it is shared with a beloved. The warmth, the security and peace of soul, the utter comfort from the touch of the other, knits the sleep, so that it

takes the body and soul completely in its healing. Paul lay against her and slept, and got better; whilst she, always a bad sleeper, fell later on into a profound sleep that seemed to give her faith.[93]

Paul is alienated from his father who does not understand him, and the younger man does not develop a meaningful relationship with the older. He becomes an artist, and seeks to please his mother with his sketches and paintings, as he had pleased her with his "budget of the day" when he was young.

> "I can do my best things when you sit there in your rock-ing-chair, mother," he said.
>
> "I'm sure!" she exclaimed, sniffing with mock skepticism. But she felt it was so, and her heart quivered with bright-ness. For many hours she sat still, slightly conscious of him laboring away, whilst she worked or read her book. And he, with all his soul's intensity directing his pencil, could feel her warmth inside him like strength. They were both very happy so, and both unconscious of it. These times, that meant so much, and which were real living, they almost ignored.

As a youth, he is drawn into romantic alliance with the neighbor-ing lass, Miriam, but his mother jealously guards her hold over him. Only after Paul meets a stronger woman, Clara—married and a few years his senior—is he able to transfer his love from his mother to another woman. With Clara, he discovers love and proves himself a man. But even so, he is not yet released from his mother's domination. When she becomes ill, he conspires with his sister to end her life. After her death, Paul achieves some peace and free-dom.

Lawrence continued to depict the sexual element in man's char-acter as a mystical force. He became the apostle of Eros in the twentieth century, as Sappho and Catullus had been in their time. *Lady Chatterley's Lover*, which originally was censored as obscene, came to represent a new pagan outlook. Lawrence rendered more graphically than any serious writer had done before the relations between Lady Chatterley and her gamekeeper Mellors:

> "So proud!" she murmured, uneasy. "And so lordly! Now I know why men are so overbearing. But he's lovely, *really*. Like another being! A bit terrifying! But lovely really! And he comes *to me!*" She caught her lower lip between her teeth, in fear and excitement.
>
> The man looked down in silence at his tense phallus that did not change.—"Ay!" he said at last, in a little voice. "Ay ma lad! Tha'rt theer right enough. Yi, tha mun rear thy head! Theer on thy own, eh? an ta'es no count o' nob'dy! Tha ma'es nowt o' me, John Thomas. Art boss? of me? Eh well, tha'rt more cocky than me, an' tha says less. John Thomas! Dost want *her*? Dost want my lady Jane? Tha's dipped me in again, tha hast. Ay, an' tha comes up smilin'.—Ax'er then! Ax lady Jane! Say: Lift up your heads o' ye gates, that the king of glory may come in."[94]

MARCEL PROUST AND MODERNISM

The Modernist movement in literature, like its counterparts in art and music, was unconventional, innovative to the point of being revolutionary, individualistic, intellectual for the most part, self-conscious, critical of the vacuity of modern life, and romantically self-indulgent. As Picasso, Kokoschka, and Mondrian, for example, sought to liberate art from its immediate predecessors, they redefined the medium and rendered it according to their own genius. So too in music: Debussy, Schönberg, Stravinsky, Copland loosened music from the harmonies and musical syntax of the past, and originated a distinct new sound. In literature, as well, a new intelligence and passion guided the writers, as D.H. Lawrence had shown the path in staking new claims and charting new courses. The likely common element in all of the art forms was the discovery of the role of the unconscious in the life and creativity of the

individual. Freud had been insistent on revealing the dominance
of the *libido* in the unconscious—and writers like Dostoyevsky,
Lawrence, and many others, not necessarily familiar with Freud's
writings, were illustrating the same truth. In another sense, the
Modernist movement of the twentieth century has been an attempt to shore up or replace the truths of mystical Christianity.

> These fragments I have shored against my ruins
> T.S. Eliot

Marcel Proust also showed the Oedipal conflict in his autobiographical novel, *Remembrance of Things Past*. Marcel recalls his
mother's influence on him—a tea cookie that she served him when
he was a boy is the subject of vivid, lengthy reminiscence of the
effect of his past upon his character. The novel also explores the
relationships among the French upper-middle class and the great
love story between M. Swann and the fallen woman, Odette de
Crécy. The poetry of his style, as well as his analytical skill, sustains the reader's interest through the long epic narrative:

> My sole consolation when I went upstairs for the night was
> that Mamma would come in and kiss me after I was in bed.
> But this good night lasted for so short a time: she went
> down again so soon that the moment in which I heard her
> climb the stairs, and then caught the sound of her garden
> dress of blue muslin, from which hung little tassels of plaited
> straw, rustling along the double-doored corridor, was for me
> a moment of the keenest sorrow. So much did I love that
> good night that I reached the stage of hoping that it would
> come as late as possible, so as to prolong the time of respite
> during which Mamma would not yet have appeared. Some-
> times when, after kissing me, she opened the door to go, I
> longed to call her back, to say to her "Kiss me just once
> again," but I knew that then she would at once look dis-
> pleased, for the concession which she made to my wretch-
> edness and agitation in coming to me with this kiss of peace
> always annoyed my father, who thought such ceremonies
> absurd, and she would have liked to try to induce me to

outgrow the need . . . And to see her look displeased destroyed all the sense of tranquility she had brought me a moment before, when she bent her loving face down over my bed, and held it out to me like a Host, for an act of Communion in which my lips might drink deeply the sense of her real presence, and with it the power to sleep.[95]

THE TRIAL

Franz Kafka's *The Trial* explored the issue of man's culpability and guilt. The book is at once a satire on a modern bureaucracy, which demeans and dehumanizes the individual and a theological quest to find the reason for man's anguish and suffering. Joseph K. is arrested one morning without prior warning and subjected to an investigative probe, though he is unable to learn the nature of his crime. Perhaps he is guilty only of original sin (in having been born), but there is also the possibility that his sin corresponds with his Oedipal development. His neighbor, Fräulein Bürstner, perhaps has an underlying significance to the crisis that befalls K—provoking (sexual) feelings in him, which he has repressed; his behavior that follows is erratic.

> He felt for her wrist again, she let him take it this time and so led him to the door. He was firmly resolved to leave. But at the door he stopped as if he had not expected to find a door there; Fräulein Bürstner seized this moment to free herself, open the door, and slip into the entrance hall, where she whispered: "Now, please do come! Look"—she pointed to the Captain's door, underneath which showed a strip of light—"he has turned on his light and is amusing himself at our expense." "I'm just coming," K. said, rushed out, seized her, and kissed her first on the lips, then all over the face, like some thirsty animal lapping greedily at a spring of long-sought fresh water.[96]

Women figure significantly in his trial. They all exploit men, and they also offer the only hope of salvation. K. becomes fearful of the way in which women use men—the janitor's wife who compels men to satisfy her sexual needs and the advocate's servant, Leni, who willfully humbles all her victims. On a psychological level, K's trial well might correspond to his immature fear of castration which he must overcome before he can become a man. Unlike his contemporary, Marcel, who regresses to childhood to evade the responsibilities of maturity, Joseph, who cannot live like a man, dies "like a dog."

LUIGI PIRANDELLO

Another early twentieth century writer who treated the desiccation of modern life in a very original and unusual manner was Luigi Pirandello. He utilized traditional themes, like love, the family, the nature of truth, art and madness. In *Six Characters in Search of an Author*, which he described as a comedy in the making, a father and mother and their four children come to witness their lives being written into a play and performed by an acting troupe. Conflict arises between the real family and the actors who play them; art can never hope to convey the profound pain of people's actual lives. The real Father declares to the Theater Manager: "Oh sir, you know well that life is full of infinite absurdities, which, strangely enough, do not even need to appear plausible, since they are true."[97] Furthermore "to reverse the ordinary process may well be considered a madness: that is, to create credible situations, in order that they may appear to be true. But permit me to observe that if this be madness, it is the sole *raison d'etre* of your profession, gentlemen." Art offers an escape for the audience, which feeds upon and is engaged by the pain of others, rendered, as with Don Quijote, through the illusions of the author.

The contrast between illusion and reality, opinion and truth, and art and life is explored in other Pirandello plays. *It Is So! (If You*

Think So) explores the peculiar relationship among a mother, daughter, and son-in-law. While the small town society looks on and gossips about the strange activities that are undertaken among this group of family members, the characters themselves act out of their own exigent needs; yet the emotional truth for Pirandello is that love, or altruism, is a saving grace when life's tragedy drives us to despair.

THE TRAGIC SENSE OF LIFE

The Modernist movement also fostered a reaction, and reaffirmation of Christian values. This was seen most prominently in Spain, the most conservative of Western societies. Miguel de Unamuno declaimed against modern culture, "Culture—oh, this culture!— Which is primarily the work of philosophers and men of science, is a thing which neither heroes nor saints have had any share in the making of."[98] He opposed the fragmentation brought about by scientific values, and the paganism of modern life. He argued in his passionate essay, *The Tragic Sense of Life* (1921) that the meaning of our lives can be restored only by return to traditional values, the philosophy of Plato, St. Augustine, the example of Jesus Christ, and the teaching of the Church. The tragic sense denies the cravings of the mortal body and arouses the hunger for immortality. Finally he pointed to the indomitable Don Quijote, the Spanish Christ figure, as an example to lead his people to the resurrection of Spanish Catholicism.

FEDERICO GARCÍA LORCA

The Spanish poet and playwright, Federico García Lorca, rendered traditional values of honor and virtue in his plays. In *The House of Bernarda Alba, A Drama About Women in the Villages of Spain*(1936), the mother of five daughters, aged between twenty and thirty nine, seals off her home from the outside world to fulfill the honor due to the memory of her husband. The women live amid strife and sexual tension. But Bernarda's absurd view of honor will not allow her daughters to mingle with any who are unworthy of their status; and it appears that all are destined to become, like Bernarda's eighty year old mother, crazy and sex starved: "I want to go to my home town. Bernarda, I want a man to get married to and be happy with!" The youngest daughter finds herself pregnant and unsuccessfully tries to conceal her condition. When Bernarda discovers the infamy, she shoots at the lover but misses; in turn, the daughter kills herself. The mother is unmoved, and she declares: "She, the youngest daughter of Bernarda Alba, died a virgin. Did you hear me? Silence, silence, I said. Silence!"[99]

Another folk drama set in rural Spain, *Yerma, A Tragic Poem*, depicts the pain of an infertile woman who seeks a cure for her barrenness. She reflects: "Men get other things out of life: their cattle, trees, conversations, but women have only their children and the care of their children." When the Happy Old Woman suggests to Yerma that she take a lover to compensate for her husband's failure, the simple village woman replies: "Where would that leave my honor? Water can't run uphill, nor does the full moon rise at noonday. On the road I've started, I'll stay."[100] Her honor is saved. In an ironic twist, Yerma's rage drives her to strangle her husband for depriving her of womanhood.

GEORGE BERNARD SHAW

There were other writers who rejected modernist assumptions. George Bernard Shaw was obdurate. Although he was a free-thinker, he opposed not only Freud but the whole romantic ethos, the divinity of sex, and the beneficent inevitability of love and marriage. He preferred to idealize the effect of love rather than reduce it to sexual passion, and maintained a metaphysical rather than a psychological interpretation. The life force was responsible for the attraction between man and woman as well as for evolutionary change. He depicted his Don Juan as a coward who was seeking to escape from women:

> Do you not understand that when I stood face to face with Woman, every fiber in my clear critical brain warned me to spare her and save myself? My morals said No. My conscience said No. My chivalry and pity for her said No. My prudent regard for myself said No. My ear, practiced on a thousand songs and symphonies; my eye, exercised on a thousand paintings; tore her voice, her features, her color to shreds. I caught all those tell-tale resemblances to her father and mother by which I knew what she would be like in thirty years' time. I noted the gleam of gold from a dead tooth in the laughing mouth: I made curious observations of the strange odors of the chemistry of the nerves. The visions of my romantic reveries, in which I had trod the plains of heaven with a deathless, ageless creature of coral and ivory, deserted me in that supreme hour. I remembered them and desperately strove to recover their illusion; but they now seemed the emptiest of inventions: my judgment was not to be corrupted: my brain still said No on every issue. And whilst I was in the act of framing my excuse to the lady, Life seized me and threw me into her arms as a sailor throws a scrap of fish into the mouth of a seabird . . . In the sex relation the universal creative energy, of which the parties are both the helpless agents, over-rides and sweeps away all personal considerations, and dispenses with all personal relations.
> *Man and Superman*[101]

PYGMALION

Shaw's attitude was in one sense a throwback to the middle ages— he was a troubadour in the service of ideal love. True love was the pursuit of perfection by the medieval knight—more so what the mythical artist Pygmalion discovered when he created the statue of Galatea and fell in love with it. Shaw explored this idea in *Pygmalion*, perhaps his most serious love comedy. Henry Higgins makes a lady out of a flower girl, Eliza Doolittle, and falls in love with his creation. But since the true artist rises above his mortal drives, he will not surrender to lust or convention. His love leads neither to marriage nor to a baby carriage—yet it is the supreme achievement of love.

Eliza Doolittle is too much a woman to accept the artist on his terms. A woman wants affection and dominance—in marriage, and she chooses the simple Freddy as the more suitable partner. The artist-teacher can accept nothing less than perfection, and so he must remain a bachelor, and worship woman as an inspiration—from afar.

Eliza's father, Alfred, a sponge and a cheat, shares Higgins's superiority to conventional morality. Alfred has no scruples about renting his daughter to Henry for his experiment—a poor, desperate man will be driven to anything—but finds bourgeois morality to be the ultimate degradation. Marriage is the triumph of expediency over idealism, as Doolittle discovers, when his sudden attainment of wealth forces him to give up happiness and principle to gain respectability.

BRAVE NEW WORLD

In *Brave New World*, written in the thirties and recently voted by some scholars and popular journals one of the four or five best books of the twentieth century, Aldous Huxley projected a world of the future six hundred years hence, in which love and religion have been displaced, and people worship by the sign of the T. The family has disappeared, and the state has taken over the birth and rearing of the young. Orgy porgy takes the place of deep lasting relationships between men and women. Though libidinal drives still are restricted, perhaps there is greater equality between the sexes. Society is hierarchal, constructed according to the needs of technology, and the individual receives the benefit of miraculous gadgets and mind-expanding chemicals. There is neither disharmony nor creativity in this mechanized dehumanized society.

A child of the two cultures—both scientific and humanistic—Huxley perceived the dimensions of the scientific revolution, and yet he appreciated the challenge to humanism in a technological age. His friendship with D.H. Lawrence brought into focus the conflict between technology and humanity, the scientific way and the artistic. Lawrence rejected the values of our technological society and believed that "more power exercised by the 'dark loins of man,' greater freedom for our instincts and our intuitions, would solve the world's troubles." Huxley recreated this conflict in *Brave New World*, where the Lawrentian Savage—non-conformist, dirty, and free remains bound to the truths of his emotional needs and rejects the antiseptic quality of the new society.

Huxley's book has had a prophetic quality as young readers are still finding it instructive and meaningful for its science no less than its anti-science prejudice. For some, the position of the Savage is preferred, and the scientist remains under suspicion. The infringement of society on the rights of the individual is condemned, and the individual's right to instinctual and emotional freedom is defended. The machine is feared as a threat to our freedom.

JAMES JOYCE

James Joyce's comic masterpiece *Ulysses*, rated by the same poll as the greatest novel of the century, recounts the story of Odysseus' journey home after the Trojan War. Joyce's anti-heroic Irish advertising salesman, Leopold Bloom, seems to bear small resemblance to his literary forebear, in this a modern study of the relations between men and women. Bloom's activities of the day are set contrapuntally to those of Homer's hero. Joyce's artistic vision is that the struggle of modern man does not occur across the seas, or in exotic lands, but it is comprised of menial, daily events. The responsibility to earn one's bread by the sweat of one's brow, and to fulfill one's responsibilities to one's family is every man's heroic struggle.

In contrast to the strong family ties that were maintained in the Homeric family, Joyce renders the ambivalent roles in the modern family. The clear roles that existed between husband and wife, parent and child no longer prevail. There is a serious generational conflict, and modern life, with its dehumanizing effect, undermines the relationship between people. Leopold and Molly Bloom lost their son Rudy in infancy—and miss the bond of a male heir. Young Stephen Dedalus is a modern Telemachus in search of a father; contemptuous of his own parent, he finds a spiritual kinship toward Bloom, as Leopold similarly finds his surrogate son in Stephen. Joyce's greatest literary achievement is rendering the character of Molly Bloom. Molly, even as Penelope, embodies the riddle of womanhood. She is complex in her feelings as wife-mother-lover, and reveals herself through her stream-of-conscious thought presented by Joyce with utmost technical virtuosity. In the last scene in the book, Molly thinks about Stephen, to whom she is somewhat sexually attracted. She daydreams using the stream of conscious about passion, frustration, and her repressed lust:

> I suppose hes 20 or more I'm not too old for him if hes 23 or 24 I hope hes not that stuck up university student sort no otherwise he wouldnt go sitting down in the old kitchen with him taking Eppss cocoa and talking of course he pretended to understand it all probably he told him he was out of Trinity college hes very young to be a professor.

Though she feels no warmth to her husband now, her recollection of their courtship evokes heart-felt memories, recalled fondly and rendered ungrammatically with elemental passion, and tinged with ambivalence toward the male of the species:

> its well for men all the amount of pleasure they get off a womans body were so round and white for them always I

wished I was one myself for a change just to try with that thing they have swelling upon you so hard and at the same time so soft when you touch it . . . show them attention and they treat you like dirt I dont care what anybody says itd be much better for the world to be governed by the women in it you wouldnt see women going and killing one another and slaughtering when do you ever see women rolling around drunk like they do or gambling every penny they have and losing it on horses yes because a woman whatever she does she knows where to stop sure they wouldnt be in the world at all only for us they don't know what it is to be a woman and a mother how could they where would they all of them be if they hadnt all a mother to look after them . . . the sun shines for you he said the day we were lying among the rhododendrons on Howth head in the grey tweed suit and his straw hat the day I got him to propose to me yes first I gave him the bit of seedcake out of my mouth and it was leapyear like now yes 16 years ago my God after that long kiss I near lost my breath yes . . . and then I asked him with my eyes to ask again yes and then he asked me would I yes to say yes my mountain flower and first I put my arms around him yes and drew him down to me so he could feel my breasts all perfume yes and his heart was going like mad and yes I said yes I will Yes.[102]

To Joyce's chagrin, embarrassment, and no doubt secret pleasure, the book was misunderstood in its time, and Molly's fantasies were deemed pornographic. The stream of consciousness technique was judged to be a means of escaping the censor's pencil. *Ulysses* was banned in the United States. In reaction, Joyce countered with a more obscure work, *Finnegans Wake*; let the censors uncover the meaning there, if they could: "Then, pious Eneas, conformant to the fulminant firman which enjoins on the tremylose terrian that, when the call comes, he shall produce nichthemerically from his unheavenly body a no uncertain quantity of obscene matter not protected by copriright in the United Stars of Ourania or bedeed and bedood and bedang and bedung to him, with this double dye, brought to blood heat, gallic acid on iron ore . . ." Joyce's pristine intention in the *Wake* was to render the history of mankind and the evolution of the family in a cyclical pattern corresponding to the circular structure of his book, where the book concludes with the opening of the first line: "A way a lone a lost a last a loved a long the . . . riverrun, past Eve and Adam's, from swerve of shore to bend of bay, brings us by a commodius vicus of recirculation back to Howth Castle and Environs," where the river is the maternal Anna Livia Plurabelle and the castle Humphrey Chimpden Earwicker and the story their family history.

It is a dream vision, a nightmarish attempt to accomplish the rendition in language of everything that Joyce knew and occupied his interest from 1922-1939. But it is playful: "The jinnies is jillous agincourting all the lipoleums. And the lipoleums is gonn boycottoncrezy onto the one Willingdone. And the Willingdone git the band up," and as unpretentious as a movie: "The movibles are scrawling in motions, marching, all of them ago, in pitpat and zingzang for every busy eerie whig's a bit of a torytale to tell." Finally it was the intense struggle of an unrepentant sinner to find his personal salvation by writing

> over every square inch of the only foolscap available, his own body, till by its corrosive sublimation one continuous present tense integument slowly unfolded all marryvoising moodmoulded cyclewheeling history (thereby, he said, reflecting from his own individual person life unlivable, transaccidentated through the slow fires of consciousness into a dividual chaos, perilous, potent, common to allflesh, human only, mortal) but with each word that would not pass away the squidself which he had squirtscreened from the crystalline world waned chagreenold and doriangrayer in its dudhud.[103]

T.S. ELIOT

T.S. Eliot's "The Love Song of J. Alfred Prufrock" also can be read as a young man's effort to achieve some kind of sexual or Oedipal resolve. Prufrock is telling the deepest secrets of his soul—perhaps an assignation, or his effort to form a relationship with a woman. No Mellors he, and she is no Lady Chatterley. For Prufrock, it is an enormous undertaking like the twelve labors of Hercules or Oedipus's solution of the riddle of the Sphinx, and he has to prod himself to keep from regressing:

> There will be time, there will be time
> To prepare a face to meet the faces that you meet;
> There will be time to murder and create,
> And time for all the works and days of hands
> That lift and drop a question on your plate;
> Time for you and time for me,
> And time yet for a hundred indecisions,
> And for a hundred visions and revisions,
> Before the taking of a toast and tea.
>
> In the room the women come and go
> Talking of Michaelangelo.
>
> And indeed there will be time
> To wonder, "Do I dare?!" and, "Do I dare?"

In his verse comedy, *The Cocktail Party*, T.S. Eliot explores the dilemma of marriage. Edward and Lavinia Chamberlayne endure frustration in married life. She feels that he is too dependent upon her, and he feels that she is domineering and unconcerned about him—until she decides to walk out on her husband. Edward now finds that he really loves his wife. Their spiritual counselor and psychiatrist, Sir Henry Harcourt-Reilly, arranges for a reconciliation between them. He tells them that neither individual can expect complete satisfaction; but at the very least marriage affords the partners the opportunity to share their isolation. There are no ideal marriages; only compromise is available. Lavinia is confused by Sir Henry's explanation:

Lavinia: Then what can we do

When we can go neither back nor forward? Edward!
What can we do?

Reilly: You have answered your own question
Though you do not know the meaning of what you have
said.

Edward: Lavinia, we must make the best of a bad job.
That is what he means.

Reilly: When you find, Mr. Chamberlayne,
The best of a bad job is all any of us make of it—
Except of course, the saints.

Sir Henry amplifies what is needed to make the best of a bad job,
to enable a marriage to succeed, and requires acceptance of the
"common routine":

Learn to avoid excessive expectation,
Become tolerant of themselves and others,
Giving and taking, in the usual actions
What there is to give and take. They do not repine;
Are contented with the morning that separates
And with the evening that brings together
For casual talk before the fire
Two people who know they do not understand each other,
Breeding children whom they do not understand
And who will never understand them.

Marriage is filled with commonplaces. He muses upon their reconciliation.

What have they go to back to?
To the stale food mouldering in the larder,
The stale thoughts mouldering in their minds.
Each unable to disguise his own meanness
From himself, because it is known to the other.

And yet he insists upon the final validity, though it is not necessarily the "best life," which is only attainable by "saints."

> It is a good life . . . In a world of lunacy,
> Violence, stupidity, greed . . . it is a good life.[104]

SIMONE DE BEAUVOIR

Simone de Beauvoir argued the cause of the new woman in her influential study, *The Second Sex.* Like the writings of Lady Murasaki and Christine de Pizan before her, the book reads like a catalogue of the suffering endured by a woman in the course of a perilous journey in a man's world. De Beauvoir, who was a companion to the French existentialist philosopher and writer Jean-Paul Sartre, argued, as early modern feminists like Mary Wollstonecraft and Charlotte Gilman had, for an end to traditional roles to be replaced by "brotherhood" between man and woman.

She recalls the remark of the seventeenth century feminist that "all that has been written about women by men should be suspect, for the men are at once judge and party to the lawsuit." She wishes to dethrone the myth of femininity and redefine what it means to be a woman.

> One is not born, but rather becomes, a woman. No biological, psychological, or economic fate determines the figure that the human female presents in society; it is civilization as a whole that produces this creature, intermediate between male and eunuch, which is described as feminine.[105]

She further argued that woman has been discriminated against, forced to remain subservient if not enslaved and compared the exploitation of woman comparable to that of the slave man in America.

> But there are deep similarities between the situation of woman and that of the Negro. Both are being emancipated

from a like paternalism, and the former master class wishes "to keep them in their place"—that is, the place chosen for them . . . Yes, women on the whole are inferior to men; that is, their situation affords them fewer possibilities. The question is: should that state of affairs continue?

ELSA MORANTE

Another reflection on a woman's experience can be seen in the work of the Italian authoress, Elsa Morante. She was born in 1912, married Alberto Moravia in 1941, and separated from him in 1962. She produced a small but impressive corpus of work consisting of four novels and several volumes of short stories and poetry. Her landscape is Italian, her sensibility Romantic, her perceptions deeply personal, and her style decidedly modernist.

For the most part, Morante's novels are more Proustian than Kafkaesque, exploring childhood sensibilities and complex family relationships. In *House of Liars*, the narrator Elisa recalls the experience with her family before she became an orphan at ten. Arturo Gerace inhabits *Arturo's Island* with his widowed father in utopian bliss. Wilhelm communicates to his son his disdain and misogyny:

> "Women want to degrade life. That's what the Hebrew legend meant when it said men were chased out of the Earthly Paradise because of a woman. It's women's fault that we're destined for nothing but birth and death, like animals. Women hate everything unnecessary, undeserved, unlimited; they're ugly creatures who want drama and sacrifice, and time, and decay, and magic, and hope—who want death. If it weren't for women, life would be one long eternal youth in a garden."[106]

When Wilhelm remarries a woman who is a contemporary of Arturo, the son finds his bliss disturbed: "I couldn't use her name when I was talking to her, and even now, when I'm writing about her—I don't know why, but I can't call her by name. Some mysterious difficulty bars me from using the simple syllables: *Nunziata, Nunziatella*. And so I'll have to keep calling her *she*, or *the wife*, or *my stepmother*, even here." He nevertheless becomes fatally attached to her, and then chooses to flee his island.

La Storia, in contrast, represents a sharp departure from her provincial interests. Though she still explores the themes of peasant life, the relationship between parents and children, and among siblings, she fully exploits the ambiguity of the term *La Storia*, the story as history, and history as a story (in the English translation *History, A Novel*). This novel, her masterpiece, renders in definitive literary form, the struggle of the Italian people through the two wars, and particularly the devastation of the Second World War. Morante escaped with Moravio to the hills of the Ciociari region in the outskirts of Rome, and the experience of living "in a miserable pigsty" influenced the creation of Moravio's war novel *Two Women* (rendered in a classic film performance by Sophia Loren) as well as *La Storia*. Morante expanded her story to the breadth of an epic.

The narrator is likely the voice of the epic poet, intruding infrequently into the events, as for example when citing the tavern used by Professor Ramondo: "I have been unable to discover the exact location of that tavern. However, somebody once told me that to reach it, you had to take a suburban tram, if not the funicular up the side of the mountain."

Iduzza Ramondo, the heroine of the novel, might be the allegory of Italian suffering in the period. In any event, she surely is a symbol. Her father, Giuseppe, was Calabrian, born to a farming family (a peasant) who moved to the city where he met and married Nora, a Jew from the ghetto of Padua, and he favored intellectual life, embraced the cause of anarchy and the habit of alcohol, which together alienated him from society. Iduzza was baptized a Catholic like her father, while he remained a resolute atheist—"The God hypothesis is useless" and an advocate of social revolution. He died in 1936 of cirrhosis of the liver.

Ida's husband, Alfio Mancuso, was born in Messina. In 1908,

he miraculously survived the devastating earthquake that afflicted the island; when escaping a whipping from his master, he climbed a palm tree, and was saved. Alfio was neither an intellectual nor an alcoholic, and he proved a comforting husband. Together they produced a son, Nino. Iduzza became a schoolteacher; but her husband died an premature death and left her at the onset of the war a widow with a fifteen year old son.

One of the central events, if not the central event of the novel is the rape of Iduzza, by a young German soldier, Gunther:

> "FARE AMORE! . . ." he shouted, repeating in a boyish outburst another two of the 4 Italian words that, in his foresight, he had made them teach him at the frontier. And without even taking off his uniform, caring nothing that she was old, he hurled himself on top of her, throwing her on that disheveled daybed, and raping her with rage as if he wanted to murder her.

> He felt her writhe horribly, but unaware of her illness, he thought she was struggling against him, and he became more obstinate for this reason, like all drunken soldiery. In reality, she had lost consciousness, in a temporary absence from him and from the situation, but he didn't realize this. And he was so charged with stern repressed tensions that, at the moment of orgasm, he emitted a great scream above her. Then, in the following moment, he peeped at her in time to see her face, filled with amazement, relax in a smile of ineffable humility and sweetness.[107]

La Storia then centers on the struggle of Iduzza to raise her two children—her second son, Useppe, born out of the rape, and fatherless, as Gunther dies soon after the event. Iduzza must give up her job teaching, and is forced to relocate to the Pietralata area in the suburbs of Rome. Nino goes off to join the partisan guerilla effort against the German occupation. She in turn must also confront the anti-Jewish laws. Though she registers as having distant Jewish ancestry, she fortunately evades the round up. On the day that the Jews are sent to Auschwitz from the railway station at Tiburtina, Iduzza is shunted off by a railway official, and miraculously escapes the fate of the 1,056 other Jews, of whom all but fifteen never returned.

The second half of the book introduces the character of Davide Segre, who befriends Nino and introduces him to the philosophy of Anarchism, which he shares with Morante. "Power," he argues, "is degrading for those who submit to it, for those who administer it, and for those who control it! Power is the leprosy of the world! And the human face, which looks up and should mirror the splendor of the heavens, all human faces, instead, first to last, are deformed by such leprous aspect! A stone, a pound of shit will be worthier of respect than a man, as long as the human race is infected by Power." Iduzza is subjected to the rantings of Davide on his political philosophy. But it is the loss of her children together with the crumbling of her Italian homeland that drives her to anarchic despair and madness.

FREDERICH DÜRRENMATT AND MAX FRISCH

Frederich Dürrenmatt and Max Frisch are two leading Swiss writers, who offered a significant perspective on the modern condition. They both are guilty of Swiss playfulness with a serious underside. Dürenmatt's *The Visit* (1956) is a drama about the richest woman in the world, Claire Zachnassian, who returns to the town of Güllen, in which she grew up, in order to seek revenge on the man Alfred Ill, who wronged her in her youth and forced her to have an abortion. She declares: "A million for Güllen if someone kills Alfred Ill." He tries to placate her: "My little sorceress! You can't ask that! It was long ago. Life went on." But she is unremitting:

> I've forgotten nothing, Ill. Neither Konrad's Village Wood, nor Petersens' Barn; neither Widow Boll's bedroom, nor your treachery. And now we're old, the pair of us. You de-

> crepit, and me cut to bits by the surgeons' knives. And I
> want accounts between us settled. You chose your life, but
> you forced me into mine . . . I want justice. Justice for a
> million.[108]

She is confident that she can buy the town with her wealth. At
first, the townspeople scoff at the cruel bargain. But the realization comes to Ill that he is doomed when the citizens begin to
make purchases on credit that they will not be able to repay. Claire
Zachnassian, the oil heiress, understands human nature and waits
patiently, knowing that they will concur and even conspire in his
demise to assure their "good fortune." And so they do.

Max Frisch writes cleverly and wryly about the loneliness of
the widower. In *Man in the Holocene*, he celebrates a seventy four
year old man, Geiger, who lives alone with his work, without being subject to any strong emotional feelings—he hardly can recall
the name of his daughter and contemplates Pythagorean Theo-
rems, the Triassic period, and the cobwebs and salamanders which
share his abode.

> Novels are no use of all on days like these; they deal with
> people and their relationships, with themselves and others,
> fathers and mothers and daughters or sons, lovers, etc., with
> individual souls, usually unhappy ones, with society, etc., as
> if the place for these things were assured, the earth for all
> time earth, the sea level fixed for all time.[109]

But he is content in what he is doing as he waits for the inevitable
landslide that will destroy his Swiss haven.

THREE CONTEMPORARY LATIN AMERICAN
WRITERS

Contemporary Latin American literature is offering a rich and
unique vision of the world from a diversity of authors in a great
diversity of states. Though having differing political and economic

organizations, these Latin nations have a common heritage, share a culture derived from native Indian and European institutions and literature, and not insignificantly influenced both by the example and the intrusiveness of its mighty North American neighbor. Its most characteristic literary form is "magical realism" in which imagination dominates and dictates to realism.

Isabel Allende, a Chilean exile now living in the United States, has proven to be a most resilient writer. She has drawn on the dual traditions of both Native American and the Spanish conquistadors, and celebrates the worlds of spirit that both depict; and she also represents the changing needs of women in her time. Her epic, *The House of the Spirits* (1985), traces the history of Chile and the progression of her own family through the twentieth century, mainly through the heroic women of the Trueba family.

Likewise, in her memorable short stories, she impersonates a modern day Scheherezade, and shows her writing witchcraft; as Eva Luna in *The Stories of Eva Luna,* she weaves a magical tapestry on the power of love: "The Proper Respect" about a couple of political and financial scoundrels who are married and joined at the hip by their bond of greed and deceptiveness; "The Judge's Wife" about a tight-laced proper woman, captured by a bandit, who finds ways to placate him after he has determined to seek revenge for the judicial actions of her husband that brought about the death of his mother; or "The Little Heidelberg" about the aged El Capitán and niña Eloísa who have danced together for forty years and never spoken a word; until the moment that El Capitán breaks the silence and asks her to marry him, which brings about her sublimation into spirit.

KISS OF THE SPIDER WOMAN

Manuel Puig renders yet another perspective on the modern, Latin-American world in his fascinating novel, *Kiss of the Spider Woman* (1979), which captures the energy and uniqueness of the homosexual consciousness. Set in a prison in Buenos Aires, the novel explores the relationship between Valentin, a macho male who is a Marxist revolutionary, and his homosexual cellmate, Molina, who is non-political. Molina is a great storyteller, and he fills the time of their incarceration with a recall of the myriad of details of Hollywood films, to the entertainment and enlightenment of his ardent companion who comes to some greater understanding of tolerance and human attachments.

The difficulty of all erotic relationships is the theme of the novel. Discoursing on homosexuality, the author explores the etiology and questions the "theory of perversion, according to which the individual would tend to adopt homosexuality just as he would any of a number of vices. But its fundamental error lies in the fact that such a miscreant deliberately adopts the form of deviant behavior which most appeals to him, whereas the homosexual cannot develop a normal sexual pattern of conduct even if he sets out to do so, since whenever he might actually perform heterosexual acts he will find himself hard put to eliminate his more profound homosexual drives."[110]

The suspicion of all erotic relations is rendered in the image of the book's title, of the spider woman who devours her mate, and the drama of the recounted films invariably deal with betrayal, and reinforce the lesson of films and life that in spite of friendship and love, there is inevitable betrayal. But the saddest is the betrayal by a political system, a totalitarian society that imposes technological fear, torture, and murder upon its innocent citizens—until they are diminished and destroyed.

LOVE IN THE TIME OF CHOLERA

Gabriel García Márquez has established himself as a leading world writer with his Chagall like novels inhabited by whimsical and fantastical creatures. There is abundant celebration of Eros in his novels. The dovetailing of magical realism and the theme of love is a characteristic of his work in two masterpieces *One Hundred Years of Solitude* (1970), an historical epic about an imaginary Latin American country, named Macondo, its evolution and demise, and *Love in the Time of Cholera* (1988). The latter novel, set at the turn of the nineteenth century, is a popular romance raised to the level of high art, tracking the story of an adolescent love between Fermina Daza and Florentino Ariza, who met and fell in love as teenagers, when she accepted his proposal of marriage on condition that she not be forced "to eat eggplant." But she changed her mind, nonetheless, as young women will, and instead married Dr. Juvenal Urbino, had children and remained with him for more than half a century.

The novel opens with the tender line: "It was inevitable: the scent of bitter almonds always reminded him of the fate of unrequited love." For Dr. Urbino's death frees his wife, who has been compared to Emma Bovary in a somewhat lukewarm marriage to a doctor, to reestablish her primary relationship. For his part, Florentino has never forgotten this love and has devoted his life to the dream of being reunited with her. A poor man by birth, he has risen to the heights of success owning a steamship company; but he still quixotically cherishes his infatuation toward his teenage love, and pursues her as ardently now as he had earlier. Though she puts him off by saying "I smell like an old woman," she will give him now what she had denied him earlier—to his greater appreciation:

> "If we're going to do it, let do it," she said, "but let's do it like grownups" . . . They lay on their backs for a long time . . . They talked to pass the time. They spoke of themselves, of their divergent lives, of the incredible coincidence of their lying naked in a dark cabin on a stranded boat when reason told them they had time only for death. She had never heard of his having a woman, not even one, in that city where everything was known even before it happened. She spoke in a casual manner, and he replied without hesitation in a steady voice: "I've remained a virgin for you." [111]

Love among the ruins, the romance of a man who lies about his virginity to please his lady-love, who both believes and disbelieves him, the triumph of love and the erotic, in this novel written near the close of a century of disease and decadence, picks up where it left off after Fermina changes her mind once again. And this romantic couple of seventy something teenagers rekindles the flame, and sails the river Magdalena on a steamship called *New Fidelity* under the flag of Cholera—so as not to be disturbed—to make up for all the lost years—a beacon to the twenty first century of the young and the young-at-heart.

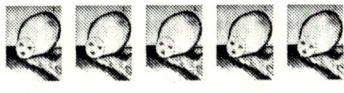

LOVE IN AMERICA

O my America! my new-found land,
My kingdome, safeliest when with one man man'd,
My Myne of precious stones, my Emperie,
How blest am I in this discovering thee!
To enter in these bonds, is to be free;
Then where my hand is set, my seal shall be.
John Donne

Amerika, du hast es besser
Als unser Kontinent, das alte,
Hast keine verfallene Schlösser
Und keine Basalte.
Dich stört nicht im Innern
Zu lebendiger Zeit
Unnützes Errinern
Und vergeblicher Streit.

Benutzt die Gegenwart mit Gluck!
Und wenn nun eure Kinder dichten,
Bewahre sie ein gut Geschick
Vor Ritter-Räuber-und Gespentergeschichten.
Johann Wolfgang von Goethe

(America, you have it better than our continent, the older.
You have no antiquated castles fallen into disrepute and
disrepair. You are not disturbed by unprofitable memories
and futile strife. Seize the present with joy, and when your
children relate their stories, create their myths, let them avoid

those of knights, robbers, and the ghosts of the past. *My translation.*)

I have nowhere seen women occupying a loftier position [than in America]; and if I were asked, to what the singular prosperity and growing strength of that people ought to be attributed, I should reply—to the superiority of their women.
Alexis de Tocqueville

The real American is not a gold chaser or money lover, as the legend classes him, but an idealist and a mystic.
Isadora Duncan

INDEPENDENCE • PURITANISM AND CHIVALRY • PIONEER WOMEN • ALEXIS DE TOCQUEVILLE • THE SCARLET LETTER • THE QUEST FOR SUCCESS • MOBY DICK • UNCLE TOM'S CABIN • WALT WHITMAN • HENRY JAMES • EMILY DICKINSON

EVOLUTION OF THE AMERICAN WOMAN • SUSAN B. ANTHONY • EMMA GOLDMAN • KATE CHOPIN • CHARLOTTE P. GILMAN • THE TWENTIETH CENTURY • DESIRE UNDER THE ELMS • BABBITT • ISADORA DUNCAN • H.L. MENCKEN • DOROTHY PARKER

PAX AMERICANA • TENNESSEE WILLIAMS • ARTHUR MILLER AND ALLEN GINSBERG • LOLITA AND THE SEXUAL REVOLUTION • PHILIP WYLIE • THE FEMININE MYSTIQUE • OH, DAD, POOR DAD • WHO'S AFRAID OF VIRGINIA WOOLF? • GORE VIDAL • THE STEPFORD WIVES • JOHN IRVING • WHAT EVERY WOMAN KNOWS • ERICA JONG • JOHN UPDIKE AND JOYCE CAROL OATES • BLACK WOMAN WRITERS

INDEPENDENCE

The United States of America established its preeminence as the world's leading industrial state and the brave new world of the imagination. Technology has made possible the achievement of the highest standard of living for a large percentage of the people—and the pleasures of this life have been sought at the expense of the spirit. This occurred in spite of the strong Christian influence that has been in evidence throughout our history—and saw the settlement of America as an "errand in the wilderness"—the extension of Christ's kingdom on earth.

The fight for independence was not so much an act of birth as an act of generational revolt against a tyrannous father. Thomas Paine used the metaphor of an Oedipal confrontation "not from the tender embraces of the mother, but from the cruelty of the monster."[112] The violence of this rebellion has infused our character and influenced our traditions of non-conformity, violence, freedom, and justice. The search for a father has been an important theme in our literature and has also been revealed in our constitutional history. Witness the limits placed on the power of the president, from the time of the founding right down to the present, and the subsequent development of final irrefutable authority in the Justices of the Supreme Court—as surrogate King and father. There also has been the seemingly ceaseless struggle between the legislative branch representing the people and the executive branch of government perpetuating ordained authority; and finally between the free press (including modern media) and our elected officials.

The United States forged its unique character out of the confrontation between reason and romanticism, between western civilization and the primitive Neolithic culture of the Indian. Was American Democracy the product of intellect, or the triumph of emotion? Was it the grafting of a great civilization on a woodland, or a pullulating new growth? Did it embody the rational idealism of Locke, Montesquieu, and Jefferson or the primitive idealism of Rousseau? As the colonies expanded in number and America realized her manifest destiny, she would establish her character and reveal her soul.

PURITANISM AND CHIVALRY

Henry Adams lamented the absence of the chivalric influence in our culture: "The Woman had once been supreme" in the old world. "Why was she unknown in America? For evidently America was ashamed of her, and she was ashamed of herself, otherwise they would not have strewn fig-leaves so profusely all over her . . . But any one brought up among the Puritans knew that sex was sin. In any previous age, sex was strength . . . Yet this energy was unknown to the American mind. An American Virgin would never dare to command; an American Venus would never dare exist."[113] The Puritan tradition in our early history did indeed require sublimation of man's passionate nature to the demands of nature and especially the Deity.

PIONEER WOMEN

The American woman was a native growth and, along with the potato and tomato, possibly the new world's greatest contribution to civilization. She came to possess a greater sense of self-worth—and enjoyed more rights than she enjoyed in the old world. Whereas Christian tradition had deprecated woman's worth, the spirit of equality elevated her social position. She came to represent "all the honest blood of womanhood, the strong New England blood of liberty."

The pioneer could not allow his woman to exist parasitically and be venerated. The woman colonist and frontierswoman worked long hours and as hard as her mate. She could not allow herself to become a lady. Moreover the chivalric adulation paid woman was related to the authoritarian-feudal structure, of which it was both an expression and a reflection. With its anti-authoritarian attitude, the American rejected all signs of rank and fawning submission.

James Fenimore Cooper was the first author to romanticize the period of settlement and the early frontier, and celebrate the character of the Indian in his *Leatherstocking Tales*. Natty Bumppo, strong, reserved and silent, possesses the characteristics that have marked heroism throughout our history and literature. The Indian lived in harmony with nature and with himself. He was individualistic, self-reliant, and his elemental virtues were an alternative and a contrast to the complexity and frequent deviousness of the white man's culture.

Natty Bumppo is ambivalent toward the white woman. She is an enigma whose presence can be both frightening and soothing. Deerslayer abruptly rejects Judith Hutter's proposal of marriage, while paddling with her in a canoe on Lake Otsego:

> "And do you so delight in violence and bloodshed? I had thought better of *you*, Deerslayer—believed you one who could find his happiness in a quiet domestic home, with an attached and loving wife, ready to study your wishes, and healthy and dutiful children, anxious to follow in your footsteps, and to become as honest and just as yourself."

> "Lord, Judith, what a tongue you're mistress of! Speech and looks go hand in hand; and what one can't do, the other is pretty sartain to perform! Such a gal, in a month, might spoil the stoutest warrior in the colony."

> And am I then so mistaken? Do you really love war, Deerslayer, better than the hearth and the affections?"

> "I understand your meaning, gal; yes, I do understand what you mean, I believe, though I don't think you altogether understand *me*. Warrior I may now call myself, I suppose,

for I've both fou't and conquered, which is sufficient for the
name; neither will I deny that I've feelin's for the callin',
which is both manful and honorable, when carried on
accordin' to nat'ral gifts—but I've no relish for blood.[114]

As Pathfinder, he proposes to Mabel Dunham—but decides that
there can be no union between their different cultures. He learns
to appreciate friendship with the white woman—as he does with
Elizabeth Temple.

The mystery of woman was also an enigma to the white man—
Cooper as well as other writers. She was a creature of radiance and
mystery who emigrated to these shores from the coasts of European romanticism, Goethe's Gretchen, Keats's *La Belle Dame Sans
Merci*. Edgar Allan Poe rendered her beauty and mystery in his
poems to *Lenore, Ulalume, Helen*; but most beautifully in his elegy
to *Annabel Lee*, the American Héloïse and Juliet:

> It was many and many a year ago,
>   In a kingdom by the sea,
> That a maiden there lived whom you may know
>   By the name of Annabel Lee;—
> And this maiden she lived with no other thought
>   Than to love and be loved by me.
>
> *She* was a child and *I* was a child,
>   In this kingdom by the sea,
> But we loved with a love that was more than love—
>   I and my Annabel Lee—
> With a love that the wingéd seraphs of Heaven
>   Coveted her and me.
>
> And this was the reason that, long ago,
>   In this kingdom by the sea,
> A wind blew out of a cloud, by night
>   Chilling my Annabel Lee;
> So that her highborn kinsman came
>   And bore her away from me,
> To shut her up in a sepulchre
>   In this kingdom by the sea.

The angels, not half so happy in Heaven,
    Went envying her and me:—
Yes! that was the reason (as all men know
    In this kingdom by the sea)
That the wind came out of the cloud, chilling
    And killing my Annabel Lee.

But our love it was stronger by far than the love
    Of those who were older than we—
    Of many far wiser than we—
And neither the angels in Heaven above
    Nor the demons down under the sea,
Can ever dissever my soul from the soul
    Of the beautiful Annabel Lee:—

For the moon never beams without bringing me dreams
    Of the beautiful Annabel Lee;
And the stars never rise but I see the bright eyes
    Of the beautiful Annabel Lee;
And so, all the night-tide, I lie down by the side
Of my darling, my darling, my life and my bride,
    In her sepulchre there by the sea—
    In her tomb by the side of the sea.

Mark Twain, on the other hand, took the woman of mysterious presence and portrayed her in drab comic tones as Miss Watson. She seeks to inculcate Huckleberry Finn with piety, reverence, and civilization. Huck, however, remains oblivious to her teachings, to the reasonableness of high culture, and prefers the simplicity of freedom.

ALEXIS DE TOCQUEVILLE

The French libertarian and social critic Alexis de Tocqueville visited the United States in the 1830's and wrote his reflections on the American character in *Democracy in America*. He particularly was impressed with the idealism he found: "Among the novel objects that attracted my attention during my stay in the United

States, nothing struck me more forcibly than the general equality of conditions."

He wrote about our political and social institutions and commented on the relationship between the sexes. He praised the romantic basis for marriage as preferable to *mariage de convenance* still practiced on the continent. "When a man always chooses a wife for himself, without any external coercion or even guidance, it is generally a conformity of tastes and opinions which bring a man and a woman together, and this same conformity keeps and fixes them in close habits of intimacy."[115]

He noted that Americans who, for practical reasons, kept their focus on commercial activities and success, were not moved to amorous quest so much as their Europeans cousins:

> The tumultuous and constantly harassed life which equality makes men lead, not only distracts them from the passion of love, by denying them time to indulge in it, but it diverts them from it by another more secret but more certain road. All men who live in democratic ages more or less contact the ways of thinking of the manufacturing and trading classes; their minds take a serious, deliberate, and positive turn; they are apt to relinquish the ideal, in order to pursue some visible and proximate object, which appears to be the natural and necessary aim of their desires.

He spoke at length about the materialistic emphasis in American civilization: "I know of no country, indeed, where the love of money has taken stronger hold upon the affections of men." He also acknowledged the strong spiritual tradition which existed since the time of the early settlers; "the energy with which they strove for the acquirement of wealth, moral enjoyment, and the comforts as well as liberties of the world, is scarcely inferior to that with which they devoted themselves to Heaven."

But American women aroused his greatest interest and praise:

An American woman is always mistress of herself: she indulges in all permitted pleasures, without yielding herself
up to any of them; and her reason never allows the reins of
self-guidance to drop, though it often seems to hold them
loosely. The Americans, believing that they had little chance
of repressing in woman the most vehement passions of the
human heart, held that the surer way was to teach her the
art of combating those passions for herself. As they could
not prevent her virtue from being exposed to frequent danger, they determined that she should know how best to
defend it; and more reliance was placed on the free vigor of
her will than on safeguards which have been shaken or
overthrown. Instead, then, of inculcating mistrust of herself, she constantly seeks to enhance her confidence in her
own strength of character. As it is neither possible nor desirable to keep a young woman in perpetual or complete ignorance, they hasten to give her a precocious knowledge on all
subjects. Far from hiding the corruptions of the world from
her, they prefer that she should see them at once and train
herself to shun them; and they hold it of more importance
to protect her conduct than to be overscrupulous of her
innocence.

He contrasted the European and American attitude toward women,
and the seeming lack of confidence that European women have in
comparison to their American counterparts:

It has often been remarked that in Europe a certain degree
of contempt lurks even in the flattery which men lavish
upon women: although a European frequently affects to be
the slave of woman, it may be seen that he never sincerely
thinks her his equal. In the United States men seldom compliment women, but they daily show how much they esteem them. They constantly display an entire confidence in
the understanding of a wife, and a profound respect for her
freedom; they have decided that her mind is just as fitted as
that of a man to discover the plain truth, and her heart as
firm to embrace it; and they have never sought to place her
virtue, any more than his, under the shelter of prejudice,
ignorance, and fear. It would seem that in Europe, where

man so easily submits to the despotic sway of women, they
are nevertheless curtailed of some of the greatest qualities of
the human species, and considered as seductive but imperfect beings; and (what may well provoke astonishment)
women ultimately look upon themselves in the same light,
and almost consider it as a privilege that they are entitled to
show themselves futile, feeble, and timid. The women of
America claim no such privileges.

American men, however, were gallant in their own way:

It is true that the Americans rarely lavish upon women those
eager attentions which are commonly paid them in Europe;
but their conduct to women always implies that they suppose them to be virtuous and refined; and such is the respect entertained for the moral freedom of the sex, that in
the presence of a woman the most guarded language is used,
lest her ear should be offended by an expression.

While the American perhaps lacked the *sang-froid* or coolness of
mind of the European, he respected the honor of his women: "As
the Americans can conceive nothing more precious than a woman's
honor, and nothing which ought so much to be respected as her
independence, they hold that no punishment is too severe for the
man who deprives her of them against her will." The marriage
bond also was held in high respect. "In America all those vices
which tend to impair the purity of morals, and to destroy the
conjugal tie, are treated with a degree of severity which is unknown in the rest of the world."

The early Puritans repressed man's libidinal nature as a temptation to be avoided for the sake of correct moral development. In
the nineteenth century, the demands of economic and industrial
development also influenced repression of man's libidinal nature.
The pursuit of love like the pursuit of perfection requires time
and, sometimes,—extraordinary patience, which the American citi-
zen could not afford because, as Tocqueville suggested, he was too
busy making money.

THE SCARLET LETTER

America did not share European romanticism toward love. Neither the excesses of *Les Liaisons Dangereuses* nor the exploits of
Casanova found a place in our literature, and while Goethe's Werther
and Byron's Don Juan pined for love, serious American literature
did not truly probe the relationship between the sexes. The two
most beautiful novels of the nineteenth century, perhaps *Madame
Bovary* and *Anna Karenina*, studied the great power of woman's
passion and desire, while our notable literature, maintaining a reputation of innocence, hardly treated love in the same way. *The Scarlet Letter* was instead a moral tale of crime and punishment.

Hawthorne's romance illuminated the conflict between the
individual's libidinous nature and society's repression. Though
Hawthorne wrote with compassion for the sinner, he did not challenge society's right to exact retribution from the adulteress; and
he perhaps exposed the hypocrisy of Puritan values. But Hester
Prynne accepts the consequences of her sin of adulterous love after
being abandoned and left alone by her husband Roger
Chillingworth, where a modern heroine would have protested her
right to realize her natural feelings after such mistreatment. The
achievement of the book is Hawthorne's revelation of the truths of
human psychology within the mythology of Puritan diabolism.
For Hawthorne, all men are sinners, or victims of the devil. Rever-
end Dimmesdale—the most saintly member of the community—
bears the mark of sinner upon his breast, the mirror of Hester's
own scarlet "A", as he confesses to his complicity in Hester's crime:

> "People of New England!" cried he, with a voice that rose
> over them, high, solemn, and majestic,—yet had always a
> tremor through it, and sometimes a shriek, struggling up
> out of the fathomless depth of remorse and woe,—"ye, that
> have loved me!—ye that have deemed me holy!—behold
> me here, the one sinner of the world! At last!—at last!—I

stand upon the spot where, seven years since, I should have stood; here, with this woman, whose arm, more than the little strength wherewith I have crept hitherward, sustains me, at this dreadful moment, from groveling down upon my face! Lo, the scarlet letter which Hester wears! Ye have all shuddered at it! Wherever her walk hath been,—wherever, so miserably burdened, she may have hoped to find repose,—it hath cast a lurid gleam of awe and horrible repugnance round-about her. But there stood one in the midst of you, at whose brand of sin and infamy ye have not shuddered!"[116]

Hawthorne is not ready to absolve men of sin. "Let God punish." cries Hester. Man must forgive. It would be some years before anyone would say that all men are sons and lovers.

The story of Hester Prynne is also of an individual alienated from a hostile society—and her effort to exist by her own law apart from others who have rejected her. St. Augustine had observed: "In the sojourning of this carnal life each man carries his own heart and every heart is closed to every heart." More so in a civilization wedded to materialism—the isolation of the individual was pronounced.

THE QUEST FOR SUCCESS

Life in America was not only a test of virtue but also a test of success. To be successful from the Calvinist perspective meant that the individual was graced by God. At the same time success was identified with material prosperity. Too often Darwin's idea of "natural selection" described the American character more accurately than Blake's vision of America (Orc) a colossus liberated in body and spirit. The carving out of the country and the fierce competition for riches and wealth brought out the best and worst of the settlers. It rewarded hard work and ambition, but also covetousness, greed, and sometimes subversion and crime. But at the same time it offered opportunity for the poor and the immigrant to

achieve a standing not available in an established nation. The na-
tive-American and the Black man were not included. Moreover, it
also encouraged a weakening of social and familial ties—as each
man strove to gain more than his neighbor and each son sought to
outdo his father. One observer noted: "A man is accounted a failure and certainly ought to be, who has not risen above his father's
station in life."

It was the test that influenced the Fultons and the Edisons,
the Girards and the Vanderbilts, the Carnegies, the Rockefellers,
and the Fords—the inventors and the industrialists. They were
driven by idealism—though it may have been mistaken or misguided. America did harness the energy of steam, electricity, and
finally atomic and nuclear power. For the individual, it was an
assertion of manhood. For society, it meant rapid industrialization.

It was no accident that technological society was the midwife
to a democratic one. Democracy recognized the rights of its citizens to equal opportunity and the claim of all to share the benefits
of "life, liberty, and the pursuit of happiness." The passion of
America was sublimated to the dynamo. Love was domination
achieved with the aid of the machine—and used to control (feminine) nature.

MOBY DICK

This was understood by Melville in the most profound work of
the nineteenth century, *Moby Dick*, and as with Hawthorne and
later Whitman, he explored the contradictions of America. "To
produce a mighty book, you must choose a mighty theme. No
great and enduring volume can ever be written on the flea, though
there be many who have tried it."

Captain Ahab, was possessed by his desire for revenge on nature (the whale) that deprived him of his limb (and now he symbolically and actually wore a leg carved from sinew of a whale);

Ahab also has been characterized as the embodiment of the will to power that Melville discerned in nineteenth-century American capitalism, pursuing the quixotic, monomaniacal purpose of subduing the white whale to his domination: "There's something ever egotistical in mountain-tops, and towers, and all other grand and lofty things; look here—three peaks as proud as Lucifer. The firm tower—that is Ahab; the volcano, that is Ahab; the courageous, the undaunted, the victorious fowl, that, too, is Ahab; all are Ahab; and this round gold is but the image of the rounder globe which, like a magician's glass, to each and every man in turn but mirrors back his own mysterious self."

And so it was with America. America's ascendancy over nature required that it sacrifice its humanity to this purpose. The story is told by the lone survivor of the Pequod, Ishmael, the ancient mariner with a moral story to tell. The great novel is a natural history of the whale—perhaps not completely dissimilar to that study which Darwin was undertaking in the same period; and there are tantalizing juxtapositions between the two men, so that the humanist's view of natural selection was indeed similar to that of the scientist. This was the allegory of America's phenomenal growth in the nineteenth century in Melville's characterization of the behavior of fast and loose fish. "A Fast Fish belongs to the party fast to it," and "a Loose-Fish is fair game for anybody who soonest catches it."

> These two laws touching Fast-Fish and Loose-Fish, I say, will on reflection be found the fundamentals of jurisprudence . . . What are the sinews and souls of Russian serfs and Republican slaves but Fast-Fish, whereof possession is the whole of the law? What to the rapacious landlord is the widow's last mite but a Fast-Fish? . . . What was America in 1492 but a Loose-Fish, in which Columbus struck the Spanish standard by way of waifing it for his royal master and mistress? . . . What are the Rights of Man and the Liberties of the World but Loose-Fish? What all men's minds and opinions but Loose Fish? What is the principle of religious belief in them but a Loose-Fish? What to the ostentatious smuggling verbalists are the thoughts of thinkers but

Loose-Fish? What is the great globe itself but a Loose-Fish?
And what are you, reader, but a Loose-Fish and a Fast-Fish,
too? [117]

Thus America's sublimated passion was not directed solely to otherworldly piety, but to material conquest.

UNCLE TOM'S CABIN

The primacy of the spirit was the argument with which the country was created. Washington, Jefferson, Jackson, and Lincoln reflected, in their somewhat diverse ways, their belief in the promise of America. Their attitude was shared by writers, like Emerson, Hawthorne, Thoreau, and Melville who, however, often were alienated from their contemporaries. Too often the individual could exercise his freedom and rights only in isolation. Thoreau went to jail to protest slavery and defended the right of civil disobedience against an unjust and unresponsive government. But it was Harriet Beecher Stowe's *Uncle Tom's Cabin* which exposed the American dilemma—the contradiction between the hope and the reality.

"The little woman who wrote the book that made this great war"—as Lincoln called her, was a passionate moralist as well as an ardent feminist, and her novel can be read not only as an indictment of slavery but a shrewd attack on male institutions and patriarchal order. There is perhaps more satire here than has been perceived. For she exposes the myth of male justice and objectivity by showing a society that utilizes the law to protect the wealth and venality of men. It is solemn male prerogative that sanctions the institution of slavery, that allows a child to be taken from its mother, and that hunts fleeing mother and child under the shield of law, a persecution of the weak and defenseless continuing (unfortunately!) to our own time.

The men in the novel range from the weak and foolish to the greedy and degenerate. Only Uncle Tom is above reproach. Weak men like Shelby lose their rights through gullibility, while evil men like Legree are driven by greed for wealth and power. Legree's proud boast of his virility is masculine bravado:

> "Look at these yer bones! Well, I tell ye this yer fist has got as hard as iron *knocking down niggers*. I never see the nigger yet I couldn't bring down with one crack," said he, bringing his fist down so near to the face of Tom that he winked and drew back.

Even Tom's friend, Miss Cissy, the daughter of a wealthy white man mated to a slave, has no rights. Although she can fascinate, manipulate, and terrify her evil master, she remains a victim:

> He was her owner, her tyrant, and tormentor. She was, as he knew, wholly, and without any possibility of help or redress, in his hands."[118]

His assertion of command and assault on Tom's goodness—in the scene where he orders Tom to beat the helpless slave so as to be part of the system of cruelty and exploitation—is the ultimate degradation committed by a male against his fellow. The novel raises the feminist complaint: Are men really in possession of that sense of fairness and objectivity that they have claimed for themselves throughout history? She throws down the gauntlet to the Freudian view that men show a greater "sense of justice, amply accounted for in the modification of the formation of their super-ego."

WALT WHITMAN

Walt Whitman, like Europe's William Blake, asserted the need for the marriage between the soul and the body, between heaven and hell. His poetry was an affirmation and vindication of the Christian paradox that held that the body and spirit were one, as he invokes in the Preface to *Leaves of Grass*:

Come, said my Soul,
Such verses for my Body let us write,
       (for we are one,)
That should I after death invisibly return,
Or, long, long hence, in other spheres,
There to some group of mates
       the chants resuming,
(Tallying Earth's soil, trees, winds,
       tumultuous waves,)
Ever with pleas'd smile I may keep on,
Ever and ever yet the verses owning—
       as, first, I here and now,
Signing for Soul and Body,
       set to them my name,
Walt Whitman

He maintained the most glorious idealist strain of any American writer in his paean to Democracy in "Song of Myself":

Walt Whitman, a kosmos, of Manhattan the son,
Turbulent, fleshy, sensual, eating, drinking and breeding,
No sentimentalist, no stander above men and women or
       apart from them,
No more modest than immodest.
Unscrew the locks from the doors!
Unscrew the doors themselves from their jambs!
Whoever degrades another degrades me,
And whatever is done or said returns at last to me.
Through me the afflatus surging and surging, through me
       the current and index.
I speak the pass-word primeval, I give the sign of democracy,
By God! I will accept nothing which all cannot have their
       counterparts of on the same terms.[119]

In celebrating the dignity of the common man and the beauty of the unrepressed self, Whitman transcended the mores of the nineteenth century and defined the milieu of modern liberation move-

ments. His beard and shaggy appearance was the garb of the out-
sider and opponent of the materialistic order and were adopted as
the emblem of the Beats, the Hippies, and the modern homeless;
and his poetic innovation, free verse, has become the dominant
mode of the free-spirited.

HENRY JAMES

Some Americans longed for a patrician society modeled on the
nobility of Europe. Americans who came into wealth frequently
aped the style and manners of the European upper class; others
valued the traditions and the order of a more stable society. In
contrast to the egalitarian idealism of Whitman, Henry James observed: "the pursuit of a social career is as reasonable an aim in life
as any other." Elsewhere one of his characters reflects on the barrenness of life in America: "The soil of American perception is a
poor little barren, artificial deposit. Yes! We are wedded to imper-
fection. An American, to excel, has just ten times as much to learn
as a European. We lack the deeper sense. We have neither taste,
nor tact, nor force. How should we have them? Our crude and
garish climate, our silent past, our deafening present, the constant
pressure about us of unlovely circumstance, are as void of all that
nourishes and prompts and inspires the artist, as my sad heart is
void of bitterness in saying so! We poor aspirants must live in perpetual exile."[120]

The American visitor to Europe—both transient and permanent—made the pilgrimage to find the high civilization and culture that were missing at home. The young traveled to complete
his education; the middle-aged to pay homage to antiquity; the
artist sought more fertile roots for his and her own growth and
development than were available at home. When the traveler was
Mark Twain, he found the stuffiness, the lack of equality, and the
artificial code of behavior a sore disappointment. Oscar Wilde allowed his characters to quip:

Mrs. Allonby: When good Americans die they go to Paris.

Lady Hunstanton: Indeed? And when bad Americans die, where do they go?

Lord Illingworth: Oh, they go to America.[121]

At the same time, Wilde also reflected on American innocence: "The youth of America is its oldest tradition. It has been going on for three hundred years."

Henry James's *The Portrait of a Lady* tells the story of an American who came to Europe to absorb continental riches. Isabel Archer brings her innocence, as well as natural ease and common sense to Europe and is well received. American women are better educated and prove to be less docile than their counterparts in Europe. Where the European woman is submissive, the American woman offers more of an intellectual challenge. Isabel is the kind of "interesting" woman that the very attractive bachelor and nobleman, Lord Warburton, has longed to find. He falls in love with her, and proposes to her on their second meeting, in the presence of his dog, offering her a title, an estate, and a moat. But Isabel prefers freedom to being married to an English Lord, and she rejects his suit.

> "Ah, Lord Warburton, how little you know me! Isabel said very gently. Gently too she drew her hand away.
>
> "Don't taunt me with that; that I don't know you better makes me unhappy enough already; it's all my loss. But that's what I want, and it seems to me I'm taking the best way. If you'll be my wife, then I shall know you, and when I tell you all the good I think of you you'll not be able to say it's from ignorance."
>
> "If you know me little I know you even less," said Isabel.
>
> "You mean that, unlike yourself, I may not improve on

acquaintance? Ah, of course that's very possible. But think, to speak to you as I do, how determined I must be to try and give satisfaction! You do like me rather, don't you?"

In his unhappiness over being rejected, he pursues the *tête-à-tête* until he sinks exasperated before her mind and ready wit.

"Do you know I'm very much afraid of it—of that remarkable mind of yours?"

Our heroine's biographer can scarcely tell why, but the question made her start and brought a conscious blush to her cheek. She returned his look a moment, and then with a note in her voice that might almost have appealed to his compassion, "So am I, my lord!" she oddly exclaimed.

His compassion was not stirred, however; all he possessed of the faculty of pity was needed at home. "Ah! be merciful, be merciful," he murmured.

"I think you had better go," said Isabel. "I'll write to you."

"Very good; but whatever you write I'll come and see you, you know." And then he stood reflecting, his eyes fixed on the observant countenance of Bunchie, who had the air of having understood all that had been said and of pretending to carry off the indiscretion by a simulated fit of curiosity as to the roots of an ancient oak. "There's one thing more," he went on. "You know, if you don't like Lockleigh—if you think it's damp or anything of that sort—you need never go within fifty miles of it. It's not damp, by the way; I've had the house thoroughly examined; it's perfectly safe and right. But if you shouldn't fancy it you needn't dream of living in it. There's no difficulty whatever about that; there are plenty of houses. I thought I'd just mention it; some people don't like a moat, you know. Good-bye."

"I adore a moat," said Isabel. "Good-bye." [122]

Ibsen's new woman had descended upon the continent from the new world. To be sure, Isabel did not serve herself well through her freedom—she made a bad marriage to an expatriate American artist Gilbert Osmond, who used her vilely—but she could not lay the blame on anyone but herself. If the new woman was true to herself by turning down proposals of marriage from English lords (and American millionaires), then perhaps only charlatans and failures would suit her.

EMILY DICKINSON

The great and serious lady Emily Dickinson lived as a recluse in Amherst, Massachusetts writing poetry that would be a profound revelation when published after her death. It is supposed that she was the victim of an unhappy love affair with a married clergyman. However, she did not describe love as Sappho did; rather she reflected her feelings as a woman through the wit and passion of her poetry—perspicuous and rational on the surface and rich with emotional longing in its heart. In one poem she imagines Death as a suitor who comes to take her for an afternoon carriage-ride to eternity:

> Because I could not stop for Death-
> He kindly stopped for me;
> The carriage held but just ourselves-
> And Immortality.
>
> We slowly drove, he knew no haste,
> And I had put away
> My labor, and my leisure too,
> For his civility.
>
> We passed the school where children strove
> At wrestling in a ring;
> We passed the fields of gazing grain,
> We passed the setting sun.

We paused before a house that seemed
A swelling of the ground;
The roof was scarcely visible,
The cornice but a mound.

Since then 'tis centuries; and yet
Feels shorter than the day
I first surmised the horses' heads
Were toward Eternity.

Or she depicts disappointment (in love!) as the breaking of a piece of ware (which she should not have valued in the first place).

It dropped so low-in my regard-
I heard it hit the ground;
And go to pieces on the stones
At bottom of my mind.
Yet blamed the fate that fractured-less
Than I reviled myself,
For entertaining plated wares
Upon my silver shelf.

Or she projects her wish for the pleasure of being a wife as preferable to being a girl.

I'm "wife"; I've finished that,
That other state;
I'm Czar; I'm "Woman" now;
It's safer so.

How odd the girl's life looks
Behind this soft eclipse!
I think that earth seems so
To folks in heaven now.

This being comfort, then
That other kind was pain;
But why compare?
I'm "wife"! Stop there![123]

EVOLUTION OF THE AMERICAN WOMAN

Other women were not content to celebrate their pain in solitary poetry, but sought to go out into the world and change people's thinking. Our Puritan ancestors had emphasized the ideal of the "virtuous woman" whose "price is far above rubies"—but the early demands of the pioneer life brought women to work alongside men. So that by the mid-nineteenth century, the women's movement in America was far advanced beyond what it was in Europe.

With the increase in industrialization, women took a more active role in the labor force. They had the "right" to work long before they could vote. And they were very much involved in the early stages of the labor movement. In the first half of the nineteenth century, women had already organized themselves as umbrella makers, seamstresses, bookbinders, tailoresses. There was a strong evangelical movement that was undertaken on behalf of women by women. But then, as Christine Stansell has written, the movement "was too absorbed in middle-class women's dilemmas in marriage, work, and property relations to learn much from working-class women." [124] Though they constituted an absolute minority (16% or two million workers in the 1870s), they tended to work long hours (16 to 18 hours a day, 80 hours a week). Marriage still represented the preferred choice for those who could choose.

The education of women along with men was one of the social reforms achieved in the American system; and the concept of a higher education for women was given impetus with the development of the land grant and state universities in the later part of the nineteenth century, and the evolution of private women's colleges

and coeducational universities. The usual profession for women
was teaching.

SUSAN B. ANTHONY

Susan B. Anthony (1820-1906) was an activist, humanitarian,
and advocate of women's rights who devoted her life to the cause of
equality. A descendant of Quakers, she brought a religious zeal
along with the egalitarian tradition of the plain people. Born on a
farm in Adams, Massachusetts, she watched her father run a fac-
tory for the manufacture of cotton with the newly invented cotton
gin, and she undertook her own role as a teacher, and later as a
social reformer. She marshaled the energy of women to serve the
cause of women's rights—despite typical opposition from men and
indifference from women.

Susan B. Anthony grew up as a witness to the industrialization in the United States when the majority of the population was
still farm dwellers; and she grew along with her country to confront the dominant challenges of her time. The rumor surround-
ing her was that even as a young girl she was a tomboy who defeated the class bully. She never backed off from a fight, and never
compromised her principles on what should be done.

The evolution of women's rights in this country did not follow
the same ideological pattern that was the case in England and
Europe—since women did not have to renounce a tradition of
chivalry in existence for half a millennium. The program of the
women's movement grew in relation to the evolving needs of the
country, and Susan B. Anthony was in complete step with this
approach.

The most important criticism that has been leveled against
her was that she did not address herself sufficiently to the needs of
working women. Indeed her vision was broader. The rights of la-
boring women became the concern of the unions and labor movement in this country; whereas she clearly took a more philosophi-

cal or a more political approach to the fight for women's rights. The advocacy of women in political affairs in America was bound up with the temperance movement, and when the Sons of Temperance refused to allow women into their organization, the Daughters of Temperance were formed. The next issue that would occupy the movement was slavery; and women (particularly Quakers) played a dominant role in the abolition movement. Anthony also published and edited a newspaper and traveled throughout the country to arouse women to involvement in political affairs.

But the greatest and the longest battle of her life was the suffragist movement—the struggle to gain the realization of the equality of women to participate in the electoral process. As late as 1870, she was handcuffed and arrested in Rochester, New York, when she registered to vote, and refused to pay the fine that would prevent her imprisonment. She also undertook battles to gain property rights for women; she argued for legal protection of women, their right to inherit property, own property, as when, for example, their husbands were incompetent.

EMMA GOLDMAN

The most radical feminist of the later nineteenth century and the first part of the twentieth century was Emma Goldman. She was born in Lithuania in 1869 of Jewish heritage, and grew up in the hotbed of Marxist teaching, revolutionary action, and philosophical anarchism. She came to America at a time when the labor movement was in the throes of conflict with the owners. She espoused the cause of anarchism, adopted a lifestyle that included living with her lovers without the sanction of marriage. When her lover was implicated in an attempted political assassination, she became a prostitute. Later, she also was arrested for her anarchism and served time in prison. She left this country and lived abroad for a year and even attended lectures of Dr. Sigmund Freud in Vienna. She returned to this country and continued her activist program, giving lectures and promoting Marxism and anarchism—until she was finally exiled from the United States. Her view was that the resolution of the injustice toward women could only be achieved in the context of a complete social revolution and included the struggle for the rights of working men. She threw herself whole-heartedly into her activities as when she incited the unemployed workers to rise up at the time of the depression of 1893:

> Demonstrate before the palaces of the rich; demand work. If they do not give you work, demand bread. If they deny you both, take bread. It is your sacred right![125]

There were also utopian experiments in which women participated with men in the founding of idealistic communities; one was the Shaker community where the monastic code was maintained and celibacy was enforced. Then there was the polygamous society of the Mormon Church; on the other hand, at Brook Farm and New Harmony, the principle of friendship between the sexes was observed (as in *Thélème*) though marriage, and even divorce were permitted. Other communities experimented with socialism, free love and uninhibited sex. The same intellectual curiosity that saw the establishment of nudist colonies influenced the community at Brockton where it was bruited that wild sex orgies were practiced. But finally in our history it was the individual woman, like the individual man, who made her mark on society.

KATE CHOPIN

Kate Chopin, a Southern writer of both French Huguenot and Creole heritage, reflected on the discontent of the American woman in the later nineteenth century. Mrs. Edna Pontellier in *The Awakening* is well married, wealthy, the mother of two children, artistic, yet she feels cheated by marriage. "Her marriage to Leonce Pontellier was purely an accident, in this respect resembling many other marriages which masquerade as the decrees of Fate."[126] An affair proves unsatisfying—which was shocking enough for the time. She wants to be free in the manner of Nora Torvald. Awakening to the cause of women's rights, she walks out on her husband. The St. Louis *Republic* felt that the book was "too strong drink for moral babes, and should be labeled 'poison'."

CHARLOTTE P. GILMAN

Charlotte Perkins Gilman was a deep thinker about the cause of women and a powerful advocate in writing of the issues of the woman's movement, which she explored in *Women and Economics* (1898). The marriage question still occupied a central point, and she questioned whether a girl's "natural instinct" and the "social environment" made the quest for a husband a matter of popular approval:

> Not at all! Marriage is the woman's proper sphere, her divinely ordained place, her natural end. It is what she is born for, what she is trained for, what she is exhibited for. It is, moreover, her means of honorable livelihood and advancement. *But*—she must not even look as if she wanted it! She must not turn her hand over to get it. She must sit passive as the seasons go by, and her "chances" lessen with each year. Think of the strain on a highly sensitive nervous organism to have so much hang on one thing, to see the possibility of attaining it grow less and less yearly, and to be forbidden to take any step toward securing it! This she must bear with dignity and grace to the end.[127]

She was a follower of Darwin in accepting the view of evolution and of Marx in accentuating the historical necessity of social change. Just as Harriet Beecher Stowe's passionate novel of social reform had spread its message throughout the world, so this grand niece of Mrs. Stowe argued that the times were ripe for women's action on behalf of themselves.

The women's movement rests not alone on her larger personality, with its tingling sense of revolt against injustice, but on the wide, deep sympathy of women for one another. It is a concerted movement, based on the recognition of a common evil and seeking a common good. So with the labor movement. It is not alone that the individual laborer is a better educated, more highly developed man than the stolid peasant of earlier days, but also that with this keener personal consciousness has come the wider social consciousness, without which no class can better its conditions.

She also wrote a utopian novel, entitled *Herland* (1915), in which she depicted an idealistic community of women in which equality has been attained by means of the extinction of the male species. Only female children are created through parthenogenetic birth, and there is no marriage, no family, and no passion. The women perform all the labor in a country that has been prospering for two thousand years. Three male stragglers land on this tropical fantasy land and they exchange stories about their respective culture. One of the hostesses asks, in a longing tone: "Do *no* women work, really?"[128]

Her marvelous short story, "The Yellow Wallpaper," describes the plight of a woman who is incarcerated in a nursery room with yellow wallpaper because of her depression, and told by her husband, who is her doctor, that she should do nothing. And so she contemplates the faded yellow-smelling wallpaper. "Dear John! He loves me dearly and hates to have me sick," she tells herself.[129] In studying the patterns and shapes on the wallpaper, she begins to see women behind bars struggling to escape. Then there is a single woman, caught in the pattern, whom she tries to rescue. She finally tears the paper off the wall, and the women behind the bars escape and crawl with her around the floor like insects on the loose. It is a witty and even humorous story, a pearl, illustrating again the lesson of comedy that derives, from personal anguish. For behind the tricks that her mind plays with the yellow wallpaper, there is the deeper meaning.

THE TWENTIETH CENTURY

Twentieth century life and literature continued to reflect the conflict between American materialism and spiritual longing. Woodrow
Wilson declared: "Sometimes people call me an idealist. That's the
way I know I'm an American. America, my fellow citizens, is the
only idealistic nation in the world." The contradiction of the American character remained. Henry Ford, who developed the "horseless
carriage" and built an industrial empire that was geared to the
profit motive, expressed a deep idealistic bent. "All that is the matter
with the world is injustice. Establish justice and everything will
be all right." He argued that "the automobile is the product of
peace."

> The development of the automobile is the greatest single
> instrument for world peace that I know of. The United
> States is made up of many nations. These people live in
> peace and understanding because there is an easy inter-
> change of ideals and ideas. There are no "remote" places in
> this country . . . No man is going to fight with a neighbor
> he knows, and likes because some temporary boss drops in
> and orders him to start a free-for-all. This is the biggest thing
> the automobile will accomplish—the elimination of war.[130]

DESIRE UNDER THE ELMS

In his tragic masterpiece, *Desire Under the Elms*, Eugene O'Neill
treated the conflict between love and the mercantile interest. Set
in New England in the nineteenth century, the play deals with
the fortunes of the Cabot family who allow greed to dominate
their thoughts and actions. Ephraim accuses his three sons by two
previous marriages of coveting his farm without knowing how to
work for it. Yet he comes home with his new possession, a wife; for
he also identifies love with ownership. Abbie's attitude does not
differ from that of her husband or stepsons. For her, love means

possessing a home, and she makes no effort to conceal her desire for land and security the first time she sees the farm:

> Abbie. (*with lust for the word*) Hum! It's purty-purty! I can't b'lieve it's r'ally mine.

> Cabot. (*sharply*) Yewr'n? Mine! (*He stares at her penetratingly. She stares back. He adds relentingly.*) Our'n mebbe! It was lonesome too long. I was growin' old in the spring. A hum's got t' hev a woman.

> Abbie. (*her voice taking possession*) A woman's got t'hev a hum.[131]

Soon a dispute arises, as Ephraim's youngest son, Eben, claims his right of inheritance to the farm that his mother brought as her dowry. Abbie discovers that her security is not so certain as she expected, as Eben accuses her of preempting his claim: "yew sold yourself fur [the farm] like any other old whore—my farm!" Moreover she further learns that her husband will not relinquish his claim to the farm even after his death—unless she provides him with an heir. She tells him: "Ye'll have a son out o' me, I promise ye."

She now turns to the son for the same reason that she married his father: to insure her possession. The play is an analogue to the *Hippolytus-Phèdre* myth where the mother falls in love with her stepson—except that Abbie shows a fiercer determination. She cajoles Eben in his mother's parlor:

> (*both her arms around him—with wild passion*) I'll sing fur ye! I'll die fur ye! (*In spite of her overwhelming desire for him, there is a sincere maternal love in her manner and voice—a horribly frank mixture of lust and mother love*) Don't cry, Eben! I'll take yer Maw's place! I'll be everythin' she was t' ye! Let me kiss ye, Eben! (*She pulls his head around. He makes a bewildered pretense of resistance. She is tender*) Don't be afeered! I'll kiss ye pure, Eben—same 's if I was a Maw t' ye—an' ye kin kiss me back 's if yew was my son—my boy—sayin'

good-night t' me! Kiss me, Eben. (*They kiss in restrained fashion. Then suddenly wild passion overcomes her. She kisses him lustfully again and again and he flings his arms about her and returns her kisses.*

With justification audience and civic leaders were outraged by this crude depiction of incest. For O'Neill, however, the incest was symbolic. While Eben's brothers Simeon and Peter go off to rape the earth, "fur the gold fields o' Californi-a," Abbie secures her fortune by taking her stepson; both are the results of Cabot greed. But the play offers a clear moral vision—first the evil of the worship of money and also the hardness of heart that afflicts those who pursue the lust of acquisition.

The attainment of true love is an effect that Abbie had not expected. She discovers that "nature'll beat ye," and love is its own reward. Through her love for Eben she finds that love is not ownership or a means to possession—but fulfillment in itself. When she does have a son, her happiness is abrogated by Eben's bitterness. She firmly declares her preference:

> If that's what his comin's done t'me—killin' yewr love—
> takin' yew away—my on'y joy—the on'y joy I ever
> knowed—like heaven t' me—purtier'n heaven—then I hate
> him, too, even if I be his Maw!

Infanticide is the one action that will demonstrate her love. It is an act of selflessness—even an expiation. For by sacrificing her child—her claim to the farm—she breaks with the Cabot way of life. She sublimates her love. To be sure, O'Neill used an outrageous metaphor to make his point. But since, for him, the greed of the Cabots is baser than incest and even child murder, it can be overcome by an act of greatest abnegation. We are made to understand Abbie's action and sympathize with her tragic downfall.

BABBITT

Sinclair Lewis's classic study of the American businessman, *Babbitt*, also depicted a man motivated by the acquisitive urge. Set in the twenties, George F. Babbitt savors his success as a businessman and the outward show of luxury and status that it affords him. He enjoys giving orders, defeating his competitors, driving his car, and playing golf, and particularly cherishes the latest conveniences of technology, a vacuum cleaner, electric cigar lighter, percolator, and toaster. A sincere businessman, he is adept at making a living rather than the art of living. His courtship and love were passionless:

> Myra was distinctly a Nice Girl—one didn't kiss her, one didn't "think about her that way at all" unless one was going to marry her. But she was a dependable companion. She was always ready to go skating, walking; always content to hear his discourses on the great things he was going to do, the distressed poor whom he would defend against the Unjust Rich, the speeches he would make at Banquets, the inexactitudes of popular thought which he would correct.[132]

After they were married, she was a convenient appendage to his mercantile interests:

> She made him what is known as a Good Wife. She was loyal, industrious, and at rare times merry. She passed from a feeble disgust at their closer relations into what promised to be ardent affection, but it dropped into bored routine. Yet she existed only for him and for the children, and she was as sorry, as worried as himself, when he gave up the law and trudged on in a rut of listing real estate.

He is naïve about life and women—he senses the emptiness of his American Dream, perhaps he should have stayed with the law. His consolation is fantasy of a fairy child that will lead him away from his banal existence.

For years the fairy child had come to him. Where others saw but Georgie Babbitt, she discerned gallant youth. She waited for him, in the darkness beyond mysterious groves. When at last he could slip away from the crowded house he darted to her. His wife, his clamoring friends, sought to follow, but he escaped, the girl fleet beside him, and they crouched together on a shadowy hillside. She was so slim, so white, so eager! She cried that he was gay and valiant, that she would wait for him, that they would sail.

ISADORA DUNCAN

The ideal of the American woman in the twentieth century was to reconcile her passion for freedom and her destiny as a woman. Strong women like the artist, linguist, and critic Gertrude Stein challenged, and even repudiated the demands that society makes upon them and chose to live as eccentric individuals or exiles. Others, like Isadora Duncan, attempted to fulfill themselves as women by expressing their femininity rather than by denying it.

"The sorrow, the pains and disillusions of Love, I transformed in my Art," she wrote in her autobiography, *My Life*.[133] She was not ashamed of her nature, and proudly related the attentions paid her by her admirers. The great Italian soldier, poet, legend Gabriele D'Annunzio courted her: "'Oh, Isadora, it is only possible to be alone with you in Nature. All other women destroy the landscape, you alone become part of it.' (Could any woman resist such homage?) 'You are part of the trees, the sky, you are the dominating goddess of Nature.'"

A true daughter of America, she followed the lineage of pioneers and Puritans—her grandparents crossed the plains in a covered wagon in '49, and she grew up possessing the healthy idealism of America. "The land of America had fashioned me as it does most of its youth,—a Puritan, a mystic and a striver after the heroic expression rather than any sensual expression whatever, and I believe that most American artists are of the same mould."

But she was critical of the Puritan influence in America and set about to challenge it: "The early settlers in America brought with them a psychic sense which has never been lost entirely. And their strength of character imposed itself upon the wild country, taming the wild men, the Indians, and the wild animals in a remarkable manner. But they were always trying to tame themselves as well, with disastrous results artistically!" She believed that American artists were restricted by this heritage. Prudery in dress and manners was still strong in the early years of the century. She found her own liberation in the dance—and became "a perfect pagan, fighting the Philistines."

She rejected "the counteracting influences of our materialistic civilization" and pursued her ideal and her passion. She sought to achieve in dance "the divine expression of the human spirit through the medium of the body's movement." She rendered the poetry of freedom as envisaged by Blake and by Whitman, and also the daring of Zarathustra. Whitman would have understood the genesis of her spirit:

> All these movements—where have they come from? They have sprung from the great Nature of America, from the Sierra Nevada, from the Pacific Ocean, as it washes the coast of California; from the great spaces of the Rocky Mountains—from the Yosemite Valley—from the Niagara Falls.

H.L. MENCKEN

Whilst the American journalist and savant, H.L. Mencken, shared Isadora Duncan's antipathy for Philistinism in America, his views on women were not in accord with hers. He acknowledged the superiority of the American woman in some ways, but not others:

> Nowhere else in the world have women more leisure and freedom to improve their minds, and nowhere else do they show a higher level of intelligence, or take part more effectively in affairs of the first importance. But nowhere else is

there worse cooking in the home, or a more inept handling
of the whole domestic economy, or a larger dependence
upon the aid of external substitutes, by men provided, for
the skill that is wanting where it theoretically exists. It is
surely no mere coincidence that the land of the emancipated and enthroned woman is also the land of canned
soup, of canned pork and beans, of whole meals in cans, and
every thing else ready made.[134]

One shudders to imagine what he would have opined in regard to
pre-packaged and frozen food and microwave cooking.

The iconoclast Mencken praised women's realism, and doubted
their intuition and their reputation for sentiment. He also dispar-
aged their good looks:

The female body, even at its best, is very defective in form;
it has harsh curves and very clumsily distributed masses;
compared to it the average milk-jug, or even cuspidor, is a
thing of intelligence and even gratifying design—in brief,
an *objet d'art*.

When the XIX Amendment to the Constitution extended the
suffrage to women in 1920, Mencken doubted that women really cared: "I believe that the majority of women . . . were not
eager for the extension, and regard it as of small value today.
They know that they can get what they want without going to
the actual polls for it." What does a woman want? "The caveman
is all muscles and mush. Without a woman to rule him and
think for him, he is a truly lamentable spectacle: a baby with
whiskers, a rabbit with the frame of an aurochs, a feeble and
preposterous caricature of God."

DOROTHY PARKER

Dorothy Parker shared Isadora's wish to be liberated from convention. Her poetry and short stories project through the form of
comedy the ambivalence of her desire for equality and freedom in

conflict with her need to be loved and wanted by a man. She understands well the differences between the sexes and portrays them in her poetry.

> Why is it, when I am in Rome,
> I'd give an eye to be at home,
> But when on native earth I be,
> My soul is sick for Italy?
>
> And why with you, my love, my lord,
> Am I spectacularly bored,
> Yet do you up and leave me—then
> I scream to have you back again?
> "On Being a Woman"[135]
>
> They hail you as their morning star
> Because you are the way you are.
> If you return the sentiment,
> They'll try to make you different;
> And once they have you, safe and sound,
> They want to change you all around.
> Your moods and ways they put a curse on;
> They cannot let you go your gait:
> They influence and educate.
> They'd alter all that they admired.
> They make me sick, they make me tired.
> "Men"

She compares the sexes in her marvelous poem, about the vigil of Penelope:

> In the pathway of the sun,
> In the footsteps of the breeze,
> Where the world and sky are one,
> He shall ride the silver seas,
> He shall cut the glittering wave.
> I shall sit at home, and rock;
> Rise, to heed a neighbor's knock;
> Brew my tea, and snip my thread;
> Bleach the linen for my bed.

They will call him brave.
"Penelope"

In her short story, "The Lovely Leave," she relates the frustration of a wife who has only a few hours to spend with her husband; but his only wishes are to savor the pleasure of being home on leave, enjoy a hot bath and polish his belt buckle.

To some people, Dorothy Parker might appear to be emotionally immature. But the poignancy of her work is contained in the deep truths that she manages to convey.

> "To be born woman is to know—
> Although they do not talk of it at school—
> That we must labour to be beautiful."
> Yeats

Perhaps some American male writers have maintained an attitude of superiority and male chauvinism. Dreiser, Hemingway, Fitzgerald, Faulkner, Miller, and Mailer all have shown women as a love-object—a crucible to be used as a test for one's manhood.

> She is a woman, therefore may be wooed;
> She is a woman, therefore may be won;
> She is [woman], therefore must be loved.
> Shakespeare

PAX AMERICANA

The aftermath of the Second World War forced America into a position of dominant world influence even before she had resolved the faults in her own character. Social injustice still existed—in spite of the strong libertarian tradition. In Joseph Heller's World

War II novel, *Catch 22*, the hero Yossarian reflects the American concern for the suffering in the world, as he walks along a war-torn street in Italy:

> What a lousy earth! He wondered how many people were destitute that same night even in his own prosperous country, how many homes were shanties, how many husbands were drunk and wives socked, and how many children were bullied, abused or abandoned. How many families hungered for food they could not afford to buy? How many hearts were broken? How many suicides would take place that same night, how many people would go insane? How many cockroaches and landlords would triumph? How many winners were losers, successes failures, rich men poor men? How many wise guys were stupid? How many happy endings were unhappy endings? How many honest men were liars, brave men cowards, loyal men traitors, how many sainted men were corrupt, how many people in positions of trust had sold their souls to blackguards for petty cash, how many had never had souls? How many straight-and-narrow paths were crooked paths? How many best families were worst families and how many good people were bad people? When you added them all up and then subtracted, you might be left with only the children, and perhaps with Albert Einstein and an old violinist or sculptor somewhere.[136]

America found herself "the policeman of the world"—a euphemism that showed idealism as well as innocence, never admitting or imagining that our position might be compared with the corrupt empires of the old world. "Pax Americana" was presided over by unlikely Caesars from F.D.R. to George W. Bush—for the most part, all hard working, genial men, guided by Puritan idealism and simplicity. The excesses of the Roman Empire were alien. Writing of Roman decadence, Gibbon had noted: "In their dress, their table, their house, their furniture, the favorites of fortune united every refinement of convenience, or elegance, and of splendor, whatever could soothe their pride or gratify their sensuality." The affluent society, on the other hand, was shared by a large proportion of the population. The hereditary aristocracy was weak. The rich mercantile class was not especially given to vice or sensuality—and perhaps the most characteristic marks of the rich in America were antipathy to communism, devotion to power, and aversion to taxes.

TENNESSEE WILLIAMS

D.H. Lawrence and Freud were important literary and cultural influences. The first young writer to emerge after the war, Tennessee Williams, was a disciple of Lawrence and an advocate of Freudian psychology. His plays taught the rehabilitative value of love to a society that still was living according to the Puritan ethic and Victorian prudery, for whom the word "sophisticated" had a sexual connotation. When Blanche DuBois in *A Streetcar Named Desire* visits her sister Stella and criticizes her marriage to a man beneath her social level, Stella responds: "But there are things that happen between a man and a woman in the dark—that sort of make everything else seem—unimportant." Happiness is identified with the freeing of the *libido*.

Williams's women in particular are revealed with great tenderness and compassion. Maggie the Cat in *Cat On the Hot Tin Roof*, one of his richest characters, advocates healthy sexual relations between husband and wife. She has a difficult job saving her husband Brick from self-hatred and impotence. But she is confident that she will be able to provide his salvation:

> Oh, you weak, beautiful people who give up with such grace. What you need is someone to take hold of you—gently, with love, and hand your life back to you, like something gold you let go of—and I can! I'm determined to do it—and nothing's more determined than a cat on a hot tin roof—is there? Is there, Baby?[137]

The greatest limitation of Williams's artistic vision is the oversimplified notion that love itself can reform the wicked and solace the weak. The knowledge and expression of our libidinal nature will not save us—and Freud himself would have asserted as much. The pressures that affect Williams's characters—the competition for place, the struggle for survival in a materialistic environment where an individual has no secure position—shape a society of violence and disorder.

Williams's use of violence, lust, incest, rape, and cannibalism give his work a melodramatic surface. But his depiction of a rapacious society cannot be dismissed as the vision of a distraught genius. Again, Blanche DuBois, the heroine of *A Streetcar Named Desire*, is destroyed by social conditions rather than by unseen fate. The chain of circumstances that brings her to her sister's doorstep—the loss of her home, her disappointment in love, her inability to function in her work are caused, or at least influenced, by a society that has insufficient compassion for the defenseless and weak. Williams implies that the responsibility for her condition rests with the values of a materialistic society. The choice is whether to succumb to nihilism and despair, as Eugene O'Neill had done in his later years, or to remain confident in the power of love to repair some of the pain of existence.

ARTHUR MILLER AND ALLEN GINSBERG

Arthur Miller in *Death of a Salesman* also showed the dehumanization derived from an excessively competitive society. Willy Loman has plied his wares for a lifetime in mad pursuit of the American dream of success—only to be cast aside after he has outlived his usefulness to the company. Like Blanche, Willy falls victim to society and to his own illusions. Gertrude Stein once observed: "Too many Americans are dependent for everything upon a job! They really don't own anything, and if the job goes, everything is gone." Willy's son, Biff, is forced to witness his father's disgrace, and he remains skeptical of the values his father accepts. When he in-trudes upon his father's tryst with a woman in a black slip in a Boston hotel, his disillusionment is complete—his future wrecked.

The writers of the beat generation—Ginsberg, Kerouac, Ferlinghetti, Corso challenged the materialism of American society—even as Thoreau, Melville and Whitman had challenged it a century earlier. Allen Ginsberg the poet of the Beat generation became the prophet of the Hippie generation. His poem "Howl" was a bitter protest against a society that failed to fulfill its democratic promise. He denounced the culture of money, technology, and its consequences, the debasement of human dignity.

Society's materialism can wreak havoc on the family as well as the individual. Willy Loman carried his pain and frustration home, and his wife and children were forced to bear it as well. The son cannot be indifferent to the suffering of his parents. In his elegy to his mother, "Kaddish," Ginsberg recounts the madness of his mother, which has been brought about by her particular pain, as well as by her identification with the suffering of the Jewish people during the Second World War. Even in her decline, she thinks of her son, as she poignantly tries to give him direction in her last letter:

> "The key is in the window, the key is in the sunlight at the window—I have the key—Get married Allen don't take drugs—the key is in the bars, in the sunlight in the window. Love, your mother"[138]

LOLITA AND THE SEXUAL REVOLUTION

In *Lolita* (1955) Vladimir Nabokov wrote the most salacious American novel of the age and heralded the inception of the sexual revolution. In his introduction, the Russian expatriate professor noted that his book would offend the "robust philistine," the "paradoxical prude," and the "cynic." But he hoped that, in spite of its eroticism, it could accomplish a socially desirable purpose. Professor John Ray, Jr., the pseudonymous editor, avers: "*Lolita* should

make all of us—parents, social workers, educators—apply ourselves
with still greater vigilance and vision to the task of bringing up a
better generation in a safer world."[139]

The story pits the "polite European" Humbert Humbert against
American civilization in a parody of Twain and James's fable of the
innocent abroad. Here the European is subjected to the corruptions of the New World, which are very different from those of the
old. Humbert is lewd and depraved. But he falls victim to a culture that he finds sterile and emasculating.

After forming an infatuation for the twelve year old nymphet,
Lolita, he marries her widowed mother in order to advance his
designs. Charlotte Haze is a bossy wife, aggressive and domineering. She condescends to her husband and as, a matter of course,
undermines his *amour-propre*—his European self-esteem. Then she
discovers his diary in which he reveals his true purpose toward
Lolita. She falls into a rage and dies in a coincidental automobile
accident. Now Humbert is free to fulfill his plans.

Humbert drives around the country with Lolita (Dolly), posing as her father. A most amusing scene occurs after Humbert
enrolls his charge in a private school; he is called down by the
head-mistress who complains of Lolita's backwardness in her sexual
maturity:

> "Let me ask you a blunt question, Mr. Haze. You are an old-
> fashioned Continental father, aren't you?"

> "Why, no," I said, "conservative, perhaps, but not what you
> would call old-fashioned."

> She sighed, frowned, then clapped her big plump hands
> together in a let's-get-down-to-business manner, and again
> fixed her beady eyes upon me.

> "Dolly Haze," she said, "is a lovely child, but the onset of
> sexual maturing seems to give her trouble."

> I bowed slightly. What else could I do?

"She is still shuttling," said Miss Pratt, showing how with
her liver-spotted hands, "between the anal and genital zones
of development."

The headmistress offers a typically American matter-of-fact resolution to Dolly's problem; to wit, teach her about the birds and
the bees. The book is as much a satire on private school education
as on American morality. She tells him:

> The Beardsley Scool does not believe in bees and blossoms,
> and storks and love birds, but it does believe very strongly in
> preparing its students for mutually satisfactory mating and
> successful child rearing. We feel Dolly could make excellent
> progress if only she would put her mind to her work. Miss
> Cormorant's report is significant in that respect. Dolly is
> inclined to be, mildly speaking, impudent. But all feel that
> *primo*, you should have your family doctor tell her the facts
> of life and, *secundo*, that you allow her to enjoy the company
> of her schoolmates' brothers at the Junior Club or in Dr.
> Rigger's organization, or in the lovely homes of our parents.

Nabokov no doubt is poking fun at American guile. Perhaps the
age of innocence has passed. Americans were at the time at once
prudish and overbearing about sex. But it is Humbert who is the
failure as both lover and father, a fuddy-duddy. The novel proves
to be a vindication of the American character—who can blame
Lolita for walking out on Humbert? His stuffiness and his hang-
ups render him unfit to understand and enjoy the sexual revolution. If one cannot experience freedom as effortlessly as Lolita, then
perhaps one should not venture from the old world.

PHILIP WYLIE

The emergence of the new woman has progressed since the war.
During the war women were called into the work force in great
numbers, and many continued to work afterwards, join unions,
and demand greater equality. In the home a wife's dependence on

mechanical gadgets also deprived her of a feeling of self-worth and identity. While some writers, like Nabokov, maintained that the American woman was too liberated, Philip Wylie assailed her as the "she" and the nefarious "mom," and furthermore opposed the whole metaphysics of chivalry:

> The absurd posturing of chivalry (and they were superficial, for the most part, in the age of chivalry itself) serve to bloat the nonsensical notion of honoring and rewarding women for nothing more than being female. Cash is heaped at the feet of the sweetheart, the bride, the wife, and especially "mom." Since money does represent a crystallization of human energy, this gave females an inordinate power . . . Women possess most of the wealth. Most of the acts of man are performed to earn back some of this money owned by women—in order to give it to other women.[140]

THE FEMININE MYSTIQUE

However, many women also objected to Wylie's own "absurd posturing of chivalry." Betty Friedan became the advocate and spokesperson of the second sex in adapting the metaphysical ideas of Simone de Beauvoir to the practical concerns of women in the United States. With American matter-of-factness, the movement has assumed a political stance. Though the position of women in the nineteenth century changed for the better, her dilemma remained:

> The feminine mystique says that the highest value and only commitment for women is the fulfillment of their own femininity. It says that the great mistake of Western culture, through most of its history, has been the under valuation of this femininity. It says this femininity is so mysterious and intuitive and close to the creation and origin of life that man-made science may never be able to understand it. But however special and different, it is in no way inferior to the nature of man; it may even in certain respects be superior. The mistake, says the mystique, the root of women's troubles

in the past is that women envied men, women tried to be like men, instead of accepting their own nature, which can find fulfillment only in sexual passivity, male domination, and nurturing maternal love.

Friedan's argument was that woman is untrue to herself by playing the role of girl friend, wife, and mother; though it could be argued that, in the game of courtship, man no less than woman is expected to play a structured part:

> When I consider life, 'tis all a cheat;
> Yet fooled with hope, men favor the deceit.
> John Dryden

OH, DAD, POOR DAD

Arthur Kopit, in a surrealistic comedy *Oh Dad, Poor Dad, Mamma's Hung You in the Closet, and I'm Feeling So Sad*, poked fun at the nefarious mom who devours her son the way her favorite plant, the Venus flytrap, and her favorite pet, a silver piranha fish, devour their prey. She carries her husband's skeleton with her in her travels, both in proof of her triumph over him and as a threat to her son Jonathan. Jonathan learns to be afraid of women, and his liberation only can be achieved when he murders his girlfriend, Rosalie. The circumstance is fantastic and absurd, but it touches a serious point in the relationship between mothers and fathers and mothers and sons.

WHO'S AFRAID OF VIRGINIA WOOLF?

Edward Albee's savage drama, *Who's Afraid of Virginia Woolf?*, brought together two themes of modern literature—the loss of feeling in a scientific society and the emancipated woman who refuses to accept a subservient role. George and Martha, two well-educated intelligent people, are incompatible and live out their lives in bitterness and mutual hatred. The play is anti-marriage as well as anti-love. It hardly has a plot—but rather is a series of confrontations between George and Martha, and between their guests and them. In the absence of nurturing virtues, only hatred remains:

> Martha: You make me sick.

> George: It's perfectly all right for you . . . I mean, you can make your own rules . . . you can go around like a hopped-up Arab, slashing away at everything in sight, scarring up half the world if you want to. But somebody else try it . . . no sir!

> Martha: You miserable . . .

> George (*mocking*) Why baby, I did it all for you. I thought you'd like it sweetheart . . . it's sort of to your taste . . . blood, carnage and all. Why, I thought you'd get all excited . . . sort of heave and pant and come running at me, your melons bobbling.

> Martha: You've really screwed up, George.

> George(*spitting it out*): Oh, for God's sake Martha!

> Martha: I mean it . . . you really have.

> George: (*barely contained anger now*) You can sit there in that chair of yours, you can sit there with the gin running out of your mouth, and you can humiliate me, you can tear me apart . . . ALL NIGHT . . . and that's perfectly all right . . . that's O.K.

> Martha: YOU CAN STAND IT!

> George: I CANNOT STAND IT!

> Martha: YOU CAN STAND IT!! YOU MARRIED ME FOR IT!![141]

George and Martha's fantasy, or ruse, of an imagined child is a desperate one—which they pitifully use to strengthen their bond. The wished-for-child serves to coalesce their marriage. The guests, Nick and Honey are in a similar situation. Honey also seems unwilling to accept the responsibility of motherhood and she remains seemingly frustrated in a regressive state of development.

GORE VIDAL

Gore Vidal projected his fantasy of the liberated woman in a most outrageous Juvenalian satiric novel, *Myra Breckinridge*. "I am Myra Breckinridge whom no man will ever possess," declares Vidal's epicene hero.[142] Myra rises—even as Aphrodite sprang from the foam of the sea—from the dismemberment of the fallen Myron, and the man-hater becomes the goddess of an age. She seeks to revenge herself on the culture that has destroyed the man in Myron. Vidal seemed to support Patricia Sexton's thesis that the institutions of our culture have the effect of feminizing the male and suggested that the feminized male and the masculinized female are one and the same—the result of oppressive cultural forces. Vidal is a satirist—and suffers the fate of most satirists in being misunderstood. His book which was anti-sex was attacked as pornography. Myra heralds the start of an age:

> The roof is fallen in on the male and we now live at the
> dawn of the Woman Triumphant, of Myra Breckinridge!

She declares her mission in view of technological progress and overpopulation:

> Yet, emotionally, I would be only too happy to become
> world dictator, if only to fulfill my mission: the destruction
> of the last vestigial traces of traditional manhood in the race
> in order to realign the sexes, thus reducing population while
> increasing human happiness and preparing humanity for
> its next stage.

Wealth and sexual prowess are the bastions of male supremacy. Myra therefore determines to deprive her uncle Buck Loner of his wealth and destroy Rusty's pride in his sexuality in order to commence the destruction of the male species. In the climax of the book she violates Rusty:

> "Lie down," I ordered. "On your stomach."

> Mystified, he did what he was told. I then tied his bound hands to the top of the metal table. He was, as they say, entirely in my power. If I had wanted, I could have killed him. But my fantasies have never involved murder or even physical suffering for I have a horror of blood, preferring to inflict pain in more subtle ways, destroying totally, for instance, a man's idea of himself in relation to the triumphant sex.

> "Now then, up on your knees."

Myra dies at the end of the novel in an automobile accident. In the sequel *Myron* (1974), Vidal described the ascension of Myron, like the Phoenix, out of her ashes. He is married to his lady-love, Mary-Ann, and settled on the West Coast where he operates a Chinese Catering Service. But the life of the bourgeoisie is not for Myron; and in his restlessness, Myra repossesses his body and seeks her liberation. She declares: "It is important that I save not only Hollywood—the source of the best of our race's dreams since those brutish paintings on the cavern walls at Lascaux—but the United States."[143] She is completely dominated by her romantic illusions of a celluloid past where the movie heroes and heroines reigned. Her fantasy of sexual domination no longer is limited to depriving the male of his virility. She wishes to secure his manhood. The question pondered in these two novels is whether the male has any future in America, or is his destiny to become a feast for Amazons?

After surveying the Breckenridges, Vidal turned away from contemporary sexual mores to create his vast historical panaroma ranging from his historical novels of Roman and early Christian times, and from the beginnings of our own country, to the age of Kennedy, and to the present dominant place of America in the world. While living most of the time in Ravello, Italy, Vidal has made frequent forays to the United States where he has contributed to the literary, political, and the intellectual life of the country, in particular exercising his acid Juvenalian wit on Talk Shows and decrying the moral and political foibles of the United States of America. In a later autobiographical memoir *Palimpsest,* (1995) he described the role of love in his consciousness, as an avowed homosexual, and identified in particular the great love of his life, an adolescent relationship with a schoolmate at St. Albans School, Jimmy Trimble, who tragically died in World War II, and whose friendship left a profound and indelible mark of Platonic love upon his personality.

THE STEPFORD WIVES

In the best-seller, *The Stepford Wives,* Ira Levin offered another projection of science fiction—a fantasy, not of transexuality but of women trapped in roles of wives and mother by male domination. The men of the suburban Stepford community have used their technological knowledge for the final solution to the woman question. It is a fairy tale of the transition by Walter and Joanna Eberhart to an insular community, and their efforts to bring an urban consciousness that will elevate the level of the community: "Sex, yes; sexism, no."[144] But they discover Ajax country, a wasteland that gets its cultural signals not from Betty Friedan or *Ms.* Magazine but from Benton and Bowles and J. Walter Thompson. They are characters from television commercials who devote their lives to wiping, washing, gossiping, and furnishing.

> They never stop,
> These Stepford Wives,
> They work like robots

All their lives.

Joanna consults a psychologist, who tells her that she is torn between the traditional image of woman and the drive for liberation. But she remains convinced that there is a sinister conspiracy to suppress the feminist woman, as her acquaintances are metamorphosed into docile, submissive wives. She becomes obsessed with the belief that the Men's Association, composed of engineers, industrialists, and technocrats has brought about the change. What is only implicit in the novel becomes a *tour de force* in the film adaptation: Joanna is programmed into a life-size replica computer Robot, and then she is physically destroyed.

In their new roles, the women are completely content with their functions and no longer suffer the anxieties that they had as feminists: Feminism, yes; feminist, no. They also enjoy better sexual relations. The creator of the machine tells Joanna with Sophoclean fatalism: "It is necessary that you become so." Whereas Huxley had projected the demise of the family in the future, Levin suggested tongue in cheek that women of the future will be programmed to fulfill their traditional roles.

JOHN IRVING

Another comic masterpiece was John Irving's *The World According to Garp* (1976), a Rabelaisian assault on sensuality and sin. There is no joy in the physical relationship between men and women, but even so, women suffer more for their lust than men. Nurse Jenny Fields takes revenge on a man who tries to touch her thighs in a darkened movie theater by slicing his "whole arm, from his shoulder to his waist . . . open like a soft melon."[145]

> In this dirty-minded world, she thought, you are either
> somebody's wife or somebody's whore—or fast on your way
> to becoming one or the other. If you don't fit either category,
> then everyone tries to make you think there is something
> wrong with you. But, she thought, there is nothing wrong
> with me.

She cohabits with a wounded soldier, Technical Sergeant Garp, who was shot in the brain while masturbating during his thirty fifth combat flight over France, and she raises a son, who is caught between his sensual desire and his fear of women. In Garp's world, women are even more distrustful of men, as symbolized by the Ellen James society, a group of feminists who cut off their tongues, as it were, to spite their faces.

In *The Cider House Rules* (1985), John Irving continued to speak out as a moralist and affirmer of humanistic values. He explores the social question relating to care of the young in a story set in an orphanage—with young people who were unwanted by their parents and by society and offers a discourse on social questions and particularly the morality and legality of the right of the fetus to life.

WHAT EVERY WOMAN KNOWS

On the other hand, the plight of modern women has been particularized by women. It appears that the more intelligent, the more self conscious she is, the more deeply she has felt the scar of existence. The girls in Mary McCarthy's *The Group* (1954) were favored by birth, education, and good looks, yet they failed to make a successful adjustment to society. The ideals of Isabel Archer no longer seemed relevant; to become a lady had scant appeal.

Sylvia Plath's autobiographical novel, *The Bell Jar* (1971) depicts the plight of a single girl coming to womanhood, and feeling that her sensitivity and intelligence make her a misfit. She cannot acquiesce to male dominance, and feels that romantic love is a game of chance. "I'd happened to be dealt to him, like a playing card in a pack of identical cards." The future holds no better promise. "I knew that in spite of all the roses and kisses and restaurant dinners a man showered on a woman before he married her, what he secretly wanted when the wedding service ended was for her to flatten out underneath his feet like Mrs. Willard's kitchen mat."[146]

The problem of sex looms large in her life. On the one hand she perceives sex as a form of suffering inflicted on women: the surrender of virginity; child-birth and child-rearing are the crosses that a woman must bear. But she divides women into two groups: those who have slept with men, and those who haven't. She yearns to be among the former. When she learns that her boyfriend Buddy Willard has had an affair with a waitress, she is driven to prove that she too can be libertine in her actions. The novel recounts her tragi-comic efforts to find a man. She only meets men who are unwilling or unable to give her the satisfaction that she seeks. Her final breakdown is related to her sexual frustration, but it is only part of her psychological problem.

Unhappiness and disorientation are also the themes explored in Renata Adler's bitter novel, *Pitch Dark* (1983), in which she used a surrealistic technique of non-sequiturs to emphasize the anomie of failed relationships. The peripatetic heroine Kate, living in her Upper East Side townhouse, is ambivalent about her life on the run—whether to go "alone, to Graham's Island," and she muses upon her adulterous liaison:

> What I wish I had not lost is the photograph of him, the only nice one. What I wish I had not lost is the ticket for my raincoat at the shoe repair shop. What I wish I had not lost is the suitcase with the letters. What I wish I had not lost is the time, or the inventory of the lost things, or the consciousness of all the things that are not lost. But nothing I had, I think, is anything Jake's wife wants or ever wanted. Nothing was lost, I think, by any of us there.

These are the manifest objects, and then there are the latent feelings:

> I look at you for signs of leaving me to find to my despair
> that one of us has already left. Maybe it's me. But, if it's me,
> I always do come back, or always have. Please don't go.
> Writing is always, in part, bending somebody's ear. As reading is. In the matter of the commas. In the mattter of the
> question marks. In the matter of the tenses. In the matter of
> the scandal on the tennis courts.

> But then, don't you see, I despaired. I simply, no, not simply, I rarely do anything simply, despaired. And then I despaired.[147]

An adulterous relationship is not a comforting solution for the needs of a free woman.

Is the alternative the Victorian ideal of acquiescence to one's duty and the satisfaction of knowing that one has done the right thing? Can Phyllis McGinley be right? She celebrated the joys of domesticity in such poems as "Eros in the Kitchen," "Song from New Rochelle," "June in the Suburbs," and "Dirge Over a Pot of Pâté de Foie Gras," and proposed that raising children can be not only the highest calling, but the source of the truest insights.

The late Anne Sexton found her sexuality a source of ambivalent emotions in such poems as "In Celebration of My Uterus" and "The Fury of Cocks." In "Welcome Morning," she declaimed:

> There is joy
> in all:
> in the hair I brush each morning,
> in the Cannon towel, newly washed,
> that I rub my body with each morning,
> in the chapel of eggs I cook
> each morning
> in the outcry from the kettle
> that heats my coffee,
> each morning,

> in the spoon and the chair,
> that cry "hello there, Anne"
> each morning,
> in the godhead of the table
> that I set my silver, plate, cup upon,
> each morning.[148]

But in "Consorting with Angels," she is tired of "the gender of things":

> I was tired of being a woman,
> tired of the spoons and the pots,
> tired of my mouth and my breasts,
> tired of cosmetics and the silks
>
> . . . .
>
> I was tired of the gender of things.
>
> . . . .
>
> Adam was on the left of me
> and Eve was on the right of me, both
> thoroughly inconsistent with the world of reason.
> We wove our arms together
> and rode under the sun.
> I was not a woman anymore,
> not one thing or the other.

ERICA JONG

Erica Jong, perhaps the most avant-garde writer of her generation, reflected all of the currents from the sexual revolution, to the women's movement, to the current idealization of love. A consummate literary artist, she has adopted the styles of her mentors from Whitman to D.H. Lawrence to Henry Fielding, and also smitten by Shakespeare.

In her best selling novel, *Fear of Flying* (1973), she recounted the escapades of Isadora Zelda Wing, namesake of the other liberated Isadora Duncan. Her flights of fantasy attempt to challenge the imagined-supremacy of such creators of fantasy as Casanova and D.H. Lawrence, in her own particular liberated woman.

Somewhere deep inside my head (with all those submerged memories of childhood) is some glorious image of the ideal woman, a kind of Jewish Griselda. She is Ruth and Esther and Jesus and Mary rolled into one. She always turns the other cheek. She is a vehicle, a vessel, with no needs or desires of her own. When her husband beats her, she understands him. When he is sick, she nurses him. When the children are sick, she nurses them. She cooks, keeps house, runs the store, keeps the books, listens to everyone's problems, visits the cemetery, weeds the graves, plants the garden, scrubs the floors, and sits quietly on the upper balcony of the synagogue while men recite prayers about the inferiority of women. She is capable of absolutely everything except self-preservation. And secretly, I am always ashamed of myself for not being her. A good woman would have given over her life to the care and feeding of her husband's madness. I was not a good woman. I had too many other things to do.[149]

She seeks to find happiness in the arms of a fellow graduate student whom she marries and divorces; a musician; a Chinese psychiatrist, Bennett Wing, whom she marries, and from whom she flees to Europe. Lolita on the loose then takes up with an Englishman and other assorted lovers. Her main hang-up is marriage. For her, "bigamy is having one husband too many; monogamy is the same."

However she cannot reconcile herself to the condition of moral uncertainty. Her liberation is accompanied by guilt and remorse. She decides that if she only stopped "blaming" herself, then her feelings of inadequacy would be relieved. But the resolution of the conflict between moral responsibilities and libidinal demands is not simple. The price of libidinal freedom for Isadora, as for most women, is a feeling of inadequacy. The book fails to resolve the issue; for she returns to Bennett's bathtub and bed. But any reconciliation would seem to be a wistful hope.

In the sequel *How to Save Your Own Life* (1977), Jong traced the career of Isadora through her success as a writer and a show biz personality. Even though she is a guru to the unliberated women, who seek her advice on how to save their own lives, she has her hands full saving herself. She glides through the world of socialites and gigolos, Hollywood stars and moguls, feminists, hangers on and takers off; and through it all, having overcome her middle class prejudices, she seeks to forge a new life style. But she finds that new freedom is old sin writ large: from adultery to casual sexual encounter to lesbian relationships to group sex.

Through it all, the central conflict in the book is whether she should have remained with her husband. The true ambivalence of her attitude to the marriage bond is rendered powerfully and movingly. She declares that "leaving" Bennett would be "the hardest thing I ever did in my life;" and she concludes that all women were obsessed with breaking up with their husbands, and that "leaving one's husband was the *only*, the cosmic, theme."[150] She loves him, loves him not, loves him, loves him *n.o.t.*! She continually returns to him to succour her wounds, yet in a fit of rage threatens to castrate him.

If she returns to hearth and tub, she no doubt will manage another cynical book showing that love is an illusion. But she chooses a new, young lover, in fulfillment of her destiny: "All my life I had written in the hope of finding my lover, my double, my friend through the printed word." But Bennett's last words like those of the ghost of Hamlet's father, haunt her future: "So leave. You'll never write another book as long as you live."

But Erica Jong continued not only to plight her troth but merrily to ply her trade. In *Fanny, Being the True History of the Adventures of Fanny Hackabout-Jones* (1980) she wrote an eighteenth century comic burlesque in the style of Fielding, which traced the life of her abandoned orphan heroine, raised and raped by her stepfather, who took up with highwaymen, witches, whores, men of letters, and pirates, and discovered that she was the natural daughter of Lord Bellars and the inheritor of the Lymeworth estate. With wit, elegance of language, alliteration and orthography, she defends the cause of womanhood and mocks the frailties of men, arguing that "the Lives of Great Men are more oft' at variance with their profess'd Philosophies than consistent with 'em; that their Habits in private mock their Statements in publick; that their bestial Behaviour in the Boudoir makes a Mockery of their Angelick Arguments in their Ethick Epistles, their Lofty Logick in their Epicks; or their Tragick Pronouncements in their Treatises." Nor does her genre deny gender. "Tis true that there are vast Diff'rences betwixt Men in regard to their am'rous Equipage (which is why Men always wish to be reassur'd to the Contrary), vast Diff'rences betwixt the Pow'rs granted by Venus, and vast Diff'rences betwixt the Native Temperaments granted by their Stars . . . but only Simpletons and Dullards dwell on these Diff'rences in Size to the Exclusion of other Qualities."[151]

JOHN UPDIKE AND JOYCE CAROL OATES

John Updike and Joyce Carol Oates—through the last decades—have been two of our most prolific authors and have created a vast body of literature combining a wide-range of interests in multiple styles and genres. It is a rare year in which there is not a book by one, or both, which provides entertainment and their unique representation and interpretation of life in America.

Updike, after graduating *summa cum laude* from Harvard in 1954, began as a cartoonist for *The New Yorker*, and early discovered his penchant for writing light verse, and thence moved to short stories, novels, and literary and cultural criticism. He has depicted all phases of modern life with particular emphasis on suburban married life in its country club and social milieu, golf (a fascination of his) and *angst*. Like virtually all American male writers, he has explored contemporary relations between the sexes, and combined a strong Puritan strain from his Lutheran childhood with a curiosity about hedonism; revealed in his best selling *Couples* (1968), the subtle short stories describing marriage in *Too Far to*

Go (1979), his historical romances *Roger's Version* (1986), a retelling of *The Scarlet Letter* from the point of view of the wronged husband, and recently Shakespeare's *Hamlet* through the love story of his mother and stepfather, *Gertrude and Claudius*. Turning in frustration against feminist critics who decried his lack of understanding of the female sensibility, he wrote a novel *S*, in the guise of an authoress. But it was *The Witches of Eastwick* (1984), in which he turned his style to a satire on the male response to women's liberation movement, as the Devil comes to suburban Eastwick to tame and exorcise the out-of-control witches, and this proved a suitable vehicle for actor Jack Nicholson's brilliant wit and talent in the classic film version (recently readapted into a musical).

Joyce Carol Oates, after graduating as class valedictorian from Syracuse University in 1960, similarly has combined a career of teaching and a life of letters, writing poetry, short stories, Gothic romances, and criticism. She has commented on the spiritual conflicts and yearnings in what she has called "Updike's American Comedies," which reflect on her work as well. She too has a vital imagination, concocting fantastic stories and characters speaking with diverse passions; and like Updike, she has sought to understand and reveal American society and deal with the outstanding social and moral issues relating to social class, and particularly the theme of violence and the wheel of love. She has written poignantly of the brutality and puzzlement of relations between the sexes. "What is this puzzle of people?" she wrote in her acclaimed short story "Puzzle," in which the heroine mourns the tragic death of her son, and blames herself for her ambivalent hatred toward her husband and the failed partnership of their marriage. "What have [couples] to do with one another? They can't help one another. They are better alone."[152] Yet at the same time, she seems to acknowledge the harshness and the selflessness, the profanity and the sanctity of the marriage bond.

BLACK WOMAN WRITERS

The emergence of the Black Woman Writers has been one of the most notable achievements of the civil rights and feminist movements at the beginning of the twentieth first century. In their own way, each reflects the unbearable life of pain endured by the black woman growing up in the south and her emergence to the light of freedom and truth; together, they speak to the triumphs and failures of the great American experiment. From such pioneers as Lorraine Hansberry and Gwendolyn Brooks to Alice Walker and Toni Morrison, the Nobel Laureate for Literature in 1993, these descendants of peoples—forcibly abducted from their homelands— carry within their bones the great experiment of America, while their hides bear the stings of American injustice. Alice Walker connects herself to the artistic heritage of her ancestors and their frustrations in her essay, *In Search of Our Mothers' Gardens*: "For these grandmothers and mothers of ours were not Saints, but Artists; driven to a numb and bleeding madness by the springs of creativity in them for which there was no release. They were Creators, who lived lives of spiritual waste, because they were so rich in spirituality—which is the basis of Art—that the strain of enduring their unused and unwanted talent drove them insane. Throwing away this spirituality was their pathetic attempt to lighten the soul to a weight their work-worn, sexually abused bodies could bear." [153] She speaks for all when she concludes on a personal note: "Guided by my heritage of a love of beauty and a respect for strength—in search of my mother's garden, I found my own."

Indeed, their experiences are not entirely unlike those of their white brothers and sisters similarly seeking their mothers' gardens, and they wish to be perceived not so much in terms of their race, but rather as authors who, like Sappho, Lady Murasaki, Christine de Pizan, Shakespeare and Emily Dickinson reflect great truths about the human condition. Maya Angelou, in her inauguration poem to honor President Bill Clinton in 1993, "On the Pulse of

Morning," celebrated the diversity of the American character, spoke of the need to recognize our common attributes and humanity, and called for a true awakening to reconciliation, and a "good morning" to all. She also has written of her feelings as a woman toward men in *Phenomenal Woman*:

> Men themselves have wondered
> What they see in me.
> They try so much
> But they can't touch
> My inner mystery.[154]

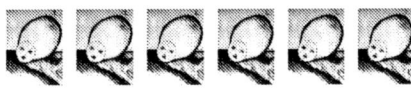

LOVE IN THE ORIENTAL WORLD

In the East my pleasure lies.
Shakespeare's Antony

Rare is the person who prefers virtue to sexual pleasure.
Confucius

Women have eight times more sexual energy than men.
The Kama Sutra of Vatsyayana

Even an outrageous man
Should not be harsh to a woman;
Remembering that
Upon her, depends the joy of sensuous
love, pleasure and virtue.
A woman is an ever holy field,
in which the Self is born.
Even the sages do not possess the power
To procreate without her.
Mahabharata

And as for the true servants of Allah, a generous provision
[in death] shall be made for them. They shall feast on fruit
and be honored in the gardens of delight. Reclining face to
face upon soft couches, they shall be served with a goblet
filled at a gushing fountain. Their drinks shall neither dull
their senses nor befuddle them. And by their side shall sit
bashful dark-eyed virgins, as chaste as the sheltered eggs of
ostriches.
The Koran

ORIENTALISM • HINDUISM • BUDDHISM • CONFUCIANISM •
JAPAN • ISLAM

ORIENTALISM

Looking eastward half a century ago, Winston Churchill described
what he saw as "a riddle wrapped in mystery inside an enigma."
His view, though of Russia, reflected a long-held, prevalent western attitude towards the east, no less than toward the orient. The
inscrutable orient has been both a magnet and a source of confusion for western man who has perceived a mixture of the exotic and
the incomprehensible. The great biological studies of today are
demonstrating that distinctions between race and gender are superficial, and dispelling the prejudicial view of superior and inferior races by showing empirically, in the laboratory, that differences among the races are no more than skin deep. The DNA code
that we all carry links all of humanity in the strongest possible
bond. While the traits of our biological composition exist in common, there is little doubt that culture and civilization have played
a significant, if not dominant, role in nurturing and shaping the
values of individuals within a society. Our present understanding
of the process of cross-fertilization and globalization illustrates the
interaction among the various communities which inhabit our global village. Each day, great sums of information—whether the daily
news, or developments in science, medicine, gossip, technology
and sports—are transmitted and immediately absorbed within the
range of both wired and wireless communication. Such cross-fertilization and interaction long have been part of the course of history. Religious teachings, ethical principles, stories and literature
have been dispersed even as military conflict and trade have flour-
ished and brought nations from the east and west into proximity
with one another though, to be sure, at a much slower rate in the
past than at present.

Orientalism evolved as a result of such cross-fertilization, as eastern religions preached the message of one world—and even one universe—bound together in one living soul. Early Persian Zoroastrism taught that life was a struggle between good and evil, and this subjective definition served different cultures and civilizations at various time. The ancient Indo-European nomadic tribes looked at a hostile world around them and sought to pacify and influence the deities by their actions, prayers, and sacrifices. In their various dialects and languages, the earliest Indian literatures provided the message of the way to serve the gods through hymn and ritual. Hinduism spread throughout the Indian subcontinent, and influenced Buddhism, which taught Enlightenment, the way of salvation. In turn, Greek philosophy, Taoism, Christianity, Zen-Buddhism, and Islam were influenced successively by eastern thought.

The common principle of these religions was that the perfection of man would be achieved through religious transformation. The shared values of *dharma*, or right action, *karma*, justice, meditation, and *nirvana* were practiced and dispersed widely in the oriental world. As in the west, there was an ambivalent attitude toward woman as both goddess and inspiration, and temptress and bane to man's perfection. Just as there existed the dichotomy between Lilith and Delilah, as evil temptresses, and the Virgin Mary as ideal of the good, the orient gave coequal expression to both woman's sexual and her idealistic nature. There was universal recognition of a woman's role as mother and wife, as the spokes of the wheel that embodied and propelled the unity and continuity of the family. On the other hand, like Eve, woman was perceived both as helpmate to her husband, and a restraint to his pursuit of perfection.

From the temple prostitutes in ancient Palestine and India to the belly dancers of the Middle East, the slave girls of the Turkish harems, the concubines of China and the far East, and the geishas of Japan, the lure of the oriental woman has captivated the imagination of men. The exotic, Oriental woman created and sustained the image of a perfumed, coquettish, submissive, concupiscent *femme fatale* with magical power over men. In ancient literature there was the depiction of the single-breasted Amazon warrior, as well as the savage Medea, cunning Circe, fascinating Calypso, and passionate Dido—all capable of extending their mastery over men. The lascivious Salomé undulating before King Herod in order to win his favor and secure the head of John the Baptist on a platter, Queen Cleopatra manipulating first the Roman general Julius Caesar, and then his protégé and successor, Mark Antony, to her cause and the cause of Egypt are famous historical images of the power that oriental women have exercised in their craft of love— down to the lovelorn ladies of Verdi's *Aida* and Puccini's *Madama Butterfly* which have propagated the western ideal of the oriental women, the fairy tale goddess, daughter, wife, and seductress.

Their beauty, their femininity, and their skill at gratifying each and all of men's desires are timeless manifestations, whether through their endemic qualities, or the mystique of their passion; and they have imposed their imprint on western sensibility and inspired men as different as Marco Polo and Rimsky-Korsakov. Art and artists have captured the beauty of the oriental woman and defined her exotic and ambivalent appeal. Irvin C. Schick suggests that she has been described "in a wealth of mutually contradictory assertions . . . as both sylph and harpy—both alluring and repulsive, crude and refined, disgustingly filthy and obsessed with bathing, unspeakably ugly and fabulously beautiful, elegant and ragged, shapeless and perfectly proportioned, graceful as a gazelle and clumsy as a duck, languorous and a beast of burden, a helpless prisoner and a scheming evil-doer."[155]

The first traveler from the west to penetrate the secrets and life of the orient was Marco Polo in the thirteenth century. In his account contained in *The Travels*, he particularly noted the modesty of oriental women:

> You must know that the young ladies of the province of
> Cathay excel in modesty and the strict observance of deco-

rum. They do not frisk and frolic or fly into a pet. They do
not keep watch at the windows gazing at passers-by or exposing themselves to their gaze. They do not offer a ready
ear to improper stories. They do not gad about to parties or
entertainments . . . In the presence of their elders they are
respectful and never utter a needless word—indeed they do
not speak at all in their presence unless addressed. In their
own chambers they remain intent on their own tasks, seldom presenting themselves to the sight of fathers and brothers and the older members of the household and never listening to suitors. [156]

Marco Polo also recounted the voracious appetite of the great Kublai
Khan to satisfy his lust. He organized his domestic affairs with the
same thoroughness that he showed in his military campaigns, and
with the same success. According to Marco Polo, he had four lawful wives, and his heir would derive from the eldest of one of them.
In addition, he enjoyed countless concubines. When he traveled,
emissaries were sent to scout the local talent, and grade the beau-
ties on a scale of 20; those who were chosen were reviewed and
graded again, and those selected were sequestered. Polo noted that
they were inspected for blemish, ensured that they were virgins,
and rejected if they failed these tests, had unpleasant breath, or
snored. Far from dishonored, the fathers "esteem it a great favor
and distinction .. that he should deign to accept them."[157] Those
who had been chosen would be guaranteed a good marriage and a
noble status, after the Khan was finished with them.

To be sure, the treatment of women in the orient has left much
to be desired. For them, life could be very harsh as they have been
accorded second class citizenship rather than anything approaching full equality, and they have been victims of cruel and inhu-
mane treatment. In Hinduism, women were subjected until recently to *suttee*, or the immolation of a wife on the pyre of her
deceased husband, and the slaying of the wife by the husband's
relatives for doubtful cause. Girls and women in China were subjected to such harsh practices as infanticide, foot binding, child

marriage, and polygamy; as well as being forced to subscribe to a pecking order of wives and concubines. Even the wise Confucius was quoted as giving the sanction for adultery and concubinage when he observed: "When the coat upon your back is old and worn, do you not take another?" Islam isolated women before marriage in the *purdah* and after marriage while their husbands could take many wives and concubines, they were restrained in the *harem*, and required to wear the veil (*chador*) when they appeared outdoors. Women have been required to preserve their virginity before marriage on pain of exclusion, while men have not. The adulterous act has exacted a harsher punishment enforced against women than against men, and some Muslim societies, particularly in Africa, still condone the practice of genital mutilation. While some of these practices are undergoing change today, Islamic women in some fundamentalist countries are still prohibited from working, or assuming leadership positions, or even appearing without the *chador*; and oriental girls are accorded lesser worth within the family, even sold, or given away.

HINDUISM

Hinduism is the most ancient of all religions that survive into the modern world. Like other eastern religions, it embraces the principles of morality and renunciation, and contains many great truths and paradoxes, profound and superficial, sacred and profane. Intriguingly, it has evolved without significant change over thousands of years from a religion that existed without a scripture or even an alphabet, a religion of cults, sacrifices, and rituals to a religion with a diversity of divinities calculated even in the millions, and great temples and stunning art. Of some controversy is its emphasis on a social stratum that limits the lower caste of people (untouchables) to a servile role in society. But the promise of transmigration of souls to a better existence in a future life, based on the acceptance of *dharma*, right action, reflects the greater laws of the gods and men, assuring that reward awaits the virtuous, and punishment will befall the sinner through the justice of *karma*. Hindus cannot only aspire to a better afterlife, but even divinity is attainable. The kingdom of Hindus encompasses not only human beings, but the world of animals—the sacred cow is well known, but serpents, monkeys, and elephants are also noted for their superior characteristics. The rituals cover the whole range of human life from greeting the morning, to the prayers several times a day contained in the *mantras*, even to which hand to use for eating, the laws of marriage, and the ceremonies of death. The truths of the religion derive from the inferences contained in the teachings in their holy texts, the *Vedas*, the *Upanishads*, and the later epics of transmitted knowledge, but no redactor like Homer, Moses, or Matthew gave formal literary shape to the sprawling stories contained in their scripture.

Hinduism is rooted in the concept of individual, ethical responsibility and, at the same time, resignation to the will of nature and the gods. The early *Vedas* are poems and hymns to nature, which accompanied sacrifice. Western minds have always had difficulty in comprehending the oriental sense of the universe, which, however, through modern science, is becoming more familiar as when, for example, the Hubble Space telescope is said to illuminate the "observable" universe, composed of some 120 billion galaxies, each galaxy containing upward of a billion stars; all of which leads one to a breath-taking awe of this metaphysical wonder. Oriental religions have always understood and taught the incomprehensibility of the infinitude of the universe.

While the Hindu view of life is seemingly rooted in renunciation of earthly desire as the ultimate truth through such individual behavior as abstinence, diet, and yoga, the practices of worship seemingly celebrate the sexual energy even while ostensibly renouncing desire. In the pre-historic past, the intercourse between the earth goddess Maya and omnipotent Indra was the beginning act that ignited cosmic energy of the universe. The union of *Purusha*, the Universal Soul, with *Prakriti*, the Cosmic substance

creates the phenomenal world of being, and their dissolution leads
to freedom and immortality; thus the sexual act has the character
of a cosmic experience. In the *Artharva Veda*, written some thirty
five hundred years ago, it is suggested that:

> Lust was born first: neither gods, nor ancestors, nor men can
> equal him. Oh Lust! You are immense as you reside in all
> living beings. I bow to you. You are a higher deity than the
> sun, moon, wind, fire. You are assimilated in all, and there-
> fore you are forever great, I bow to you.[158]

While the practices of worship serve as a reminder of the restriction on desires, the ancient art and sculpture give expressive suggestion to the role of the erotic in human existence—underlying
the potency of the universe. Artists were free to express such voluptuousness in stone, representing the myths and stories of the
gods, and depict the apsarases, or divine nymphs, virile serpents
and snakes in erotic embrace, and show the presence in the holy
sanctuaries of the lotus *yoni* and the phallic *lingam*. Woman sym-
bolizes the earth with her life-giving power and goodness and nour-
ishment, and her power was perceived not only in outward appearance, but in her inner strength. The Hindu gods are represented in love and embrace, or even idealized hermaphroditic form
having the qualities of the both male and female, as in the Shiva
Ardhanari stone sculpture.

While Brahma (the Creator) may be far above such human
intercourse and desires of the flesh, the manifestations of other
gods are represented in consort with women. Kama (the God of
Love, Desire) is in eternal conflict with *dharma*. When Kama
tempted Shiva during his meditation, the disturbed god reduced
him to ashes with the fire of his burning eye, so that lust became
bodiless, and desire lost its physical form and found its outlet
through the pores of the body. Yet the touch of the goddess Kali
animated Shiva (the Destroyer), and the tender marital embrace
of Shiva and his wife Parvati, another incarnation of Kali, symbol-
izes not only procreation and the fecundity of the universe, but

the pleasure and duty found in marriage as well. Lakshmi, who is represented as the consort of Vishnu (the Preserver) for her part was seen as the goddess of prosperity and good fortune. The relationship between Krishna and his consort Radha is celebrated in Hindu poetry and art; and while he is represented as a dutiful husband washing the feet of Radha, he is also depicted as mischievous in his licentious pursuit of mortal woman for personal gratification.

The situation of women within the structure is ambiguous. The goddesses enjoy an almost equal status with the gods, recognizing the power and seductive influence that they exercise. The literature, which has as its principle teaching the attainment of perfection, also recognizes the sacred duty of marriage and the central role of the family in perpetuating Hindu values.

The great literary epics of the Hindus, the *Mahabharata* and *Ramayana* composed between 400 B.C. and 400 A.D, trace the relationship between man and divinity. These seemingly disconnected stories of the gods have, as their purpose, the teaching of religion, morality, as well as statecraft. The stories recount even in an entertaining way the myths and legends of the gods and reflect the potential for humans to aspire to attain divine wisdom and status.

While gods enjoy the highest status, they are ever-present in the human, animal, vegetable and mineral kingdom; since one never knows where divinity will be found, therefore everything in nature must be treated as holy. Even as western science recognizes the common denominator of atoms within the disparate elements in the universe, so too the Hindu ancient belief holds this interconnectivity. But metempsychosis avers that in the process of transmigration, the soul will return in another life in another form, based significantly on our virtues or vices in this life. *Karma* is thus the judgment on our actions, by which the gods hold us inalterably accountable. Moreover, one never knows who is contained in the present incarnation of a person, creature or thing. The *Mahabharata* celebrates such interconnection between all the ele-

ments of the universe whether in human, animal or divine form.
Pandu, King of the Pandavas, leaves his wives in order to go hunting, and while he witnesses two deer engaged in the act of intercourse, he slays them:

> When Pandu drew near, the stag looked up at him and,
> with tears in his eyes, asked, "Why have you done this?"
> Pandu replied: "Kings may hunt deer; it is no crime." "Not
> for hunting do I blame you," answered the deer. "But for
> your cruelty in killing us while we made love I curse you!
> You have brought grief when I was happy. You have made
> my love useless—and yours shall be the same. Death will
> strike you down when you next make love." [159]

Out of fear of this prophecy, Pandu refuses to make love to his
wives. However, the gods take pity on him and through miraculous incantation of a magical spell of love, five sons are born immaculately, and he enjoys adoptive paternity. His five sons in turn
share one wife, the beautiful Draupadi, among themselves; she is
the symbol of family stability. The great epic tells of their adventures and conflict with their cousins, the Kuravas, for control of
Bharata, the empire of India; and the humiliation of the Pandavas
when their wife Draupadi is lost in a game of dice and forced to be
surrendered to her enemies; and the wars that occur between them.
Draupadi, however, remains faithful to her husbands, and goes
with them when they enter the forest for a twelve year exile and
retreat to cleanse and purify themselves in preparation for the battle.
The great battle between the warring cousins is the subject of the
most renowned section of the poem, *Bhagavat Gita*.

While in the forest, one of the brothers Arjuna is invited into
the palace of Indra, where he pursues his meditation and learns
the arts of war; here he also is tempted by the divine nymph,
Urvasi:

> With her beauty and grace and the charm of her movement
> of her eyebrows and of her soft voice and her face radiant as
> the moon, she seemed to challenge the moon himself as she

glided along. And as she went, her deep, finely tapering
black nippled breasts, adorned with a golden necklace, and
rubbed with the fragrant salve of sandalwood, trembled up
and down . . . And Arjuna spoke, "O thou foremost apsarases
I bow my head before thee in greeting. I wait upon thee as
thy servant."[160]

Because he remains unmoved and cool to her advances, he arouses
the ire of the gods for his asceticism and lack of human emotion,
even as his father had alienated the gods by similar callousness. As
punishment for his pride, he is compelled to pass time in the
company of women as a eunuch in order to perfect his character.

Similarly the *Ramayana*, "the Fortunes of Rama," the other
classic epic of India, recounts Prince Rama's pursuit of perfection
through the practices of *dharma* and holiness. The prince is the
heir apparent to the throne of Ayoda, and the epic recounts his
preparation for his rule through his heroic exploits and various
encounters with the corruption of the world, which test his character and steadfastness. The story, told by Valmiki, begins on the
morning after the evening of the recitation of the *Mahabharata*,
and contains great adventure, romance and faith. Rama himself is
a reincarnation of Vishnu, and so his life is a model for the faithful
to emulate. The poem also celebrates the unique love between
Prince Rama and his faithful bride and consort Sita, "the Star of
Beauty." She too partakes of divinity, having been born directly
from a furrow of the earth; and the prince courts and wins her love
by his feat of strength in stringing the powerful bow, and together
they endure a remarkable series of adventures.

Sita was a fair young girl. Her dark eyes were like the eyes of
a doe, her lips were full, her long dark hair was falling down
her back clear to her ankles, and it was fragrant from being
scented over incense smoke. She had a red brow-mark and
lines of red and white sandalwood paste on her arms; the
soles of her feet were dyed red with lac; she wore crimson
robes and silver veils light as air, belts of embroidery and fine
chains swaying as she walked, jeweled diadems and bell

anklets, new barley shoots behind her ear, bridal garlands of
jasmine, and seven strands of pearls around her neck and
falling over her full round breasts. But who describes Sita?
All this was forgotten when she looked at you. When she
smiled, what else existed?[161]

Here the love recounted is between a husband and wife, even to a
greater extent than in the earlier epic. Rama and Sita endure many
hardships and remain together when Rama has to endure an exile
of fourteen years in the forest until he is restored to his rightful
throne. Their courtship, true friendship and married love all are
celebrated, and Sita remains faithful to her husband when she too
is abducted by the demon King Ravana, the monster with ten
heads and twenty arms, who deceptively tries to win her love from
Rama—by promising her riches, and even by producing a replica
of her husband's skull to suggest that he is dead. But she remains
true to her vows until Rama overcomes the wicked monster king.
Now her fidelity while in captivity is questioned, and she is tested
by ordeal of fire and proven innocent. Mother Earth however re-
claims her because of the insult done to her integrity, but not
before she leaves Rama with their twin sons. She represents in
Indian literature the standard of the "Most Faithful Wife" even as
Odysseus and Penelope and Romeo and Juliet are memorialized in
their bond of truest love.

Kama (Desire) is a god as well as a philosophical principle of
libidinal pleasure; sensual as well as sexual love binds men and
women together even as the universe is interconnected with this
supreme universal energy. Dated some two thousand years ago,
the *Kama Sutra* by Vatsyayana is a treatise which, according to
tradition, derived from a poem written for Shiva while he was engaged in intercourse with his divine consort, Parvati. This frank
and pornographic work teaches the role of good manners, cleanli-
ness, even food, charms, magic, incantation, tattooing and perfume as a stimulant and aphrodisiac to the attainment of the pleasure of the flesh in marriage. Since in Hindu tradition, parents

choose the mates for their children, it remains for the husband and wife to discover love, and each other. Marriage is a sacred rite, which is best accomplished by members of the same caste, with the insistence that the bride be a virgin, and ensures parents of descendants who can carry on the family name, and offer sacrifices to their ancestors. Accordingly, sexual pleasure is a discovery that is fundamental for the male as well as the female, and there are practical ways of accomplishing this objective.

These are the sixty four arts of love recounted in the manual, dealing with such things as touching, kissing and embracing, all of which idealize marriage, women and love: "Men and women being of the same nature feel the same kind of pleasure, and therefore a man should marry such a woman as will love him ever afterward."[162]

The work is very pragmatic, and deals with every phase of the relationship between a man and a woman. From courtship to marriage, and love making, the work is filled with aphorisms and practical advice about understanding and sustaining relationships. This classic work has lost none of its depth and wisdom though it is not without its amusing observations and folk wisdom. "Man is divided into three classes: the hare man, the bull man, and the horse man, according to the size of his lingam. Woman also, according to the depth of her yoni, is either a female deer, a mare, or a female elephant."[163]

The writer insists on equality between the partners: "Whatever things may done by one of the lovers to the other, the same should be returned by the other; that is, if the woman kisses him, he should kiss her in return; if she strikes him, he should also strike her in return."[164] If, on the other hand, the man does something unpleasant to the woman like biting her, "she should angrily do the same to him with double force."[165] Moreover, a woman should have the right of choice: "A girl who is much sought after should marry the man she likes, and whom she thinks would be obedient to her, and capable of giving her pleasure."[166] As for the wife, "whether she be a woman of noble family or a virgin, widow, remarried or a concubine, [she] should lead a chaste life, be devoted to her husband, doing everything for his welfare."[167]

The work finally is reminiscent of such western works as Ovid's *The Art of Love*, and Andreas Capellanus' *The Art of Courtly Love*, with which it bears similarities as well as comparisons, and could well serve as a contemporary love manual; in fact a modern version has been written by a psychologist for women.[168] It is an ever-present source of guidance to those who have freely chosen each other and seek a lasting, binding relationship.

BUDDHISM

China has had the longest, most uninterrupted civilization, even containing the fossil remains of Peking Man, which existed in time between the Java and Neanderthal race some five hundred thousand years ago. Chinese civilization has historical records of some four thousand years, defined in a series of different dynasties in different regions, all of which have made their unique contribution to its culture and its history. Though marked by a continual history of what western society has termed oriental despotism, China has created down to our own time an efficient, though regimented society, in which the needs of its citizens and service to the state have been given their proper recognition. Among its lasting achievements were the 1500 mile Great Wall constructed in the third century B.C. to protect its northern borders, as well as early advances in medical science such as understanding the role of infection in the spread of disease, and the importance of the pulse in assessing health care. China also has shown the way in the cultivation of plants and gardens, the invention of porcelain, gunpowder, paper and ink, and silk and fabric dyeing. In the field of aesthetics, China recognized the necessary harmony in the space of nature outside the home, and even emphasized the use of space and ambience within the home in the now popular mode of *feng shui*. Even today, their medicinal herbs, and soothing, healthful green

tea, as well as their ubiquitous manufacturing of everything and
anything have contributed to the advancement of world civilization. But undoubtedly the major event in the history of China was
the influence of Buddhism.

Buddhism evolved from Hinduism in India in the sixth century. Siddhartha Gautama (566-480 B.C.), who came to be known
as "Buddha," the Great Teacher, was born in Nepal, the son of a
Rajah, but it was taught that his birth was "immaculate," without
human sexual congress, by divine intervention in the form of an
elephant mating with Queen Maya. Siddhartha himself was
tempted by Mara the prince of evil, even as Jesus was tempted by
Satan. The beliefs of *dharma*, *karma* and *nirvana* were derived from
Hinduism, but given their particular form by the belief in the
path of seeking truth that Buddhism advanced. As with Hinduism and Christianity, the desires of the flesh were seen to be a
corrupting influence and, like the holy men of Christianity and
Hinduism, the celibate monks were the great perpetuators of the
religion. To emulate Buddha was to become the Buddha. Buddhism taught that original sin was not a result of our sexual nature
but rather of our ignorance of truth; and both Buddhism and
Taoism, which derived from it, showed the path toward Enlightenment through restriction and denial of sensual gratification.

Whereas Hinduism did not have a single author, Buddhism,
like the other great Chinese belief, Confucianism, was identified
with a single great teacher, and it has been suggested that the life
and legends of Prince Rama had some literary influence on the
virtue and stories associated with Prince Buddha. Buddha himself
did not leave a written testament, and the scripture of Buddhism,
like that of Confucianism as well as Christianity, was created by
his disciples and contained in the Tripitaka. There are no accurate
histories, but it is agreed that Buddha lived the life of a prince,
married and fathered a son before he arrived at his view of Enlightenment (*Bodhi*) and disengagement from the material world. He
is credited with rejecting the excessive ritualistic and metaphysical

bent of Hinduism in favor of the message of loving-kindness and beneficent living.

In important respects, the teachings of Siddhartha were rooted in Hindu values of asceticism and renunciation of the flesh. But Buddha rejected that Brahmanism which he colorfully character- ized as "wriggling like eels," and presented the Enlightenment as a path equally available to rich and poor. He preached and insti- tuted the Four Noble Truths, which deal with the need to recog- nize the ubiquity of pain, and its cause which derives from craving and attachment, as well as the Eightfold Path of Enlightenment that teaches the way out of the maize to the achievement of peace, or *nirvana*.

Buddha also rejected the excessive speculation and class rigid- ity of Hinduism, and derided the emphasis on the role of the supernatural in human affairs. Though Buddha was thought to be the son of God and the redeemer of the world, unlike Christ he was not to be symbolically ingested by the believer with the wafer and the wine, for Buddhism eschewed such materiality; and some Buddhists point out that although Buddha's teachings were com- parable to those of Christ, he was not considered a deity. Bud- dhism also disdained the excessive sensuality and sexuality associ- ated with Hinduism in favor of a strict puritanical and ascetic code. The Buddhist monks, who carried beggars' bowls and main- tained strict conformity to their oaths of poverty and deprivation of the desires of the appetite, spread their message far and wide. Buddhism was integrated into Chinese society by the first cen- tury, and its influence was widespread throughout the orient in such countries as Tibet, Mongolia, Burma, Sri Lanka, Thailand, Cambodia, Laos, Korea, Vietnam, and Japan.

Strikingly, the mystical truths of Buddhism are sources of modern wisdom and knowledge in some areas such as contempo- rary physics. Like Hinduism, Buddhism taught that the universe expresses its perfect rhythms and harmonies thorough the divine dance, and the teacher is the proper recipient of this gift of knowl- edge, which is beyond rational understanding. Gary Zukav, in his fascinating study, *The Dancing Wu Li Masters*, suggests that the ambiguities contained in modern particle physics rather precisely reflect the ancient mystical truths and teaching of Buddhism, which described patterns of organic energy in the universe. As with Shiva's dance in Hinduism, the *Wu Li* masters represented the world as a cosmic dance, a metaphor that captures its rhythms, harmony, and incomprehensibility. *Wu Li*, the Chinese characters for Physics, have five overlapping meanings: one meaning is "patterns of organic energy," a second is "Enlightenment", a third meaning is "I clutch my ideas," a fourth meaning is "my way." and finally there is the profound truth of "nonsense," all of which wittily accord and overlap with the brilliance together with obscurity of our own imperfect understanding of physics.[169]

Buddhism has not created a great body of literature and art, as it has focused on renunciation of the flesh and the world. While the lotus existed wherever Buddha walked, the sculpture and art associated with Buddhism eschewed the erotic aspect of Hindu art. Nevertheless there are famous sculptures particularly in the Mahayana branch in which Buddha is seated cross-legged with a beatific view on his face and a posture of meditation suggesting the power of enlightenment, and even some that represent Buddha in a cosmic embrace, but they are untypical. The art and scripture celebrated the life and teachings of Buddha, as well as the mystical beauty of nature, just as Chinese court painters depicted life of the aristocratic court, but did not particularly celebrate the human male and female form itself. The major tradition of art and literature was court centered, and embodied Confucian as well as Buddhist principles.

CONFUCIANISM

Along with Buddhism, the teachings of Confucius (541-479 B.C.), a contemporary of Siddartha, have existed in tandem in China and other Buddhist nations down to the present day—both as com-

peting and complementary systems of truth. We recall the famous
distinction between the late Chairman Mao Tse-tung (1893-1976)
and his prime minister Chou En-lai (1898-1976) reflecting what
was described as Mao's Buddhist remoteness and aloofness compared to Chou's punctilious civility and Confucian ethical rationalism.

Unlike Prince Buddha who derived from a noble family,
Confucius was brought up in more humble circumstances, the
son of a provincial governor who left the boy fatherless at aged
three. Pursuing the life of a mandarin scholar and civil servant, he
came to a profound understanding of the nature of social organization and the relationship between the ruler and the ruled from his
practical experience. Though repudiated and forced into exile in
his later life for what were thought to be controversial teachings,
his impact after his death was significant. "The Master took four
subjects for his teaching: culture, conduct of affairs, loyalty to su-
periors and the keeping of promises."[170] The essential moral principles contained in the *Analects* have guided the path of China.
Confucius taught the virtues of observance of filial piety, respect
for elders, modesty, seriousness, acceptance of the golden rule, and
service to the truth. He taught that precision in language is not
only an aesthetic ideal, but a moral requisite. "If language is incor-
rect, then what is said does not concord with what was meant; and
if what is said does not concord with what was meant, what is to
be done cannot be effected."[171] The standard of ethics and morality that he established has played a dominant role not only in
China, but throughout the nations of the oriental world until today.

The teachings of Confucius were also contained in parables
evolved from the *Analects*, and sometimes retold in folk literature
where his disciple, Tzu Lu, became his butt. In one such story,
Confucius and Tzu Lu were walking through the hills, and
Confucius directed Tzu Lu to fetch water. Tzu Lu confronted a
tiger near the water and killed it by seizing its tail, which he put in
his pocket, and returned with the water. Then he asked Confucius

how a superior would kill a tiger. Confucius responded: "A superior man would kill a tiger by seizing its head." "And how," Tzu Lu inquired, "would an ordinary man kill a tiger?" "An ordinary man would kill a tiger by seizing its ears," declared the Master. Tzu Lu continued to probe as to how an inferior man would kill a tiger. "An inferior man would kill a tiger by grabbing its tail," responded Confucius. Upset with himself, and the prescience of Confucius, Tzu Lu discarded the tiger's tail and concluded that Confucius had sent him on a mission of death. In revenge, he picked up a stone and placed it in his pocket, intending to use it against the Master. "How would a superior man kill a man?" he asked. Confucius responded: "A superior man would kill a man with his pen." Tzu Lu continued, "and how would an ordinary man kill a man?" "An ordinary man would kill a man with his tongue," responded the Master. Tzu Lu inquired how an inferior man would kill a man. "An inferior man would kill a man with a stone." Impressed by the greatness and wisdom of Confucius, Tzu Lu threw away the stone.[172]

As in Plato's view, literature was subordinated to the ideal of society reflecting an order based on the cardinal teachings of Confucianism; namely that human society is ordered by the same principles as the world of nature. The upper class has the responsibility to set the example, to rule and lead, and the lower class has the obligation to obey and follow—even as in the order of nature, where day follows day, season follows season, rain falls, and crops, plants and trees grow, the snows melts, and the rivers flow into the sea. Confucius warned that when the leaders fail in their obligations, the proper order is upset, nature will force society to correct itself, and the leadership will be overthrown.

While there is no word for poetry in Chinese, there were religious hymns, oral narrative and stories that existed within Confucian teaching. The Chinese language is devoid of articles, pronouns and prepositions and therefore the style typically has been compact and formalistic, and subject to much critical commentary. The third century author Lu Chi described the role of the writer:

Taking his position at the hub of things, the writer
contemplates the mystery of the universe . . .
His spirit gallops to the eight ends of the universe;
his mind wanders along vast distances. In the end,
as his mood dawns clearer and clearer, objects
clean-cut now in outline, shove one another forward.
He sips the essence of letters; he rinses his mouth
with the extract of the Six Arts.[173]

Literature for the most part was diadactic, embodied moral principles, taught virtue and duty. But now and then, it celebrated
universal themes of attraction and love, themes of longing of a
man toward a woman and a woman toward a man, as in an excerpt
from David Hawkes's translation of the classic allegorical poem of
the first century, *Hsiang chün:*

The goddess comes not, she hold back shyly,
Who keeps her delaying within the island,
Lady of the lovely eyes and the winning smile?
Skimming the water in my cassia boat,
I bid the Yüan and Hsiang still their waves
And the Great River make its stream flow softly.
I look for the goddess, but she does not come yet.
Of whom does she think as she plays her reed-pipes? [174]

Hsiao-shuo the word for fiction literally means small talk, and prose
fiction consisted of different forms of chit-chat, including mythology, stories about gods and ghost used interchangeably, parables,
dreams, and dialogues which illustrated Buddhist and Confucian
doctrines. Furthermore, literature was enhanced by beautiful calligraphy, scroll art, and a musical intonation. There was a formal
literary tradition, *Ku Wen*, the courtly style, which was judged by
rhetorical correctness and poetic elegance; and there was the popular
tradition, *Pai Hua*, written in the colloquial style for the larger,
untutored audience.

For example, there is the rather typical, charming "Story of Ying-Ying," composed in the T'ang period (608-917). A virtuous man, a gentleman and a scholar, Chang woos the beautiful Miss Ts'ui. After he expresses his sincere avowal of love to her maid, who is initially shocked by his forwardness, she passes the message on to her mistress. The young people exchange verses, and Miss Ts'ui suggests in a poem, "Bright Moon on the Night of the Fifteenth," that she might be willing to see Chang.

> I await the moon in the western chamber
> Where the breeze comes through the half-opened door.
> Sweeping the wall the flower shadows move;
> I imagine it is my lover who comes.

Seizing the hint, he climbs her bedroom window and, though she puts him off at first, finally he captivates her. Now the obligation of his studies requires that he leave her, and she finds herself abandoned, and suffers the guilt of a jilted lover. Both she and Chang go on with their lives and marry others. Chang on a visit to her town, some time later, begs for a chance to see her. She, however, has not yet forgiven him, and secretly sends him another missive:

> Emaciated, I have lost my looks,
> Tossing and turning, too weary to leave my bed.
> It's not because of others I am ashamed to rise;
> For you I am haggard and before you ashamed.[175]

The story, with its tentative happy ending, is both pleasing and instructive, and warns of the implications of the double standard, for it is easier for a man, than a woman, to break the bonds of romantic love without dire emotional consequences. While serving as a Buddhist or Confucian lesson on the dangers that beset young people, it also celebrates the universal truth of youthful passion. Miss Ts'ui has a child by her present husband whose name is Ying Ying, and she bestows the story's title.

Realistic writing and lyrical poetry were rare but not unknown.

The great Chinese poet Li Po (701-762) served as a court poet also in the T'ang dynasty, followed Taoism, preached Confucian values, but is remembered today as a rebel who, while he enjoyed the favors of many women, and wrote of military victory and the pleasures of the grape, regaled and saluted the lovely, young maidens of Wu in his most memorable lyric. But more typically he celebrated solitude and nature in, for example, "Dialogue in the Mountains":

> You ask me why it is
>   I lodge in sapphire hills;
> I laugh and do not answer—
>   the heart is at peace.
> Peach blossoms and flowing water
>   go off, fading away afar.
> And there is another world
>   that is not of mortal men.[176]

Kuan Han-ching writing plays as well as poetry during the Yüan dynasty (1277-1367), describes with light-hearted lyricism yet Confucian propriety the realistic feelings of a woman receiving advances from an unwanted suitor.

> It was quiet outside the gauze-green window
> And nearby, no one was to be seen;
> He knelt down anxiously—
>   Searching for a kiss.
> "You ingrate," I said, and turned away:
> Even though I scolded him,
> I half resisted—
>   And half yielded.[177]

In another poem, he describes the virtues of the woman whom he is pursuing. Speaking in his own voice, he attempts to persuade his wife, Hung Niang, to allow him to take her as his concubine:

> Her hair is black
> Her cheeks, rosy.
> It's a shame that she is a maid.

> Her manners are those of a girl from a rich family
> And are equal to those of Hung Niang.
> She always has a smile for me and talks elegantly.
> She is like a flower which understands me.
> If I should have her as mine,
> > Will you be jealous?

To which proposal, though acknowledging his free will in such weighty matters, she replies in a poem, reminding him of his aristocratic responsibility and duty:

> I hear you've been casting your eyes on a beauty,
> This is totally unlike King Kuan, your kin and a brave man;
> Should you set up a separate household for her,
> I would be terribly jealous.[178]

Permission denied! Touched by his wife's polite persuasiveness, Kuan Han-ching fulfilled his Confucian responsibility, and purportedly gave up the smiling, dark-haired, flowery beauty.

Later in Chinese literature, during the Ming Dynasty (1368-1644), the voice of romantic feeling was given even greater recognition, as when Feng Meng-long (1574-1646) allowed himself to rhapsodize in defense of the power of love:

> Do not talk idly of romance if you don't know the game;
> a world is hidden there within love's name.
> If one knew all of love that was in love to know,
> the epithet 'romantic' should be no cause for shame.[179]

His contemporary, the playwright T'ang Hsien-tsu (1550-1616) similarly spoke of love's rich rewards of pain:

> Has the world ever seen a woman's love to rival that poor Tu Li-niang? Dreaming of a lover, she fell sick; once sick, she became more deeply attached; and finally after painting her own portrait as a legacy to the world, she died. Dead for three years, still she was able to live again when in the dark

underworld her quest for the object of her dream was fulfilled. To be as Li-niang, is truly to have known love.[180]

Yet she too is permitted love only in a dream, and only in death
can she achieve fulfillment.

In the classic Chinese novel of the eighteenth century, which
has been rendered into a television masterpiece series, *Dream of the
Red Chamber*, the epic life a noble family is presented in its spiritual and realistic dimension, and the claim of love is given some
recognition. The story began eons ago when the goddess undertook to repair the dome of heaven out of a mountain of stone, but
neglected a single stone, which bemoaned its fate and sought counsel
from a Buddhist monk and Taoist priest. After warning of the dire
consequences, they turned the stone into a precious jade so that
the humble stone could learn for itself what life in the human
world would be like.[181] Centuries later, the idealistic hero Pao-yü
(Precious Jade), is born with this precious stone in his mouth.
While he seeks to lead an exemplary life, he is confounded, in a
Confucian parable, by the vanities and corruptions of the world.
The author, a member of an aristocratic Ts'ao family, and the book,
mixing fiction and autobiography, both celebrates and satirizes
the life style of this proud feudal family, symbolized by the red
chamber (with, what, some Chinese scholars have noted, is a sly
pun on a bordello) with its materialism, love of money, greed,
luxury, dogmatism and rigidity. Pao-yü reluctantly goes along with
the standards of the society, even when it denies him the passionate love that he feels for his own love choice, a lady of lower status,
Lin Tai-yü (who dies of rejection and a broken heart). Instead he
marries Hsüeh Pao-ch'ai, whom his family has chosen for him.
The novel ends with the dissolution of the family in a manner of
Buddhist retribution, and hero's escape from this world to the life
and peace of a monk. Here again the moral, Buddhist theme of the
Four Noble Truths is reiterated:

This is a tale of sorrow
And of fantasy;
Our life is but a dream
Laugh not at mortals' folly.[182]

JAPAN

Though living on comparatively small isolated islands like Ireland or Madagascar, which broke off from the Asian mainland at the end of the glacial ice age some fifteen thousand years ago, Japan has made a significant contribution to world culture through the industry and adaptability of its people. Existing within the long shadow of Asia, the Japanese nation has tenaciously protected its independence and developed the code of the Samurai Warrior that would shield it from incursions throughout its history from larger neighbors which sought to annex or dominate.

While jealously guarding their autonomy, the Japanese have remained rather open-minded to foreign influences. During their history, they demonstrated their susceptibility to the great advancements around them from the ancient cultures and religions, as well as ancient and modern art, literature, and architecture. They have shown their ability to adapt and improve whatever they touched with their native genius, from the ideographic Chinese writing system with thousands of characters to a simpler phonetic alphabetic form, to mastery of modern science and technology, modern engineering and electronics, represented for example by the exquisite Japanese automobile. They are masters of modern capitalism and its subtleties, renowned for their management style, which is studied and copied world over. Yet they have grafted capitalism to Confucian principles, and showed a greater sense of community and social responsibility in protecting their citizens from its vagaries in ways that western societies would more usefully emulate rather than ridicule.[183]

The native religion is Shintoism (the Way of the Gods), and its beautiful shrines are symbols of nationalism and reverence for ancestors. The source of power is matriarchal, deriving from the power of the sun goddess, Amaterasu. The omnipotent power of the sun in its purity and eternality gives legitimacy to the Japanese imperial house. The religion also teaches great respect and love of nature, and exists alongside the imported influence of Confucianism and Buddhism from the mainland. The radiant beauty of the islands with their myriad of trees and pacific mountains belies the dangers that they have had to confront not only from the outside, but from such natural disasters as fires that have frequently burned out of control and consumed the buildings made from the beautiful wood that fills the land, as well as incessant earthquake activity.

Zen-Buddhism, which followed the establishment of Buddhism late in the first millennium, reenforces the oriental dichotomy between the material and the non-material world, and points to the path that leads from the material, physical world to negation of passion and self. Zen derives from the word for meditation, in Buddhism, wisdom *Ch'u*, and in Hinduism, *dhyana*. In Zen, the truth is coaxed by challenging the intellect with the aphoristic *koans* that are intended to sharpen the mind to perceive the truth, *dharma*, and lead to *satori*. When the Zen monk asked: "How may I enter the Way?" the Master replied: "Do you hear the sound of the torrent? There you may enter." Another time walking in the mountains, the Master asked: "Do you smell the mountain laurel?" "Yes," replied the monk. "Then I have held nothing back from you," the Master declared. "What is Zen?" the Master is asked. It is passionate wisdom, "Boiling oil over blazing fire."[184]

This sense of detachment and idealization has found its development in an acute sensibility and aesthetic sense, which is the essence of Zen in its representative form in Japan. Zen achieved a distinctly Japanese flavor as a modification of Buddhism and influenced almost every aspect of Japanese life from the simple beauty of flower arrangement and calligraphy to the sword and tea ceremonies, landscape gardening, art and architecture. The Japanese throne room today is minimalist and most elegant, and contains a single chair and table that can serve as a model for any well-designed office in the world.

This controlled simplicity and elegance are found in poetry and literature in, for example, the tradition of Haiku, as in these three typical poems by the eighteenth century poet, Kobayashi Issa (1763-1827):

> Climb Mount Fuji,
> O snail,
> but slowly, slowly.

> All the time I pray to Buddha,
> I keep on
> killing mosquitoes.

> In spring rain
> A pretty girl
> yawning.[185]

As with musical notation, which are mere scrawls to the novice, there is a depth of meaning intended for those who can appreciate and feel it.

Along with Buddhism, the Confucian principles of ethics have been maintained, as on the mainland, with stern authority. There has been an overt denial of the libidinal drive as something unworthy of the upper ruling class, but only appropriate to the common class. Japan shares with other Oriental nations a condescending view toward women. The five infirmities, according to one ancient text, pointed to women's "indocility, discontent, slander, jealousy and silliness—and placed them in a greatly inferior position to men."[186] Nevertheless, of particular note was the participation of women in the act of composing literature, denied them in most other oriental cultures.

In the oldest anthology of Japanese poetry the *Manyōshū* (Collection of Myriad Leaves) in the eighth century, a poem by Lady Kasa reflects her feelings of love:

In the loneliness of my heart
I feel as if I should perish
Like the pale dewdrop
Upon the grass of my garden
In the gathering shades of twilight.

It has been suggested that her poem is answered by the poet Otomo Yakamochi, who was perhaps her friend and shared her grief:

Rather than that I should thus pine for you,
Would I had been transmuted
Into a tree or a stone,
Nevermore to feel the pangs of love.[187]

Sei Shonagon, a contemporary of Lady Murasaki, also achieved a reputation in letters. Very little is known of her life, and her work *The Pillow Book* survives from a manuscript published five hundred years after her death. A lady-in-waiting to the Empress Sadako, Madame Shonagon recorded her notes of observations on the Heian court hierarchy in the last decade of the tenth century. An astute observer and author, she looks forward to such essayists as Francis Bacon, Michel de Montaigne and Henry David Thoreau, who also recorded their pithy yet assiduous observations. She has provided a memorable account of the stiff formality and restricted life in the court at Kyoto, from which she sought relief in her notes and diary. With proper modesty, she terms her observations—contained in an elegant scroll with delicate art work—stuffing for the padding of a pillow.

Yet she offers accurate descriptions of the dress and habits of the court, as well as her own prejudices and dislikes. "When I make myself imagine what it is like to be one of those women who live at home, faithfully serving their husbands—women who have not a single exciting prospect in life yet who believe that they are perfectly happy—I am filled with scorn."[188] She records her thoughts and prejudices, which include a fondness for sparrows, horses, and plum blossoms. She disdains the lower classes, distrusts men, favors page boys with long hair, and muses that preachers would be more effective if they were handsome, and she doesn't like to see people yawn. Once when she had been away for two days, the Empress expressed a sorrow at her departure, and Madame Shonagon responded with a poem of her own:

> How sadly have I viewed those long spring days
> From my poor dwelling-place,
> When even one who lives above the clouds
> Has found them hard to bear!

However she receives her comeuppance from the Empress for perhaps exceeding the boundaries of her position by addressing her so directly. "I did not like your poem, and my ladies also criticized it severely."[189] In like manner, her contemporary, Lady Murasaki in her diary also ridiculed her "most extraordinary air of self-satisfaction," and found "those Chinese writings of hers that she so presumptuously scatters about the place . . . full of imperfections."[190]

Lady Murasaki herself was certainly among the greatest literary artists in Japan's history, as well as one of the greatest authors of the Middle Ages. Her father held high office and pursued a life of letters, but chose early retirement from the world in order to take vows as a Buddhist priest. She herself married a military man and had two daughters, one of whom also pursued letters. Widowed at twenty six, she became a lady-in-waiting in the very formal court of Emperor Akiko, a girl of merely sixteen years old. Her *The Tale of Genji* was the major prose work of the Heian period (795-1185). Using her own persona, she wrote what is thought to be an autobiographical novel with the admixture of fiction and truth which provides a graphic record of life in the Japanese court with its "depravity and decorum," reflecting both the values and the moral laxity of that society.

The hero of the novel, Lord Genji, the shining one, is an illicit son of the emperor, who loves his father with great loyalty and sees his daughter in turn become the empress. He is no stranger to courtly amours, and he neglects his spouse (*kita no kata*) Nyosan, who is his niece (daughter to his half brother, the former Emperor, Suzaku). She in turn becomes susceptible to the attentions paid to her by the courtier Kashiwagi, who visits her alone in her bedroom, in order to declare his affection, and then falls asleep in her bed. After spending such an evening alone with him, Princess Nyosan is filled with shame:

> There is in many high-born women an abundance of natural appetite that the good manners instilled in them since childhood render invisible to the common eye. But upon the mildest provocation this tendency will manifest itself in most surprising ways. With Nyosan, however, this was not the case. Her innocence was every bit as great as it seemed. The experiences of that fatal night had left in her mind no impression but that of the most abject terror. She could not convince herself that all was safely over, and hardy daring to appear even among her own people, she spent week after week in the darkness of the back rooom. She felt that something was wrong with her, and at last unaided by any outside person, she realized what was amiss.[191]

Ultimately she has no choice but to retire from the world and take the vows of a nun, with Genji's acquiescence and approval. Similarly Lady Murasaki, adopted by Prince Genji as a young maiden in life as in the novel and who later became his confidante and lowly second wife, was no stranger to the pangs of "despised love." Lady Murasaki recounts the story of their relationship and value of this bond of friendship, and particularly shows her ability to weave together a narrative that provides an inquiry into the marriage question, and the plight of women of the time, which doesn't end with her death as the novel proceeds even beyond.

Once again, the conflict between worldliness and Buddhist aloofness underlies this epic story, and passionately represents the view that inappropriate actions are destined to be punished by unseen powers—"the fruit of *karma* or the punishment of present crimes [follows] lest we should doubt if Gods and Buddhas can indeed make manifest their will."[192] This medieval romance pre-dated the literary tradition and themes for the next thousand years, from Chaucer's depiction of the idealized life in the court society of England in the fourteenth century to Shakespeare's and later Dostoyevsky's profound rendition of human nature, to the auto-biographical style of Marcel Proust, the subtle literary skill and erudition of James Joyce and the representation of women's issues of Simone de Beauvoir.

As Japanese literature evolved into the Kabuki and the No drama, it reflected the same principles of the conflict in human nature between obedience to authority and human desire. For ex-ample, in the No play *Kurozuka*, a monk visits the moor of Adachi and requests lodging from a woman. She agrees to let him stay in her home, but instructs him not to look into her bedroom. When she leaves, the monk struck by curiosity looks into the bedroom, and discovers a carnage of corpses and blood. He seeks to escape, but now the witch pursues him as a fury, until only the power of his prayers frees him from her grip. This story reflects an older fairy tale, "The Bush Warbler's Home," where a woodcutter walk-ing in the forest comes across a mansion which he enters. He is asked by the beautiful patroness to watch over the abode while she goes away on errands, and she admonishes him not to look into the adjoining rooms. After the lady leaves, the woodcutter looks around the house and discovers three pretty girls who glide away when he approaches. He visits other rooms and sees great trea-sures, including a bird's nest with three eggs. When he acciden-tally drops the nest, the three eggs hatch into three birds that fly away. The lady returns to criticize the woodcutter for the havoc he has wrought on her daughters, and she too is transformed into a bush warbler and flies away. The mansion then disappears, and the woodcutter is left standing alone in the forest. It is a clear Buddhist, Confucian parable about the danger of entering a lady's forbidden, closed chambers.

Finally, the Japanese also instituted the unique concept of the Geisha, a distinctive Japanese creation, a lady of entertainment

immaculately coiffed and dressed, and versed in the arts of providing both intellectual and spiritual pleasures.[193] A recent photo
spread in a popular magazine showed a notable variation on the
lady of entertainment, lying supine on a dining room table, stark
naked amidst a party of male adult Japanese revelers who benignly
ate their sushi with chopsticks off her pleasing palette.

ISLAM

Islam was the religion created by the prophet Muhammad (570-
632) in the seventh century, which in less than a decade captured
the Arabian peninsula, as well as Egypt, Syria, Persia, Damascus,
Antioch, Jerusalem, and within a century reached from the walls
of Constantinople in Turkey to the Barbary coast and Iberian peninsula; and over a thousand years would stretch from the Pillars of
Hercules to the suburbs of Vienna, the Balkans, Constantinople,
Afghanistan, India, the Indonesian islands and Malaysia, encom-
passing an empire greater than that ruled by Cyrus the Great,
Alexander the Great, the Roman Empire, Genghis Khan, Attila
the Hun, the Holy Roman Empire, the British Empire, or Napoleon. Its legacy has been a significant body of religious and mystical work, advances in medicine, in mathematics, including the
Arabic numeral system that made possible computation which
would have been impossible with mere Roman numerals, the development of textiles and pottery, and an advanced mercantile,
commercial network. There was an important literary tradition as
well as unique architecture and stunning Mosaic art. Mosques and
palaces in the various countries in which Islam took hold, the
Kaabah at Mecca, the Dome of the Rock in Jerusalem, the Alhambra
in Spain, and the Taj Mahal in India are a few of its outstanding
architectural masterpieces.

The followers of Islam, the faithful Muslims who "submitted"
to Allah, succeeded in transmitting the prophecy and message by
persuasion—but mainly by the sword. Claiming ancestral descent

from Abraham, the father of Judaism, and maintaining the blessedness of Jesus while rejecting his ascension from the dead, Islam taught that Allah took Jesus onto himself as a great human being and prophet like Muhammad. The Prophet, or Messenger of God, derived much of his teaching from the other Semitic religions, and Islam was perceived by his followers as inheriting the mantle of Judaism and Christianity. But in fact the struggle between Islam and its confederate religions was an intense and competitive one for more than a millennium.

While there was no single country or city that defined Islam as Rome defined Christianity, and Jerusalem was the cynosure of Judaism, a center developed and thrived wherever Islam took hold and, with its great military and administrative organization and religious energy, transmitted its values and teachings. Throughout the middle ages, Islam hung like the sword of Damocles over Europe; Muslims decried Christians and Jews as infidels and idolaters, and Christians debased Islam as a "fardel of blasphemies" and a "gallimaufry of errors." It has been averred that "Islamic institutions of polygamy and divorce, as well as certain religious motifs such as Paradise, were insistently interpreted by Christian polemicists as incontrovertible proof that Islam is a sensuous religion which grants its adherents boundless sexual license . . . and that it is therefore a false faith."[194] Edward Said observed in his book, *Orientalism*: "Not for nothing did Islam come to symbolize terror, devastation, the demonic, hordes of hated barbarians. For Europe, Islam was a lasting trauma. Until the end of the seventeenth century, the 'Ottoman Peril' lurked alongside Europe to represent for the whole of Christian civilization a constant danger, and in time European civilization incorporated that peril and its lore, its great events, figures, virtues, and vices, as something woven into the fabric of life."[195] At the same time, the value of economic relations between the great powers of the world was a strong bond of peace that existed and has persevered till this day.

The *Koran* was the sacred text of Islam, which set down the teachings of Muhammad as related to him by the angel Gabriel.

"No, your compatriot is not mad. He saw him on the clear horizon. He does not grudge the secrets of the unseen; nor is this the utterance of an accursed devil."[196] The writing is passionate and filled with exhortation about the Mercy and Compassion of Allah to the faithful, and the death and destruction that will befall the faithless. "On the day of Judgement, the heavens shall become like molten brass and the mountains like tufts of wool scattered in the wind. Friends will meet, but shall not speak to each other. To redeem himself from the torment of that day, the sinner will gladly sacrifice his children, his wife, his brother, the kinfolk who gave him shelter, and all the people of the earth, if then this might deliver him. But the fire of Hell shall drag him down by the scalp, shall claim him who had turned his back on the true faith and amassed riches and covetously hoarded them."[197]

Islam preached submission to a paternalistic Allah, a militant if not vengeful deity, unlike the pacific, oriental religious leaders. Muhammad was a practical man of affairs who understood business and the law and, to his followers, lived a life of piety and purity. Perhaps when he was a camel driver of twenty five years old, he married the twice-widowed Khadija, the love of his life who was some fifteen years his senior, and took control of her affairs. Theirs was a marriage of love, friendship and respect, as their businesses prospered; and to her he confided his visions, which she encouraged, and indeed she was an early convert, along with his adopted son, Ali. He remained faithful to her for the whole of their twenty six year marriage. Their only surviving child, their daughter Fatima, married Ali, from whom the dynasty of the Shiite branch of Islam has descended.

After escaping his enemies who planned to murder him in Mecca, he made his historic *hegira* to Medina in 622, where he was embraced as a prophet, military strategist, general, and law giver. After the death of Khadija when he was fifty one, Muhammad took for himself several concubines in addition to eleven wives, including the beautiful, young Jewish princess, Safiya, after he slew her husband Kinana ibn al-Rabi, the prince of Khaybar, and despoiled and looted the kingdom. He died at the age sixty two, a revered and all-powerful leader.

Muhammad was an ambitious man and exemplary hero who had many facets. He empowered the inhabitants of the Arabian deserts with his rhetoric and passionate mission to them, converting slaves into loyal soldiers, who together spread the word and the faith of Allah. Muhammad not only combined the prophetic and leadership qualities of Moses and Jesus, but also the military and political savvy of Alexander, Julius Caesar and Augustus Caesar. His teachings were full of moral firmness, but there also was a fanaticism contained in the instruction to spread the word of Allah to the heathen wherever he resided. As Jesus came bearing a sword, so Islam taught that "Paradise lies beneath the shadow of your swords."

The Koran was a great literary text written with energy and passion in the Arabesque style by Muhammad on everything from parchment to palm leaves over the last twenty three years of his life, and collated after his death into a 114 disjointed suras (chapters). Its teaching not only encouraged literacy among its followers hundreds of years before the Reformation, but it gave world status to the evolving Arabic language, transmitted in the beautiful Arabic script and accompanied by chant that captivated the listeners. Muslims were required to accept their individual responsibility to fulfill word of Allah as represented by the Five Pillars of Islam; these included accepting Allah, fulfilling the duty of prayer, fasting during the month of Ramadan, giving alms to the poor, and making at least one pilgrimage to Mecca.

There was no intermediary between Allah and the faithful who could pray directly to him. Comparing the Koran to other ancient scriptures, Michael Cook has noted: "There were four Vedas—each transmitted in different Brahmin lineages—together with a mass of associated material that would be included on a broad definition of the canon. There were two Homeric epics . . . transmitted in the same lineage . . . When the Biblical canon was eventually settled, there were thirty-nine books of the Old Testament

and twenty-seven of the New; there was also a great deal of apocry-
phal material which appeared in some people's Bibles but not in
others. There was enough of Buddhist Tripitaka to take up 130,000
blocks when the Chinese printed a translation of it in the late
tenth century; today the Pali canon fills several shelves in a library.
In Confucian China, there were differing views as to the exact number and identity of the classics. The Koran, in contrast to all this,
is a single book of well-defined content between two covers." [198]

Though it preached a severe morality, Islam also had a strong
sexual undertone to it, distinguishing it from Christianity and
those religions of the Orient that taught the forswearing of earthly
pleasures for the spiritual rewards of the afterlife, and encouraged
celibacy. Even more affirmatively than Judaism, Islam upheld the
duty of a man to marry. Muhammad set one example by remaining faithful to one woman for most of his life and another, in his
later years, when he engaged in polygamy, sanctioned by Muslim
law. The Eden of Islam, the resurrection after death to which every
follower was entitled, decreed the resurrection of the body no less
than the soul for an absolute fulfillment of physical desire. Unlike
the ascetic ideal associated with Christian conception of heaven,
Islamic paradise was one place in which every fantasy and sensual
pleasure could be indulged by men.

In the sublunary world though, sexual relations were strictly
interdicted before marriage, and women were enjoined to observe
modesty and preserve their virginity for their husbands. They were
not encouraged to seek education or work, and were precluded
from holding public office or leadership roles. Rather they were
trained in the arts of serving their husbands; for a woman was
assured of Paradise "if her husband is pleased with her." Islamic
law offered women protection in marriage, including equal rights
to sue for divorce, and the right to inherit. But while a woman
could only have one husband at a time, a man could possess even
a thousand wives, if he could afford to keep them. Women were
given as child brides and sold as concubines, and there was an
important slave trade in women, along with other commerce. The

punishment for either an adulterer or an adulteress was the same and harsh, a hundred stripes with the lash.

The Caliphs and Sultans who had extended the realms of Islam reaped, as their reward, pleasure domes and harems, and Islam gained a reputation for voluptuousness and gross sexual exploitation. The slave trade and bacchanal entertainments performed in palaces before the Sultans, and even for the crowd, created in the western mind both a jaundiced and fantasy view of Islam. European travelers were eager to discover the extravagances of eroticism practiced in the Islamic east and duly returned with purloined art work and stories. Gustave Flaubert, writing of his travels to the Middle East in the nineteenth century, commented: "The oriental woman is a machine and nothing more; she does not differentiate between one man and another. Smoking, going to the baths, painting her eyelids, and drinking coffee, such is the circle of occupations around her existence. It is we who think of her, but she hardly thinks of us."[199]

In the literature as well, there appeared a frankness about sex that would not occur in European literature for many centuries. The romance and love of King Solomon and the Queen of Sheba were woven into their great tapestries and art, and integrated into the literature. Certainly its greatest literary achievement was the *Arabian Nights, or The Thousand and One Nights*. The stories, which represented a great anthology of world literature and drew from the diverse lands of the Islamic world, were transmitted orally for hundreds of years and consigned to print only in the eighteenth century.

These fantastic stories—like all great literature—showed the subtle and profound intearaction between the role of fate and character in life; they described the elevation of poor orphans and hard working people through the virtue of effort and faith, the power of the jinn, the power of love, the power of the dream, the power of Allah. They were edifying and instructive, offering practical wisdom about a range of matters including the rules of conduct and behavior, the ways of the world, and the path to happiness and heaven. The stories were set not only in palaces but in bazaars, on the seas, in forests, and included a complete class of characters ranging from kings, emirs, and caliphs to eunuchs, dervishes, druggists, weavers, carpet makers, hunchbacks, mermaids, bakers, merchants, rabbit catchers, cooks, dyers, chamberlains, slave girls, and fishermen. While there were both treacherous and virtuous characters, poetic justice and virtue always prevailed at the end of the tale.

They embodied the best qualities of humanism and the teachings of Islam, including a surprising tolerance toward other cultures and religions within the Islamic pale. There were beast fables and erotic tales as well, but mostly the stories celebrate the virtues of faith, humility, diligence, kindness, hard work, charity, love and, above all, fidelity to Allah. Perhaps most characteristically, the stories fostered the Islamic attitude toward relations between men and women, husbands and wives and their children, and spawned fairy tales and adventure stories that have found their place in world literature in diverse sources from Chaucer and Boccaccio to Shakespeare, the Brothers Grimm, Hans Christian Andersen, and a myriad of Disney animations, including the recent, popular *The Lion King*.

The Thousand and One Nights begins with the tale of the mighty King Shahryar of the lands of China and India who discovered the infidelity of his wife and became disillusioned with marriage and women. His experience mirrored that of his brother Shah Zaman, who also discovered upon his taking leave, that his wife was involved in improper relations with his blackamoor servant. Through his disappointment and disillusionment, King Shahryar foreswore any permanent bond with a wife, and decided that he would enjoy a woman for an evening, to be followed by her execution the following dawn (before she could betray him). Now there was this maiden Scheherazade, the daughter of the Vizier whose responsibility was to execute the sentences on the maidens, and she decided to take upon herself the task of saving the daughters of Islam

from the cruel fate of this unhappy king. She pleaded with her
father to give his permission for her to attend King Shahryar.

> "Oh Allah!" he cried in his fury. "Have you lost your mind?
> I won't let you expose yourself to such danger. How can you
> be so unwise and foolish? I want you to know that unless
> you have experience in worldly matters, you'll be prey to
> misfortune." "I must do this," she responded. "Come what
> may!"[200]

Insistent on getting her way, the maiden, who was wise, well versed
in science and poetry, and a proper and comely court lady, was
betrothed to the melancholy king; and using her mother wit, she
managed to survive the fatal sentence by weaving together these
wondrous stories, and leaving him hungry for more each dawn.

She related the stories of poor Ali Babba, who uncovered the
magical words to a kingdom of riches, "Open sesame!" and was
granted the wealth stolen by the forty thieves, and the amazing
voyages of Sinbad the Seaman, who traveled the empire in search
of experience and recounted his diverse adventures. Then there
was the most marvelous story of Aladdin and his magic lantern.
The poor orphan son of a tailor, deprived of his father like
Muhammad himself, was able to enlist the power of the jinn and
the gifts of his own diligence. When he first saw the beautiful
princess, Lady Badar al-Budur, he aspired to marry her. His mother
cautioned him about his ambition to marry the royal princess, but
he insisted that his mother represent his request.

And Scheherazade noticed that the dawn was approaching and
ceased telling her story. When the next night arrived, however, she
acceded to the king's desire to hear the continuation of the tale.
The story was stretched over more than a fortnight, and she related how Aladdin's mother presented her son's suit, and ultimately
how the boy was given the opportunity to rise above his station
and achieve all the goals of his dreams. When he finally married
Lady Badar al-Budur, he proved worthy of her love, not only by
his gallantry, good looks, generosity, and military prowess, but

also by enlisting his jinn to secure him the most beautiful jewels and the most beautiful palace for his wife and the king, his father in law. Then the wicked, envious sorcerer conspired to steal his magic lantern by manipulating Lady Badar al-Budur, and then abducting her. Aladdin left no stone unturned in his effort to rescue her and subdue the villain and regain the copper lantern, his wife, and his rightful possessions; and in time, he even became king. Hard work and faith will secure for any man the blessings of Allah.

Another edifying story was that of the shrewish princess Al-Datma whose beauty and high station brought many suitors to her, but it was bruited abroad that she would marry no man unless he could defeat her in a medieval joust, cheek by jowl. Moreover, if the man were overcome, the penalty would be that he would be branded on his head with a crude inscription that he had been mastered. Now Prince Behram ibn Taji, son of the king of Persia, was determined to win the beautiful princess for himself, and agreed to confront her in a joust. But during the battle, she confounded him by removing her visor and showing her face, which so captivated him that he was defeated and had to submit to being branded. But his determination did not forsake him, and he returned disguised as an old man, and connived to trick her into believing that if she married him, he would divorce her immediately after he had bestowed upon her a great treasury of jewels. Once married, he revealed himself to her as the young prince who had undertaken these labors to earn her love. She, like Petruchio's Kate, was pleased to have been so tamed.

Scheherazade thus never completed any story through the night until the dawn rose, and the king bewitched by this woman, in this allegory of marriage, came to appreciate his wife, and stayed his sentence for the length of a thousand and one nights of her tales. At the end of three years, she surprised him by presenting to him the three sons whom he had sired and she had sequestered. His heart melted, and his misogyny was cured. Touched by this love, he now married her in a royal wedding, and even persuaded his brother to overcome his disillusionment with women too, by marrying her sister, Dunazade, which he did. "Thereafter, Scheherazade went to King Shahryar and Dunazade to King Shah Zaman and each king enjoyed the company of his beloved consort, and the hearts of the people were comforted."[201] Next, the king took it upon himself to publish the thirty volumes of her stories as the reward for her fidelity and love.

In the nineteenth century, Edward Fitzgerald translated the *Rubaiyyat* by the Persian scientist and poet of the twelfth century, Omar Khayaam. The original collection was addressed to a court audience rather than to the popular, mass audience of *The Arabian Nights*. The poems are the work of a court scholar who defines his profession as a tentmaker and celebrates the issues that all poetry has revered, the conflict between youth and age, optimism and pessimism, memory and desire, time and eternity:

> The Moving Finger writes, and having writ,
> Moves on: nor all your Piety not Wit
> Shall lure it back to cancel half a Line,
> Nor all your Tears wash out a Word of it. (LXXVI)

The work reflects the sensibility of the middle years of Khayaam (and Fitzgerald) with its admixture of disappointment and wisdom, as it explores the contradictions that literature can represent between faith and doubt, pleasure and sorrow, science and poetry, blasphemy and mysticism, truth and illusion, life and death:

> Ah, fill the Cup—what boots it to repeat
> How Time is slipping underneath our Feet?
> Unborn Tomorrow and dead Yesterday,
> Why fret about them if Today be sweet! (XXXVII)

According to the legend, the poet was the victim of a unfulfilled love for a lady of the court, Halima Begum, whose father had promised her to another in infancy.[202] The poem touched the modern consciousness with its acute intelligence and celebration of love, and represented an aspect of Orientalism that was quite attractive—an appreciation of life and love, together with lack of reserve, which proved to many a refreshing change from the prevailing Victorian morality. It brought about a revival of Orientalism in the western world, and contributed, in an important manner, to shaping the modern sensibility:

> Ah my Belovéd, fill the Cup that clears
> Today of past Regret and Future Fears:
> Tomorrow! Why, Tomorrow I may be
> Myself with Yesterday's sev'n thousand Years. (XXI)

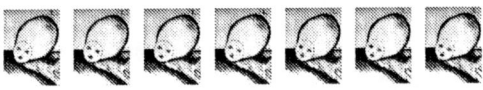

WAITING FOR GODIVA

The worship of God is: honoring his gifts in other men, each according to his genius, and loving the greatest men best: those who envy or calumniate great men hate God; for there is no other God.
William Blake

No man is an Island, entire of itself . . . Any man's death diminishes me because I am involved in mankind. And therefore never send to know for whom the Bell tolls; it tolls for thee.
John Donne

It is doubtful whether men were in general happier at a time when religious doctrines held unlimited sway than they are now; more moral they certainly were not.
Sigmund Freud

No civilization can be perfect until exact equality between men and women is included.
Mark Twain

At century's end, feminists can no longer say of consumer culture with such ringing confidence that "what it does to everyone, it does to women even more." The commercialized, ornamental "femininity" that the women's movement diagnosed now has men by the throat. Men and women both feel cheated of lives in which they might have contributed to a social world; men and women both feel pushed

into roles that are about little more than displaying prettiness or prowess in the marketplace.
Susan Faludi

THE INFORMATION AGE OF COMPUTERS AND TECHNOLOGY • ARMAGEDDON/CHAOS • AN ANATOMIE OF THE WORLD • RELIGION AND SCIENCE • ROMANCE AND PORNOGRAPHY • HUMANAE VITAE • THE DECLINE OF THE WEST • THE NEW PHILOSOPHY CALLS ALL IN DOUBT • THE NEW COCKS OF THE WALK • WHAT GOES AROUND COMES AROUND • THREE HAPPY ENDINGS • LADY GODIVA

THE INFORMATION AGE OF COMPUTERS AND TECHNOLOGY

The Y2K virus came and went, and essentially proved a dud. But perhaps not so with the "love bug virus," the theme of this book, which has proven its memorable potency as the herald of the new century, the information age of computers and technology. President Kennedy ushered in the New Frontier, and enunciated his noble ideal for the Boomer generation and America in his Inaugural Address in 1961: "I do not believe that any one of us would exchange places with any other people or any other generation." And then in his Second State of the Union in 1963: "And while no nation has ever faced such a challenge, no nation has been so ready to seize the burden and glory of freedom."[203]

ARMAGEDDON/CHAOS

Science continues to achieve its greatest feats of knowledge in history—sending spaceships to Mars and far into our solar system and beyond, creating far-reaching new technologies and products, extending mortality, improving food production, conquering disease, probing and exploring the ultimate truths of the physical, chemical and biological sciences, lowering the levels of poverty and raising the standard of living. Yet poverty, disease, and suffering persist; and indeed the path to destruction occurs with the same speed as our spaceship earth makes its way within our galaxy to its inevitable rendezvous with the hereafter in time and space—and perhaps to inevitable demise. Nature seemingly maintains its ultimate, perfect control over man—freedom being like the quest of Tantalus in the Greek myth, to drink the water ever receding beyond his palate, and to enjoy the fruit ever beyond his grasp. The medieval construct of a Faustian pact with the Devil, in which the rewards of success in this life must be paid for in an eternity of damnation, and the Enlightenment notion of man, as a well-functioning machine like a clock or an engine, have been overwhelmed by the explosion of knowledge, in this, the information age—as we define ourselves with a computer chip capable of processing vast sums of information—the beneficiaries of intellectual contributions from Plato and Gutenberg to Galileo, Newton, Darwin, Einstein, McLuhan, and the breathtaking advances of science in our time.

AN ANATOMIE OF THE WORLD

In respect of these new frontiers, our time perhaps is not unlike the seventeenth century when the convergence of the Renaissance, Reformation and Scientific revolutions first unleashed the great energies of the modern world, and set us on the course of possibilities that we are now reaping. "I am a little world made cunningly," wrote the poet and Christian Humanist John Donne, in describing the complexity of the human being. Shakespeare similarly expressed mixed feelings about human potential: "What a piece of work is a man, how noble in reason, how infinite in faculties, in form and moving how express and admirable, in action how like an angel, in apprehension how like a god! the beauty of the world!

the paragon of animals! and yet to me what is this quintessence of dust?" Both Donne and Shakespeare, like Leonardo da Vinci, were masters of all the knowledge of their time—hence they were Renaissance Men. At the same time, they were doubtful and disturbed by fear of the unknown, and expressed ambivalence about the impact of change, as in Donne's *An Anatomie of the World*:

> And new Philosophy calls in in doubt,
> The element of fire is quite put out;
> The Sun is lost, and th' Earth, and no man's wit
> Can well direct him where to look for it.
> And freely men confess that this world's spent,
> Where in the Planets and the Firmament
> They seek so many new; then see that this
> Is crumbled out again to his Atomies.
> Tis all in pieces, all coherence gone.
> All just supply and all relation.
> Prince, subject, father, son are things forgot,
> For every man alone thinks he hath got
> To be a Phoenix, and that then can be
> None of that kind, of which he is, but he.
> This is the world's condition now.[204]

George Herbert (1593-1633), like Donne a poet and an Anglican minister, also was cognizant of the new philosophy, and sought to incorporate it into his writing. In his classic poem, "The Pulley," published in an anthology called *The Temple*, he showed prescience as well as metaphysical wit in suggesting that science would not be a barrier to worship and faith, but a pulley, using the notion of the interaction of mechanical forces and energy, in the leverage used by God to pull and draw man to his ways:

> When God at first made man,
> Having a glass of blessings standing by,
> "Let us," said He, "pour on him all we can;
> Let the world's riches, which dispersed lie,
> Contract into a span."

And so God endowed man with Strength, then Beauty, Wisdom, Honor, and Pleasure:

> When almost all was out, God made a stay,
> Perceiving that, alone of all His treasure,
> Rest in the bottom lay.

He then decided to withold rest from man, and rationalized his decision:

> "For if I should," said He,
> "Bestow this jewel also on My creature,
> He would adore My gifts instead of Me,
> And rest in Nature, not the God of Nature:
> So both should losers be."

And he concluded with a dark pun:

> "Yet let him keep the rest,
> But keep them with repining restlessness;
> Let him be rich and weary, that at least,
> If goodness lead him not, yet weariness
> May toss him to My breast."[205]

Like Donne, Herbert was writing as a humanist, possessing what T.S. Eliot aptly termed "a unified sensibility," versed in science as well as in letters and religion, and able to embrace these ambiguities along with his faith. This was a time in which the notion of scientific progress did not yet exist, and the word "progress" had no other meaning than travel such as a royal journey rather than a reflection on an imaginable future, the *sine qua non* of our philosophy of science; for us, a future that we believe will be better and offer marked improvement to our lives through increased mortality and eradication of devastating diseases.

RELIGION AND SCIENCE

Those ancient adversaries, religion and science—faith and reason, continue to play a warring role for the love of man, as the twin brothers Jacob and Esau fought for dominance, even in Rebecca's womb. Religion asserts its dominant claim for the soul, and offers the consolation of inner harmony for acceptance of the order of things; while science promises its glittering rewards in the here and now: shopping malls and fancy cars, high definition television, compact disc players and improved plumbing and energy resources.

Religion is perhaps the most conservative force in our society—and questions the impetus for change. If things do not change, then they cannot get worse, and the end can be postponed. The modern preachers, like those prophets of old, speak out against "whoring" with other gods, which is a pointed reference to the twin faults of science—its offering of alternative gods and its gainsaying those types of sexual restrictions that have proven to be the building blocks of our culture.

The role of love and sex is very much in the forefront of contemporary life—as has been the case from Biblical times—with television playing a critical role in the dissemination of information. The ever-growing influence of cable television and the internet provides a ubiquitous forum for all points of view. The Supreme Court has recognized the rights of the channels devoted to Epicurean and hedonistic fantasies if not lifestyles to maintain their access to the viewing public. Thus, Christian ministries offer their messages just one touch away from ladies frolicking in tight-fitting wet suits and male and female strip shows accompanied to choral applause. Then there is omnipresent love making represented on screen and explicit language almost everywhere on television except perhaps for the Disney Channel and Wall Street Week.

Will hedonism or piety finally gain the hearts and minds of the present and immediate future society? In the startling image in *Revelations*, the end of the world, Armageddon, is the reign of the whore of Babylon, who takes men into her grip and deprives them of their vitality.

ROMANCE AND PORNOGRAPHY

Romance and pornography are two popular forms of escapist entertainment that tantalize and titillate with pleasing fantasies. The first romantic movie with Rudoph Valentino was based on E.M. Hull's pornographic novel *The Sheik*, and it was not the first time that romance and pornography were intertwined; for, as Irvin Schick has pointed out, "the distinction is admittedly fuzzy."[206] The definitions have been undergoing changes in the last seventy years, since the ban on James Joyce's *Ulysees* was lifted by Judge John M. Woolsey in 1933. A modern conservative critic, Robert Grant, protests that "pornography effectively legitimizes lust, by freeing it from moral scruple," and argues for a return to censorship: "Not to repress pornography is to connive at the degradation of love; it is to unhinge a culture and a whole much deeper conception of the personal than any known to liberalism."[207] Others argue that pornography like sex is a matter of working out power relationships. Jane Miller has compared the genres of Romance and Pornography and assessed their differing, yet comparable appeals to men and women:

> Romance .. has in common with pornography the facelessness of the sexual partner, the infinitely generalizable lover, divested of the particular and the real. Different organs of the body are employed for "knowing" that partner: the heart in the first, the genitals in the second. Yet the fantasies they spell out are finally quite different. . . . Romance soothes women and mediates for them the painful ambivalence they internalize about men's power over them in the world by proposing to reduce men to their level, inducing dependence in a man on a woman, a dependence viewed by other men as groveling and abject. Pornography, on the other hand, reasserts for men images of conquest and control, desperate consolation for childhood losses and adult defeats.[208]

Not only pornography, but also libertinism and recreational sex are the vogue of the moment. Sex sells not only from *Baywatch* to *Sex and the City*, but in fashion and advertising. One need only visit any major city in the world and witness the same underground attractions. While the crisis of the AIDS virus is influencing attitudes and behavior—and abstention and caution are the order of the day—the danger of epidemic through the transmission of a virus through sexual contact remains a frightening concern, particularly in the homosexual community. If, as the men of the cloth have maintained through the centuries, God had been interested in enforcing morality, then it could well be accomplished through control of the sexual drive. The fear of transmission of disease though sex is the greatest curb on relations since St. Paul uttered the strictures of Christianity on the pain of loss of heaven, and St. Augustine admonished "switching off the itch of lust." While skeptics remain unconvinced about the activities of viruses according to a divine plan of Nature, the actual dangers represent a powerful curb on behavior and standards of conduct.

HUMANAE VITAE

Pope Paul VI, in his 1968 Encyclical *Humanae Vitae*, blamed the media and technology for weakening the family bond and destroying values which are antithetical to man's spiritual perfection. "Everything in the modern media of social communications which leads to sense excitation and unbridled customs, as well as every form of pornographic and licentious performance, must arouse the frank and unanimous reaction of all those who are solicitous for the progress of civilization and the defense of the supreme good of the human spirit."[209] He affirmed the unambiguous dignity of the marriage bond.

> Marriage is not, then, the effect of chance or the product of evolution or unconscious natural forces; it is the wise institution of the Creator to realize in mankind his design of

love. By means of reciprocal personal gift of self, proper and
exclusive to them, husband and wife tend toward the communion of their beings in view of mutual personal perfection, to collaborate with God in the generation and education of new lives.

He further argued that the use of technology (contraception) has
vitiated the sanctity of the family by placing pleasure in marriage
before responsibility.

The Church, calling men back to the observance of the
norms of the natural law, as interpreted by her constant
doctrine, teaches that each and every marriage act (*"quilibet
matrimonii usus"*) must remain open to the transmission of
life. In defending conjugal morals in their integral whole-
ness, the Church knows that she contributes toward the
establishment of a truly human civilization; she engages
man not to abdicate from his own responsibility in order to
rely on technical means; by that very fact, she defends the
dignity of man and wife.[210]

While maintaining his leadership of the Church of Rome, Pope
John Paul II has perhaps shown himself more conciliatory toward
technology. Though rigorously opposed to any rationalization of
birth control, he has, for example, defended modern physics, as-
serting the admissibility of the Big Bang Theory with Christian
doctrine, while insisting that what happened before the Big Bang
belongs to the domain of religion.[211] Though opposing elevation
of women to priestly roles, he defends, in the year 2000, organ
transplants as an aid to human betterment, but not cloning as a
technological effort at reproduction that displays interference with
the divine plan.

Absent great spiritual direction, the legacy of the humanities
in the twentieth century has been that of perpetuating much doubt,
disillusionment, and despair. From the characterization of a heart
of darkness, the waste land, and the decline of the west at the start
of the century, the humanistic tradition of the past century has

harped on the negative and predicted the end of civilization, punctuated by wars with lethal chemicals of mass destruction and inherent moral corruption.

THE DECLINE OF THE WEST

A survivor of displacement and the horrors of the Second World War, Samuel Beckett described the breakdown of modern life in his terse, black comedy, *Endgame*, which projects great destruction or nuclear devastation and the demise of the nuclear family. All humane values have been destroyed—and communication within the family has failed. Hamm accuses his father Nagg: "accursed progenitor" and "accursed fornicator" of the greatest injustice of all: "Scoundrel, why did you engender me?" In an ironic parody of God's answer to Job from the whirlwind, Nagg answers Hamm from the garbage bin which he inhabits.

> It's natural. After all I'm your father. It's true if it hadn't been me it would have been someone else. But that's no excuse.

Nagg and his mate Nell live out their dwindling years without hope or meaning, in a parody of love:

> Nell: What is it, my pet? Time for love?
> Nagg: Were you asleep?
> Nell: Oh no!
> Nagg: Kiss me.
> Nell: We can't.
> Nagg: Try.
> (*Their heads strain towards each other, fail to meet, fall apart again.*)

When Nagg dies, he is unmorned by his son. The blind Hamm requires the ministration of his "son" Clov. But there is no bond:

> Hamm: You don't love me.
> Clov: No.

Hamm: You loved me once?
Clov: Once.

In what may be called hopeful despair, Hamm suggests: "But humanity might start from there all over again! Catch him, for the love of God!"[212] The sins of the father are visited on their children, even to this age. Clov in the end leaves Hamm to blindness and old age.

There was a similar brooding pessimism in Oriana Fallaci's memoir, *Letter to a Child Never Born*, which explored the thoughts of a woman about pregnancy in our post-industrial age and questioned the value of bringing a child into the world: "A lot of women ask themselves why they should bring a child into the world. So that it will be hungry, so that it will be cold, so that it will be betrayed and humiliated, so that it will be slaughtered by war or disease?"[213] Here sexual differences do not necessarily matter.

> If you're born a man, you won't have to worry about being raped on a dark street. You won't have to make use of a pretty face to be accepted at first glance, of a shapely body to hide your intelligence . . . and you'll be able to disobey without being derided, to love without fear of pregnancy, to take pride in yourself without being laughed at. But you'll run into other forms of slavery and injustice: life isn't easy for a man, you know.[214]

For a girl though, it might be harder:

> From now on you must prepare to defend yourself, to be quicker and stronger, and to throw others down from the terrace. Especially if you're a woman. This too is a law: unwritten but obligatory. It's either you or me, either I save myself or you save yourself: these are the terms of this law.[215]

To marry or not to marry; to go against man's law, the laws of the Church, God's law; to choose to abort, or to bear the responsibility for one's actions. For a Catholic, the trial is more fierce, and one must cope with one's own conditioned moral doubts. These were her central concerns.

THE NEW PHILOSOPHY CALLS ALL IN DOUBT

What should we teach our young? Writing a little more than a decade ago, Allan Bloom, as formerly mentioned, upheld the need for vitality of the humanistic tradition, "to don regal and courtly garments, enter the courts of the ancients and speak with them" as the only true path to education. He remained firmly committed to the old knowledge, criticizing the direction of education and the absence of self-knowledge, and he challenged the new philosophies that were, in his view, vitiating education: "with rare exceptions, [college] courses are parts of specialties and not designed for general cultivation, or to investigate questions important for human beings as such. The so-called knowledge explosion and increasing specialization have not filled up the college years but emptied them."[216] He not only opposed emphasis in such areas as African-American and Women's Studies, but showed true naïveté or myopia, in failing to assess the incoming revolution in computers, as he heaped ridicule on "the latest item . . . computer literacy, the full cheapness of which is evident only to those who think a bit about what literacy might mean."[217]

The extent to which he failed to understand the impact of the computer and the changes being wrought by the new technologies showed not necessarily a lack of imagination; but rather better illustrates the true rate of acceleration in the pace of knowledge in the last decade. If humanists are guilty of demanding that the clock stand still, as the Inquisition by the Church of Rome in 1633 sought to suppress Galileo's physics, or William Jennings Bryan, at the Scopes Trial in 1925, sought to undermine Darwin's theory of evolution, then perhaps some scientists can be accused of lacking the historical perspective of the *philosophes* of the eighteenth century, who brought to science a humanistic bent. There are notable biologists, chemists, physicist, mathematicians and technicians, whose narrow specialization and reductionism offer a somewhat limiting view of science that seems to be a dominant force in our culture today.[218]

THE NEW COCKS OF THE WALK

Today our society has been described as bifurcated into two cultures—the scientific and the humanistic. As the new knowledge has taken us beyond anything we could have imagined, men of science have taken the helm in divining the future.

Earlier in the last century, the Austrian philosopher Ludwig Wittgenstein (1889-1951) deconstructed language, and questioned its ability to provide the basis and substance of meaningful discourse. Similarly today deconstruction in the laboratory is thought to yield the ultimate truths, and we look deeply to decipher our character and behavior from biological understanding of our genes, which contain not only the guide to our future, but our past inheritance—the role traditionally assigned to religion and the arts. Scientists today have the ear of culture and the media, receive grants and awards, publish books, garner Nobel Prizes, and enjoy celebrity status on the Talk Show circuit. No wonder they are cocky.[219] Biologists and physicists and mathematicians provide the ultimate meanings of life, which in the past had been provided by poets such as Homer, Dante, Goethe, and literary artists were recognized for their gift of not only understanding but imagining the world. Is scientific knowledge the only kind of knowledge that can be tolerated in our society?

Is it necessarily accurate to argue that the key to unraveling aesthetic pleasure is to find the location on the brain which receives excitation, or that music is inexplicable because it has no evolutionary purpose? Will the DNA molecule ever explain language and religion, or can the pleasure of viewing art be reduced to finding the locus on the retina where such stimulation exists?

WHAT GOES AROUND COMES AROUND

Evolutionary biologists, like their medieval counterparts, are seeking to discover the final truth in the decoding the grail of the DNA molecule. Geoffrey F. Miller, in his recent book *The Mating Mind*, argues with conviction that sexual choice has been the dominant influence in shaping the evolution of human nature eons before literature or the internet were invented, and that we are the outcome of this biological process of genetic screening. Accordingly, relations between the sexes have been the dominant influence on humanity, and the story of love is the history of pre-civilization as well as civilization. He authors a wonderful script about "Courtship in the Pleistocene," which suggests that "our ancestors lived in areas of sub-Saharan Africa that contained mixtures of open savanna, scrub, and forest. Instead of caves or jungles, picture Africa's broad, flat plains, with their fever trees and acacias, their wet and dry seasons, their hot days and cool nights, their plentiful hoofed herds and rare, emaciated predators, the incandescent sun, and millions of scrabbling insects."[220] Drawing from such diverse sources as paleontology, archeology, anthropology and primatology, he reasons that pre-Neanderthals engaged in courtship practices—of choosing mates by flirting, dating and mating, that one might find in an upscale bar or pub, in which one seeks an indicator of someone's intelligence, kindness, creativity, and humor: "if an individual made you laugh, sparked your interest, told good stories, and made you feel well cared for, then you might have been more disposed to mate."[221] Afterwards their marriages also paralleled our own. "During the days, women would have gathered fruits, vegetables, tubers, berries and nuts to feed themselves and their children. Men would have tried to show off by hunting game, usually unsuccessfully, returning home empty-handed to beg some yams from the more pragmatic womenfolk. Our ancestors probably did not have to work more than twenty or thirty hours a week to gather enough food to live. They did not have weekends or paid vacation time, but they probably had much more leisure time than we do."[222] It would take perhaps a million and half more years till our species—maintaining the same value system, instituted chat rooms on the internet, and evolved into soccer moms, and outdoorsmen of leisure, and even couch potatoes.

To be sure, the dependence of the species on love is confirmed by science, religion, and literature. People still fall in love, form relationships, get married and have families. They may be using the internet and chat rooms, and computer dating services beyond the imagination of the Pleistocene couple, but perhaps Miller is right: things haven't changed. Love is the mark, the distinctive fact of evolution, and provides the key to our happiness as well as to our immortality. Choosing love should also be a moral action, and perhaps we ought to approach our love objects with intelligence as well as emotion.

Having come this far in this odyssey, we have noted the beauty of love, and perhaps can also understand the intelligence that underlies this passion. Intelligence can and should make a difference in the way we define and maintain relationships. As a young cub reporter, my first beat was covering cases in the Coney Island Court. I remember the judge presiding over a series of divorce cases at one point turned to no one in particular, perhaps to me by now a regular in his courtroom, and said with exasperation, "You'd think these people had never loved each other in the first place." Mixed marriages between men and women of different cultures and races, are growing by leaps and bounds, and promise to be the distinctive feature of lives—and perhaps to lead to greater tolerance, in the Twenty First century. Homosexual relations, while not mainstream, are accepted. There are still too many teenage pregnancies, young people seem terrified of making premature commitments, and finally couples perhaps do not work hard enough at maintaining relationships once they have begun to sour.

Surely, there will always be complex problems in personal relations and for the species, and there always be interesting and difficult moral questions. Such as the famous case of Baby M. where a mother was engaged to receive artificial insemination and agreed to give up the child at term. However, the mother recanted having bonded with her offspring, and refused to surrender the child. Solomon's wisdom was required to determine who should have the prevalent claim: the seed-bearer or seed-provider. Even absent intercourse, the experience of parenting creates diverse pressures on the partners involved and underlines the importance of cooperation within the nuclear and extended family. But the story of love recounted here deserves a happy ending.

THREE HAPPY ENDINGS

In the dominant myth relating to the relationship between men and women, the male is supposed to subdue his woman through his wit and persistence. In his famous sex comedy, *The Taming of the Shrew*, Shakespeare pits the obstinate, insistent man against the obdurate, unbending woman. Kate is an over-indulged, spoilt hussy until Petruchio takes her in hand and makes her his wife.

Petruchio: Good morrow, Kate; for that's your name, I hear.

Katherina: Well have you heard, but something hard of
　　　　hearing: They call me Katherina that do talk of me.

Petruchio: You lie in faith; for you are called plain Kate,
And bonny Kate, and sometimes Kate the curst;
But Kate, the prettiest Kate in Christendom
Kate of Kate-Hall, my super-dainty Kate,
For dainties are all Kates, and, therefore, Kate,
Take this of me, Kate of my consolation—
Hearing thy mildness prais'd in every town,
Thy virtues spoke of, and thy beauty sounded,
Yet not so deeply as to thee belongs,

Myself am moved to woo thee for my wife.

Katherina: Moved! In good time: let him that moved you
    hither
Remove you hence. I knew you at the first
You were a moveable.

Petruchio: Why, what's a moveable?

Katherina: A join'd stool.

Petruchio: Thou hast hit it: come sit on me.

Katherina: Asses are made to bear, and so are you.

Petruchio: Women are made to bear, and so are you.
II.i.182-200

Later after Petruchio succeeds in taming the shrew, or many would say that Kate subdues Petruchio, she expresses or feigns the proper duty of a wife:

> Thy husband is thy lord, thy life, thy keeper,
> Thy head, thy sovereign; one that cares for thee,
> And for thy maintenance commits his body
> To painful labor both by sea and land;
> To watch the night in storms, the day in cold,
> Whilst thou liest warm at home, secure and safe;
> And craves no other tribute at thy hands
> But love, fair looks, and true obedience—
> Too little payment for so great a debt.
> Such duty as the subject owes the prince,
> Even such a woman oweth to her husband;
> And when she is froward, peevish, sullen, sour,
> And not obedient to his honest will,
> What is she but a foul contending rebel
> And graceless traitor to her loving lord?

I am ashamed that women are so simple
To offer war where they should kneel for peace,
Or seek for rule, supremacy, and sway,
When they are bound to serve, love, and obey.
Why are our bodies soft, and weak, and smooth,
Unapt to toil and trouble in the world,
But that our soft conditions and our hearts
Should well agree with our external parts?
Come, come, you froward and unable worms!
My mind hath been as big as one of yours,
My heart as great, my reason haply more,
To bandy word for word and frown for frown;
But now I see our lances are but straws,
Our strength as weak, our weakness past compare,
That seeming to be most which we indeed least are.
V.ii 146-164

Scholars will continue to dispute whether Petruchio tamed Kate, or Kate tamed Petruchio, but long-married married folks certainly no doubt have gleaned the truth.

Chaucer in "The Wife of Bath's Tale" in *The Canterbury Tales* presents another insightful story. Set in the age of romance, when knights were knights and ladies were themselves, King Arthur ruled, and the Elf Queen and her fairies thrived and danced in the meadows. A young knight commits rape on a virgin and is brought before the King for punishment. The mandatory sentence for such a crime is death. But the Queen and the ladies of the court take pity on the handsome chevalier, and the King defers to his wife. She offers the knight an opportunity to find the solution to a riddle. If he succeeds, his life will be spared: "What is the thing that women most desire?" He is given a year and a day for his quest, and then, on his oath as a knight, he must return.

The knight searches nigh and far for the answer. He asks men and women, young and old, rich and poor, wise and foolish. He hears many answers: honor, joy, pleasure, wealth, gorgeous clothes, and fun in bed, marriage, frequent marriages, flattery, and freedom. He also learns that women want to be thought well of, not have their vices exposed, not be criticized, and be thought capable of keeping a secret. Yet he fears he has not found the answer that will satisfy his peevish interrogator.

The knight returns to the court at the expiration of the assigned term with notable Freudian despair. Suddenly he encounters a vision of twenty four dancing ladies, who disappear at his approach. Only a foul looking, hag remains, and she inquires about his dilemma. Upon hearing his plight, she declares that she will supply the answer; but in return he must swear to do whatever she commands him. He agrees, whereupon she "crooned the gospel in his ear."

He now appears before the queen and declares that he knows the answer to the riddle. The court is spellbound with anticipation. The queen asks, "What thing is it that women most desire?" The knight responds: "A woman wants the self-same sovereignty/ Over her husband as over her lover,/ And master him; he must not be above her." The court is awed; the truth is received. His head is spared.

The story does not end here. Now the hag demands her fee: she wants the knight to marry her. Reluctantly he fulfills his obligation. After they are married, the poor knight is disconsolate, and the hag asks her unhappy mate whether he would prefer an old and true wife or a young and possibly faithless one. But he has learned from his near-encounter with death and gained wisdom as well as knowledge. He rises to the moment:

> "My lady and my love, my dearest wife,
> I leave the matter to your wise decision.
> You make the choice yourself, for the provision
> Of what may be agreeable and rich
> In honor to us both, I don't care which;
> Whatever pleases you suffices me."
> "And have I won the mastery?" said she,
> "Since I'm to choose and rule as I think fit?
> "Certainly, wife," he answered her, "that's it."
> "Kiss me," she cried. "No quarrels! On my oath

And word of honour, you shall find me both,
That is, both fair and faithful as a wife;
May I go howling mad and take my life
Unless I prove to be as good and true
As ever wife was since the world was new!
And if tomorrow when the sun's above
I seem less fair than any lady-love,
Than any queen or empress east or west,
Do with my life and death as you think best.
Cast up the curtain, husband. Look at me.[223]

She is transformed into a young and lovely woman, and he gives her "a hundred thousand kisses," and they live in perfect bliss. The moral is plain. If you want her to be ever young, and your life to be every blissful, then she must have mastery over you. And she of course must make you believe that you have mastery over her.

LADY GODIVA

And then there was Lady Godiva, in one sense a variant on the oriental story of the virtuous Scheherazade. According to legend, in 1040, Leofric, Earl of Mercia and Lord of Coventry imposed higher taxes on his tenants, and his wife, Lady Godiva, besought him to remove them. He said he would do so, if she rode naked through the town. Accordingly Lady Godiva took him at his word and made her historic journey on a white horse through Coventry. Everyone waited for Lady Godiva, prohibited from looking. Only peeping Tom was recorded as having violated the interdiction, and is remembered in legend with opprobrium. Robert Graves points to Godiva as a manifestation of the qualities of the White Goddess, the most ancient divinity and moon goddess, whose intuition and inspiration have served as the force of poetry, beauty and truth from earliest times.[224]

Today women are taking their proud role in society, perhaps a far cry from the "bra burners" of the nineteen sixties and the later "top-free seven" from Rochester who strode about unencumbered to bring attention to themselves as much as to their cause. From business and the arts to scholarship and sports, whether soccer, golf, basketball, tennis, swimming, and Olympic events, women from the entire globe, and American women in particular, are setting an important example and a leadership role, and performing with skill, tact, and their unique sensibility. A baker's dozen and counting are the number of women filling the United States Senate today, quietly showing the way to bi-partisanship, seeking the larger, global picture, and advancing social justice with distinction. Perhaps it is just a matter of time before some new Godiva will coax the current earls of Mercia and bring about the perfection to which Mark Twain alluded at the head of the chapter; and usher in a greater era of understanding, compassion, and tolerance, "with liberty and justice for all," to accompany our scientific progress, and this outcome—Godot himself—would no doubt deem worth waiting for.

ENDNOTES

[1] *Pantagruel* (Paris: Editions Gallimard, 1965), Book 2, Chapter 8 (*My translation*).

[2] Wolfgang Wickler, *The Sexual Code: The Social Behavior of Animals and Men*, trans. Francisca Garvie (New York: Anchor Books, 1972).

[3] Admiral Jacques-Yves Cousteau as early as the seventies initiated the form of television documentary in his wonderful marine study, "The Tragedy of the Sockeye Salmon."

[4] Helene Deutsch, *The Psychology of Women* (New York: Grune & Stratton, 1945), pp. 90-91.

[5] See Rosabeth Moss Kanter's classic study, "Women in Organizations: Sex Roles, Group Dynamics and Change Strategies," in *Beyond Sex Roles*, ed. Alice G. Sargent (St. Paul's: West Publishing Company, 1977), p. 382.

[6] *Ibid.*, p. 319.

[7] *The Psychology of Women, op. cit.*, p. 15.

[8] *I Ching*, trans. John Blofeld (New York: Dutton, 1968), p. 159.

[9] *The Complete Works of Montaigne*, trans. Donald Frame (Stanford: Stanford University Press, 1957), p. 241.

[10] *The New York Times* (February 23, 1987), p. 45.

[11] "To be properly understood," writes Todd Gitlin, "television has to be seen as the place where force-fields intersect: economic imperatives, cultural traditions, political impositions. For television is not an apparatus invading us from without. Its very technology, like other technologies, emerges from a matrix of commercial interests, within a culture of privatized individuals. And it makes its home comfortably in American history. Alexis de Tocqueville, that most observant Frenchman of a century and a half ago, would have found TV familiar in many ways. American culture, he observed in the 1830's, already was given to comfortable, sensational, mass-

produced amusements, 'vehement and bold,' 'untutored and rude,' aiming 'to stir the passions more than to charm the taste.' Television's spectacles have roots in centuries-old myths, just as they recycle and transform them. Television is a screen on which the absurdities and abominations of our politics are displayed in living color." These tendencies have only been exaggerated since the introduction of Music Television. *Watching Television* (New York:Pantheon Books, 1987), p. 4.

[12] Allan Bloom, *The Closing of the American Mind: How Higher Education Has Failed Democracy and Impoverished the Souls of Today's Students*, (New York: Simon and Schuster, 1987), pp. 47, 21.

[13] *The Triumph of Vulgarity: Rock Music in the Mirror of Romanticism* (New York: Oxford University Press, 1987), p. 108.

[14] Charles Butler, *The Feminine Monarchy* (Oxford: I. Turner, 1634).

[15] Kate Millett, *Sexual Politics* (New York: Doubleday, 1970), p. 356.

[16] Mary Ellman, *Thinking About Women* (New York: Harcourt, Brace and World, 1968), p. 54.

[17] *The Female Eunuch* (New York: McGraw Hill, 1971), p. 42.

[18] Millett, *op. cit.*, p. 341.

[19] Jill Johnston, "On a clear day you can see your mother," *The Village Voice* (May 6, 1971), 37ff.

[20] *Sisterhood is Powerful* (New York: Vintage, 1970), p. 514.

[21] Leonore Tiefer, *Sex is not a Natural Act* (Boulder: Westview Press, 1995), p. 203.

[22] Sarah Blaffer Hrdy, *Mother Nature: A History of Mothers, Infants, and Natural Selection* (New York: Pantheon Books, 1999), p. 109.

[23] Susan Faludi, *Stiffed: The Betrayal of the American Man* (New York, William Morrow, 1999), p. 14.

[24] The Biblical account of creation is perhaps less insidious than critics such as Jane Miller suggest: "The image of Eve being created out of Adam's (presumably redundant) rib is one of the most insidiously potent metaphors of Christian cultures." *Women Writing About Men* (New York: Pantheon Books, 1986), p. 189. The Biblical redactors actually changed a far more anti-feminist myth—that of the giant Marduk clefting the female dragon, Tiamat, in two, from whose dismemberment the world was made. Tiamat is metamorphosed into abstract Chaos, and the story of Adam and Eve

becomes a fairy tale of idealized sexual innocence. All references are to the King James Bible.

[25] *The Homeric Hymns and Homerica*, trans. Hugh G. Evelyn-White (London: Loeb Classical Library, 1954), p. 123

[26] *The Iliad*, trans. Richard Lattimore (Chicago: University of Chicago Press, 1952).

[27] *The Odyssey*, trans. Robert Fitzgerald (New York: Doubleday Anchor, 1963).

[28] *Poems and Fragments*, trans. Guy Davenport (Ann Arbor: University of Michigan Press, 1965), #15, #20

[29] David M. Robinson, *Sappho and Her Influence* (New York: Cooper Square, 1963), "Ode to Aphrodite" (Tucker) p. 49.

[30] *The Oresteia Triology*, trans. George Thomson (New York: Dell, 1965), p. 42

[31] *Medea*, trans. Frederic Prokosch, in *Drama on Stage* (New York: Holt, Rinehart, and Winston, 1961).

[32] *Lysistrata*, trans. Charles T. Murphy, in *Greek Literature in Translation* (New York: Longman's, 1944).

[33] *Great Dialogues of Plato*, trans. W.H.D. Rouse (New York: New American Library, 1972) p. 87.

[34] *De Rerum Natura*, trans. W.H.D. Rouse (London: Loeb Classical Library, 1937), p. 3.

[35] *The Poems of Catullus*, trans. James Michie (New York: Random House, 1969), p. 25.

[36] *The Odes and Epodes*, trans. C.E. Bennett (London: Loeb Clasical Library, 1955), p. 161.

[37] My translation.

[38] *Epigrams*, trans. Walter C.A. Ker (London: Loeb Classical Library, 1961), I, 247.

[39] *The Art of Love and Other Poems*, trans. J.H. Mozley (London: Loeb Classical Library, 1952), p. 13.

[40] *The Satyricon of Petronius Arbiter*, trans. W.C. Firebaugh (New York: Washington Square Press, 1966), pp. 98-100.

[41] *Juvenal and Persius*, trans. G.G. Ramsay (London: Loeb Classical Library, 1956), p. 107, *passim*.

[42]*Meditations*, trans. Meric Casaubon (London: Everyman's Library, 1929), pp. 23, 105.

[43] Maurice Valency, *In Praise of Love* (New York: Macmillan, 1958), p. 22.

[44] *Confessions of St. Augustine*, trans. Rex Warner (New York: New American Library, 1963), pp. 69, 70.

[45] *The Consolation of Philosophy*, trans. Richard Green (Indianapolis: Bobbs-Merrill, 1962), p. 4.

[46] *Aucassin and Nicolette*, trans. Eugene Mason (New York: E.P. Dutton, 1958), pp. 6-7.

[47] Quoted in *In Praise of Love, op. cit.*, p. 163.

[48]*Ibid.*, pp. 108-109.

[49] *The Art of Courtly Love*, trans. John Jay Parry (New York: Frederick Ungar, 1961), p. 2.

[50]*Lays of Marie de France*, trans. Eugene Mason (London: J.M. Dent, 1911), p. 24.

[51] *The Book of the City of Ladies*, trans. Earl Jeffrey Richards (New York: Persea Books, 1982), p. 256.

[52]*Ancrene Wisse*, ed. J.R.R. Tolkien (Oxford: Early English Text Society, 1962), p. 3.

[53]Evelyne Sullerot, *Women on Love*, trans. Helen R. Lane (New York: Doubleday, 1979), p. 52.

[54] *The Divine Comedy*, trans. Carlyle-Wicksteed (New York: Modern Library, 1950),pp. 569-570.

[55]*Decameron*, trans. Frances Winwar (New York: Modern Library, 1930), pp. 414-415.

[56] *The Canterbury Tales*, ed. F.N. Robinson (Boston: Houghton Mifflin, 1957), ll. 1347-1352, 2987-2983.

[57] *The Canterbury Tales*, trans. David Wright (New York: Random House, 1965) pp. 145-146; 181.

[58] *The Five Books of Gargantua and Pantagruel*, trans. Jacques Le Clercq (New York: Modern Library, 1936), pp. 421, 154-155.

[59] *The Complete Works of Montaigne, op. cit.*, 680, 286, 647, 682.

[60]*John Donne and William Blake* (New York: Modern Library, 1941), p. 3.

[61]In the famous retort to Ben Jonson's criticism that his idealization of his patron's daughter in *"The Anniversarie"* poems "was profane and full of

blasphemies. That..if it had been written of the Virgin Mary, it had been something," Donne argued that he "described the idea of a woman, and not as she was." He was justifying a tradition that had existed for more than a thousand years, but which was now being questioned by rationalism and a naturalistic outlook. Ben Jonson, *Selected Works* (New York: Random House, 1938), p. 990.

[62] *The History of that Ingenious Gentleman Don Quijote de la Mancha*, trans. Burton Raffel (New York: W.W. Norton, 1995), p. 12.

[63] *Madame de Staël*, ed. Morris Berger (New York: Doubleday, 1964) p. 222.

[64] *Six plays by Corneille and Racine*, trans. Paul Landis (New York: Modern Library, 1931), pp. 53-55.

[65] *Eight Plays by Molière*, trans. Morris Bishop (New York: Modern Library, 1957), pp. 35, 87.

[66] *Complete Poems and Major Prose*, ed, Merritt Y. Hughes (New York: Odyssey Press, 1957).

[67] *Complete Plays*, ed. Gerald Weales (New York: Anchor Books, 1966), p. 329.

[68] *Clarissa* (London: Everyman's Library, 1932), III, 370-371. The original quaint title was *The History of a Young Lady Comprehending the Most Important Concerns of Private Life and Particularly Shewing, the Distresses That May Attend the Misconduct Both of Parents and Children, in Relation to Marriage.*

[69] *Candide, or Optimism*, trans. John Butt (Baltimore: Penguin, 1968), p. 136.

[70] Samuel Shellabarger, *Lord Chesterfield and His World* (Boston: Little Brown, 1951), p. 356.

[71] *The Complete Justine and Other Writings* (New York: Grove, 1965), p. 455.

[72] *The Portable Blake*, ed. Alfred Kazin (New York: Viking, 1946), p. 305.

[73] *Romanticism and Its Discontents* (New York: Farrar, Straus and Giroux, 2000), p. 3.

[74] *The Descent of Man* (New York: Appleton and Company, 1898), p. 634.

[75] *Byron*, ed. Peter Quennel (London: Nonesuch Press, 1964), pp. 223-224.

[76] *The Sorrows of Young Werther*, trans. Elizabeth Mayer (New York: Vintage Boooks, 1971), p. 14.

[77] *Faust* (ll. 1699-1702), trans. Louis MacNeice (New York: Oxford University Press, 1951), p. 59.

[78] *Madame Bovary*, trans. Francis Steegmuller (New York: Modern Library, 1957), p. 183.

[79] *The Flowers of Evil*, trans. Marthiel and Jackson Mathews (London: Routledge & Kegan Paul, 1955), p. xviii.

[80] *Anna Karenina* (New York: Harper and Brothers, 1959), p. 556.

[81] *Dombey and Son* (New York: Oxford University Press, 1982), p. 169.

[82] *Cassandra, An Essay* (Old Westbury: The Feminist Press, 1979), p. 37.

[83] *The Subjection of Women in Three Essays* (Oxford: Oxford University Press, 1975), p. 451.

[84] *Pride and Prejudice* (Boston: Riverside Editions, 1964), p. 6.

[85] *The Complete Major Prose Plays*, trans. Rolf Fjelde (New York: Farrar Straus, Giroux, 1978), pp. 192-193.

[86] *Six Plays of Strindberg*, trans. Elizabeth Sprigge (New York: Doubleday-Anchor, 1955), p. 43.

[87] *Civilization and Its Discontents*, trans. Joan Riviere (London: Hogarth Press, 1957), p. 61.

[88] *Beyond the Pleasure Principle*, trans. James Strachey (London: Hogarth Press, 1950), p. 53.

[89] "The Interpretation of Dreams," in *Basic Writings*, trans. A.A. Brill (New York: Modern Library, 1938), p. 308.

[90] "Dostoyevsky and Parricide," in *Collected Papers*, ed. James Strachey (New York: Basic Books, 1959), V, 235.

[91] "Some Psychological Consequences of the Anatomical Distinction Between the Sexes," *Collected Papers, op. cit.* V, 196-197.

[92] *Civilization and Its Discontents, op. cit.*, p. 75.

[93] *Sons and Lovers* (New York: Viking Press, 1970), p. 67.

[94] *Lady Chatterley's Lover* (New York: Grove Press, 1959), p. 252.

[95] *Remembrance of Things Past*, trans. C.K. Scott Moncrieff (New York: Random House, 1924), I, 10-11.

[96] *The Trial*, trans. Willa and Edwin Muir (New York: Alfred Knopf, 1960), p. 38.

[97] *Six Characters in Search of an Author*, in *Naked Masks*, ed. Eric Bentley (New York: E.P. Dutton, 1950), p. 216.

[98] *The Tragic Sense of Life*, trans. J.E. Crawford (New York: Dover, 1954), p. 393.

[99] *Three Tragedies*, trans. James Graham-Luján and Richard L. O'Connell (New York: New Directions, 1955), p. 211.

[100] *Ibid.*, p. 151.

[101] *Selected Plays* (New York: Dodd Mead, 1948), III, 631-632, 637.

[102] *Ulysees* (Modern Library, 1934), pp. 760ff.

[103] *Finnegans Wake* (New York: Viking Press, 1939), pp. 9,20, 185-186.

[104] *Complete Poems and Plays* (New York: Harcourt Brace, 1952), pp. 356ff.

[105] *The Second Sex*, trans. H.M. Parshley (New York: Alfred A. Knopf, 1958), p. 267.

[106] *Arturo's Island*, trans. Isabel Quigly (New York: Alfred A. Knopf, 1959), p. 138.

[107] *History*, trans. William Weaver (New York: Vintage Books, 1984), pp. 58-59.

[108] *The Visit*, trans. Patrick Bowles (New York: Grove Press, 1962), p. 39.

[109] *Man in the Holocene*, trans. Geoffrey Skelton (New York: Harcourt Brace Jovanovich, 1979), p. 8.

[110] *Kiss of the Spider Woman*, trans. Thomas Colchie (New York: Vintage Books, 1980), p. 98.

[111] *Love in the Time of Cholera*, trans. Edith Grossman (New York: Penguin Books, 1988), p. 338-339.

[112] *Common Sense and Other Political Writings* (Indianapolis: Bobbs Merrill Company, 1953), p. 21.

[113] Henry Adams, *The Education of Henry Adams* (Boston: Houghton Mifflin, 1961), pp. 384-385.

[114] James Fenimore Cooper, *The Leatherstocking Saga* (New York: Pantheon Books, 1954), pp. 267-268.

[115] *Democracy in America*, trans. Henry Reeve (London: Oxford University Press, 1946), p. 468.

[116] *The Scarlet Letter* (New York: Modern Library, 1950), pp. 289-290.

[117] *Moby Dick* (New York: Modern Library, 1950), pp. 395-397.

[118] *Uncle Tom's Cabin* (New York: Coward McCann, 1929), pp. 331, 393.

[119] *Leaves of Grass and Selected Prose* (New York: Modern Library, 1950), p. 43.

[120] Peter Buitenhuis, *The Grasping Imagination* (Toronto: University of Toronto Press, 1970), pp. 69-70.

[121] *A Woman of No Importance*, in *The Works of Oscar Wilde* (London: Collins, 1957), p. 421.

[122] *The Portrait of a Lady* (Boston: Riverside Editions, 1956), pp. 96-97.

[123] *Selected Poems* (New York: Modern Library, 1996), p. 172.

[124] *City of Women: Sex and Class in New York, 1789-1860* (New York: Alfred A. Knopf, 1986), p. 220. Today, Sarah Blaffer Hrdy estimates that "economic reality" requires that families have more than one wage earner. "Most mothers, even if they want to, do not have the option of staying home to care for their babies." *Mother Nature, op. cit.*, p. 109.

[125] *Living My Life* (New York: Dover, 1970), I, 123.

[126] *The Awakening* (New York: Garrett Press, 1970), p. 46.

[127] *Women and Economics* (New York: Harper Torchbooks, 1966), pp. 87-88.

[128] *Herland* (New York: Pantheon, 1979), p. 61.

[129] *The Yellow Wallpaper* (Old Westbury: Feminist Press, 1973), p. 21.

[130] Ann Jardim, *The First Henry Ford: A Study in Personality and Business Leadership* (Cambridge, Mass.: M.I.T. Press, 1970), pp. 71-72.

[131] *Plays of Eugene O'Neill* (New York: Modern Library, 1982), III, 221-222.

[132] *Babbitt* (New York: Harcourt Brace, 1922), pp. 89-90.

[133] *My Life* (New York: Liveright, 1972), p. 108.

[134] *In Defense of Women* (New York: Alfred Knopf, 1918), pp. 15-16.

[135] *Dorothy Parker* (New York: Viking Portable Library, 1954), p. 334.

[136] *Catch 22* (New York: Modern Library, 1961), p. 403.

[137] *Cat on a Hot Tin Roof* (New York: New Directions, 1955), p. 197.

[138] *Kaddish and Other Poems* (San Francisco: City Lights, 1961), p. 31.

[139] *Lolita* (New York: G.P. Putnam's Sons, 1955), p. 8.

[140] *Generation of Vipers* (New York: Rinehart & Co., 1942), pp. 47, 50.

[141] *Who's Afraid of Virginia Woolf?* (New York: Atheneum, 1969), pp. 151-152.

[142] *Myra Breckenridge* (New York: Little Brown, 1960), p. 1.

[143] *Myron* (New York: Random Houses, 1974), p. 42.

[144] *The Stepford Wives* (New York: Random House, 1972), p. 9.

[145] *The World According to Garp* (New York: E.P. Dutton, 1976), p. 8.

[146] *The Bell Jar* (New York: Harper & Row, 1971), pp. 93-94.

[147] *Pitch Dark* (New York: Alfred A. Knopf, 1983), pp. 21-22, 59.

[148] *Complete Poems* (Boston: Houghton Mifflinf, 1981), p. 455.

[149] *Fear of Flying* (New York: Holt, Rinehart and Winston, 1973), p. 228.

[150] *How to Save Your Own Life* (New York: Holt, Rinehart and Winston, 1977), p. 56.

[151] *Fanny* (New York: New American Library, 1981), p. 41.

[152] *Marriages and Infidelities* (New York: Vanguard Press, 1972), p. 53.

[153] *In Search of Our Mothers' Gardens* (New York: Harcourt Brace Jovanovich, 1983), p. 233.

[154] *Phenomenal Woman* (New York: Random House, 1995), p. 4.

[155] Irvin C. Schick, *The Erotic Margin, Sexuality and Spatiality in Alteritist Discourse* (London: Verso, 1999), p. 95.

[156] *The Travels of Marco Polo*, trans. Ronald Latham (New York: Penguin Books, 1958), pp. 196-197.

[157] *Ibid.*, p. 123.

[158] quoted in Vinod Verma, *The Kamasutra for Women: The Modern Woman's Way to Sensual Fulfillment and Health* (New York: Kodansha International, 1997), p. xx.

[159] *Mahabharata*, trans. William Buck (New York: New American Library, 1973), p. 18.

[160] quoted in *The Kama Sutra of Vatsyayana: The Classic Hindu Treatise on Love and Social Conduct*, foreword by John W. Spellman (New York: Penguin Books, 1962), pp. 33-34.

[161] *Ramayana*, trans. William Buck (Berkeley: University of California, 1976), pp. 56-57.

[162] *The Kama Sutra of Vatsyayana, op. cit.*, p. 93.

[163] *Ibid.*, p. 89.

[164] *Ibid.*, p. 103.

[165] *Ibid.*, p. 111.

[166] *Ibid.*, p. 150.

[167] *Ibid.*, p. 163.

[168] See Vinod Verma, *The Kama Sutra for Women, op. cit. passim.*

[169] Gary Zukav, *The Dancing Wu Li Masters* (New York: William Morrow, 1979), p. 33.

[170] *The Analects of Confucius*, trans. Arthur Waley (New York: Vintage Books, 1938), p. 128.

[171] *Ibid.*, p. 171.

[172]Lu Hsun, *A Brief History of Chinese Fiction*, trans. Yang Hsien-Yi and Gladys Yang (Westport: Hyperion Press, 1973), pp. 77-78.

[173]David Hawkes, "The Quest of the Goddess," *Studies in Chinese Literary Genres*, ed. Cyril Birch (Berkeley: University of California Press, 1974), p. 67.

[174]*Ibid.* p. 45.

[175]*Traditional Chinese Stories*, ed. Y.W. Ma and Joseph S.M. Lau (New York: Columbia University Press, 1978), pp. 140, 145.

[176]*An Anthology of Chinese Literature*, ed. and trans. Stephen Owen (New York: W.W. Norton, 1996), p. 403.

[177]Lai Ming, *A History of Chinese Literature* (New York: John Day, 1964), p. 227.

[178]*Ibid.*, p. 238.

[179]*An Anthology of Chinese Literature, op. cit.* p. 855.

[180]*Studies in Chinese Literary Genres, op cit.* p. 242.

[181]Tsao Hsueh-Chin, *Dream of the Red Chamber with a Continuation by Kao Ou*, trans. Chi-Chen Wang (New York: Twayne Publishers, 1958), pp. 1-3.

[182]*A Brief History of Chinese Fiction, op. cit.*, p. 307.

[183]For example, the noted economist and business professor, Lester C. Thurow, badgers and letures the Japanese on television and in print for defying the laws of the marketplace in showing softness toward workers: "In the economic cleanup, it must rain on the just and unjust alike," and he argues that managers and workers must be ruthlessly disposed of, laid off, for the benefit of the bottom line without concern for the human consequences. "What must be done is like pulling a thornbush from the ground with your bare hands. The bush must be grabbed ruthlessly and pulled quickly with great strength. There will be an initial jolt but it will quickly pass." (Do not such attitudes relate to the environment that fosters, though it does not create, the catastrophic bankruptcy of the Enron Corporation in 2002?) *Building Wealth* (New York: Harper Collins, 1999), p. 61.

[184]*Zen Buddhism: Selected Writings of D. T. Suzuki*, ed. William Barrett (New York: Doubleday-Anchor, 1956), p. xv.

[185]*The Essential Haiku*, trans. Robert Hass (Hopewell, New Jersey: Ecco Press, 1994) pp. 155, 165, 171.

[186] Kenneth G. Henshall, *A History of Japan From Stone Age to Superpower* (New York: St. Martin's Press, 1999), p. 58.

[187] Donald Keene, *Landscapes and Portraits, Appreciations of Japanese Culture* (Tokyo: Kodansha International, 1971), p. 27.

[188] *The Pillow Book of Sei Shonagon*, 2 vols. trans. Ivan Morris (New York: Columbia University Press, 1967), I, 20.

[189] *Ibid.*, p. 245.

[190] *Ibid.*, p. xiii

[191] Lady Murasaki, *The Tale of Genji*, trans. Arthur Waley (New York: Modern Library, 1960), p. 661.

[192] *Ibid.*, p. 257.

[193] The Geisha continues to elicit fascination to the western imagination as evidenced by the continuing popularity of Arthur Golden's *Memoirs of a Geisha* (New York: Vintage, 1997), a novel that is based in part on interviews with past and present Geishas.

[194] *The Erotic Margin, op. cit.*, p. 87.

[195] Edward W. Said, *Orientalism* (New York: Pantheon, 1978), pp. 59-60.

[196] *The Koran*, trans. N.J. Dawood (Middlesex, England: Penguin, 1968), p. 17.

[197] *Ibid.*, p. 57.

[198] Michael Cook, *The Koran, A Very Short Introduction* (Oxford: Oxford University Press, 2000), pp. 141-142.

[199] quoted in *The Erotic Margin, op cit.*, p. 123. Flaubert, the inveterate observer, elsewhere documented the "following fact: some time ago a santon (ascetic priest) used to walk through the streets of Cairo completely naked except for a cap on his head and another on his prick. To piss he would doff the prick-cap, and sterile women who wanted children would run up, put themselves under the parabola of his urine and rub themselves with it." *Orientalism, op. cit.*, p. 103.

[200] *Arabian Nights*, trans. Richard F. Burton (New York: Signet, 1991), p. 13.

[201] *Ibid.*, p. 582.

[202] *The Original Rubaiyyat of Omar Khayaam*, trans. Robert Graves and Omar Ali-Shah (New York: Doubleday, 1968), p. 45.

[203] *The State of the Union Messages* (New York: Chelsea House, 1966), III, 31444.

[204] *John Donne and William Blake, op. cit.*, pp. 171-172.

[205] *The Poems of George Herbert*, ed. Arthur Waugh (London: Oxford University Press, 1958), p. 144.

[206] *The Erotic Margin, op. cit.*, p. 144.

[207] Robert Grant, *The Politics of Sex and Other Essays* (New York: St. Martin's, 2000), pp. 95-96.

[208] Jane Miller, *Women Writing About Men* (New York: Pantheon, 1986), p. 161.

[209] *Encyclical of Pope Paul VI: Humanae Vitae* (Glen Rock, New Jersey: Paulist Press, 1968), p. 16.

[210] *Ibid.*, pp. 7, 9, 14.

[211] The physicist Stephen Hawking describes an audience with Pope John Paul II in which "he told us that it was all right to study the evolution of the universe after the Big Bang, but we should not inquire into the Big Bang itself because that was the moment of Creation and therefore the work of God." *A Brief History of Time* (New York: Bantam Books, 1990), p. 116.

[212] *Endgame* (New York: Grove Press, 1958), pp. 6, *passim*.

[213] *Letter to a Child Never Born*, trans. John Shepley (New York: Washington Square Press, 1982), p. 11.

[214] *Ibid.*, pp. 17-18.

[215] *Ibid.*, p. 51.

[216] Bloom, *op. cit.*, p. 340.

[217] *Ibid.*, p. 341.

[218] For example, at a conference sponsored by The New York Academy of Sciences held at Rockefeller University in June 2000, devoted to the topic "The Unity of Knowledge: The Convergence of the Human and Natural Sciences," the convergence was not particularly tangible, as the lead scientist declared in the keynote address: "There is knowledge that the natural sciences offer, and then there is all other knowledge."

[219] At the turn of the century, a survey by *The New York Times* questioned many leading intellectuals about the future, and there was hardly a humanist in the lot. Humanists such as historians and social scientists are playing a marginal role in guiding the direction of society compared to the role that they played even in the recent past, which reflects our current enamor with science. They do not seem to have positions of influence compared to their scientific brethren, are not consulted very much notwithstanding, for example, Allan Bloom's protestations, the charming conversational style of

the beloved Harold Bloom, and the obscure illuminations of Jacques
Derrida.

[220]Geoffrey Miller, *The Mating Mind, How Sexual Choice Shaped the Evolution
of Human Nature* (New York: Doubleday, 2000), p. 181.

[221]*Ibid.*, p. 188.

[222]*Ibid.*, p. 181.

[223]*The Canterbury Tales*, trans. Nevill Coghill (Baltimore, Md.: Penguin Books,
1951), pp. 301, 304, 309-310.

[224]Robert Graves, *The White Goddess, A Historical Grammar of Poetic Myth*,
enlarged ed. (New York: Noonday Press, 1966), pp. 403-405.

ACKNOWLEDGEMENTS AND AFTERWORD

Grateful acknowledgement is expressed to the following copyright holder: From Freakers' Ball. Words and Music by Shel Silverstein. Copyright © 1972 Evil Eye Music Inc. New York, N.Y. Used by Permission

It seems in retrospect like a fortuitous circumstance that, in my first summer as a graduate student at Columbia University, the course most conveniently fitting into my schedule was *Virgil's Minor Poems: The Eclogues and Georgics*, offered by the Classics Department. With some little college Latin and less Greek, I entered the seminar, and began a discovery of Classics. That same year, I was introduced to the enigmatic writing of James Joyce and Old English and the rich tradition of English and Comparative Literature, and performed a translation of the *Aeneid* for my Language requirement. At the time, Columbia boasted the presence of scholars of stellar attributes who influenced me greatly, and included Eric Bentley, Maurice Valency, Mark Van Doren, Marjorie Hope Nicolson, Gilbert Highet, W.T.H. Jackson, Moses Hadas, Lionel Trilling, Jacques Barzun, William York Tindall, and Northrop Frye (as Visiting Professor), for whose courses, I recall fondly, we could either register, or just audit. I earned my Ph.D at New York University where I enjoyed and benefited from my association with J. Max Patrick, Leon Edel, John Gassner, Elkin Calhoun Wilson, and R.C. Harrier. Earlier at Brooklyn College, I had the good fortune to have been taught and influenced by Margaret M. Bryant, Harry D. Gideonse, William Gerhard, Randolph Goodman, Bernard Grebanier, and particularly fondly recall the late Edgar Z. Friedenberg. My father Percy of blessed memory was my first mentor, and my mother Gertrude introduced me to Shakespeare.

Funding for secretarial expense was graciously made available to me at the inception by the late Vice President and Dean Francis B. McGarry, a devoted educator and a liberal administrator at East Stroudsburg University. Barbara Benninger ably typed the first draft; Gary Krawford prepared the second draft in word-processing form. Lorraine Lang Smith, my student and cartoonist for the college newspaper during the period that I served as faculty adviser, prepared for me a set of illustrations from which I selected the cover. Lisa Modica, Kori Klyman, Nick Kuckel, Rachel Davey, James Stevens, and the fine staff at Xlibris have provided most helpful professional and creative support -- the best "A" team for which a writer could hope.

As Professor of English and Chair of the Committee on International Education, I have enjoyed an association with many international students from virtually all of the countries, religions and cultures that I have dealt with in the book, and I would acknowledge their contribution—exemplified by my Chinese teacher, Wei Chen. My children Adam and Orna Jacqueline provided assistance at various stages of development, and always their intelligence, love and friendship. I also would like to acknowledge the services of the Academic Computing Center of East Stroudsburg University, and the various libraries and staffs—always considerate—including The New York Public Library, the Columbia University Libraries and my own university library.

I learned, while living abroad during my Sabbatical year, to miss and appreciate the services of public libraries in this country, which are nonpareil. I would like to thank my friends, past and present, at the Livingston Library for their continual help and warm support. I also would like to thank the thousands of my students who have honed my style, and my many colleagues, mentioning Robert J. Willis who contributed to formulating the title, as well as you, my ideal reader, for making the task the pleasant resolve that it has been.

Livingston, NJ—East Stroudsburg, Pa. January 21, 2002
Ronald.Meyers@po-box.esu.edu

INDEX

Advance Peeks at Godiva

"Starting with the birds and the bees, the book covers ground from the earliest glimmers of love among animals to the most complex manifestations of passion in the present day . . . the torch has been handed down."

MAURICE VALENCY, Author *In Praise of Love*

"Herein .. a lucid catalogue of passions traced through the ages across the far reaches of our global village, a headlong plunge down the multi-cultural slopes of love and destiny, desire and fate. Ronald J. Meyers presents in the lapidary style of his cherished authors, Horace, Li Po, Montaigne, and James Joyce, an urbane examination of Cupid's stray darts of amorous human endeavor, impaling with wit and charm the random targets the human heart has too often hit and missed. Whether read as an e-book or an elegant paperback or hardcover, it is a remarkable book deserving a notable place on your laptop, cocktail table, or library shelf, an adornment to your mind and heart, the story of love's adventures not to be missed."

CRAIG STRETE, Screenwriter/Author

"WOW Ronald!"

ERIC BENTLEY, Author/Scholar

"A delightful and imaginative guided tour through the written history of our primary emotion that I am sure will appeal to any reader who has even been either blessed or afflicted by LOVE."

SHEILA RAESCHILD, Feminist/Author

"All you want to know about love, ancient and modern, you will find in Ronald J. Meyers' encyclopedic, compact and engaging narrative."

RANDOLPH GOODMAN, Theater Historian

"WAITING FOR GODIVA, A GUIDE FOR THINKING WOMEN AND MEN TO THE STORY OF LOVE is an ambitious conspectus of a subject so large that Professor Meyers earns merit for merely attempting it. As it turns out, the book is an instructive compendium of both old and new insights, by way of narrative and commentary, into the human response to Aphrodite/ Eros through the centuries of western and oriental civilizations.

Upon this subject of subjects, Professor Meyers offers the reader a constellation of viewpoints, including his own; and the total effect reaffirms Virgil's great summation in the seventeenth canto of Dante's _Purgatorio_: 'Love is the seed of everything Good within you, but also of everything within you that deserves punishment.'

Until we understand this, as Professor Meyers well knows, we walk in darkness. And it is to such a conclusion that his enterprising study makes a useful and entertaining contribution."

BERNARD SPIVACK, (late) Renaissance and Shakespeare
Scholar

Ronald J. Meyers teaches Literature and Writing at East Stroudsburg University in Pennsylvania. He also has taught at Pratt Institute, New Jersey Institute of Technology, Rutgers, Temple University, Hunter College, Brooklyn College and, for the Pennsylvania Consortium of International Education, at Oxford University and the University of Pavia. He has delivered and/or published numerous papers on a wide range of topics relating to literature, education, and cultural studies. He enjoys membership in such associations as The New York Academy of Sciences, the Dramatists Guild, the International Association for the Fantastic in the Arts, and the Global Awareness Society. He is long married, has two married children, all with loving spouses, and five sweet, sprouting grandchildren.

Printed in the United States
22818LVS00002B/45